D0907789

Humana Festival '99
The Complete Plays

Humana Inc. is one of the nation's largest
managed health care companies
with more than 6 million members in its health care plans.

The Humana Foundation was established in 1981
to support the educational, social, medical and cultural development
of communities in ways that reflect
Humana's commitment to social responsibility
and an improved quality of life.

SMITH AND KRAUS PUBLISHERS
Contemporary Playwrights / Collections

Act One Festival '95

Act One Festival '95

EST Marathon '94: The One-Act Plays

EST Marathon '95: The One-Act Plays

EST Marathon '96: The One-Act Plays

EST Marathon '97: The One-Act Plays

EST Marathon '98: The One-Act Plays

Humana Festival: 20 One-Acts Plays 1976–1996

Humana Festival '93: The Complete Plays

Humana Festival '94: The Complete Plays

Humana Festival '95: The Complete Plays

Humana Festival '96: The Complete Plays

Humana Festival '97: The Complete Plays

Humana Festival '98: The Complete Plays

Women Playwrights: The Best Plays of 1992

Women Playwrights: The Best Plays of 1993

Women Playwrights: The Best Plays of 1994

Women Playwrights: The Best Plays of 1995

Women Playwrights: The Best Plays of 1996

Women Playwrights: The Best Plays of 1997

Women Playwrights: The Best Plays of 1998

If you require pre-publication information about upcoming Smith and Kraus books, you may receive our semi-annual catalogue, free of charge, by sending your name and address to *Smith and Kraus Catalogue, 4 Lower Mill Road, North Stratford, NH 03590. Or call us at (800) 895-4331, fax (603) 922-3348. WWW.SmithKraus.com.*

Humana Festival '99
The Complete Plays

Edited by Michael Bigelow Dixon
and Amy Wegener

Contemporary Playwrights Series

SK
A Smith and Kraus Book

A Smith and Kraus Book
Published by Smith and Kraus, Inc.
PO Box 127, Lyme, NH 03768
WWW.SmithKraus.com

Manufactured in the United States of America

Cover and Text Design by Julia Hill Gignoux
Layout by Jennifer McMaster
Cover artwork © James Bozzini

First Edition: October 1999
10 9 8 7 6 5 4 3 2 1

Library of Congress Cataloguing-in-Publication Data
Contemporary Playwrights Series
ISSN 1067-9510

Contents

Acknowledgments

The editors wish to thank the following persons for their invaluable assistance in compiling this volume:

Ilana Brownstein
Beth Burgess
Jennifer Cox
Preston Dyches
Emily Gnadinger
Adrien-Alice Hansel
Brandi Harrison
Sara Kmack
Kae Koger
Jeff Rodgers
Sara Skolnick
Alexander Speer
Kathy White

Eric Askanese
Charmaine Ferenczi
Ronald Gwiazda
Mary Harden
Morgan Jenness
Joyce Ketay
Carl Mulert
Bruce Ostler
Jack Tantleff

And participants in
the Audience Project
at Actors Theatre of Louisville

Foreword

Theatre, it strikes me, is no more nor less than the study of the human condition. It helps us, we hope, to become more human and perhaps better humans by bringing us together to tell stories of our kind, to celebrate us at our best and to empathize with us at our worst. Theatre powerfully reminds us where we have been and where we might be going. It points out the complexities and ambiguities of living a life and reminds us we have embarked on both a difficult and fascinating journey. Great plays do not oversimplify, nor do they pander; they assist us in thinking about and feeling what it means to live.

Theatre has both an affirming and critical role. As affirmation it celebrates our insights, ethics, deeds and compromises. It marks that which we have done well and applauds our plans as they affect our fellow creatures. People enjoy affirmation and will seek it out. In its critical role, theatre dissects and satirizes, questions and defines our failures, our misguidedness, our arrogance and our shortsightedness. People will accept such implied criticism in a well-told tale, but they are unused to paying money for bad news.

A theatre institution must accept and creatively energize both roles. It is a burden and a joy to accept this responsibility, and a theatre must be firm in its resolve because to do one without the other is to misunderstand the human condition we depict.

To pursue these goals we must seek to be the best storytellers we can, for the tale badly told will not find its mark. And we must tell all the stories, entertaining and painful, that can deepen our understanding.

We must tell the stories of the past so we may learn from the past, the stories of the present so we may know our effect on others and our surroundings, and the stories of the future so we may hope.

We must invest in the future by stimulating a new literature for the stage that serves our purposes described above. We have these responsibilities not only to ourselves and our community but to a larger community, our far-flung profession, and its powerful and necessary role in world culture.

Jon Jory
Producing Director
Actors Theatre of Louisville

Editors' Note

Each year we begin the process of assembling the Humana Festival of New American Plays with this question: How will we find the plays? This year, our initial answer was the same as it has always been: Let's read hundreds of full-length scripts and thousands of ten-minute plays, and try to respond imaginatively to the varied genius of American playwrights. So we did, and in that process discovered many of the remarkable works that appear in this collection, and which are appearing in theatres around the country even as this volume hits the bookstores.

However, this year our search was also fueled by a new methodology, as we encouraged playwrights to experiment with new genres. When playwrights were invited to partake in our non-traditional projects, they embraced the opportunity enthusiastically. American playwrights, it turned out, were not only interested in new creative challenges, they were eager to embark on shared adventures with the audience. So Jon Jory gave the go-ahead for a series of dramatic experiments with time, space and technology: a car play, phone plays and the T(ext) Shirt Project.

Inevitably, this publication of those experiments looks vastly different from the live events. For one thing, this book is unlikely to drive off with you in the backseat, whisper in your ear, or shrink in the washing machine. For another, the plays in this book are in sequence, while this year's Humana Festival was a lively three-ring circus of performances taking place in three theatres, parked on the curb out front, overheard on phones in the lobby, and displayed on the attire of audience members. From February through March, this Humana Festival boldly declared that playwriting could go anywhere and, to much acclaim, it did.

This book adds another ring to the circus by connecting playwrights directly with readers. Without a production on stage (or on a phone, car or t-shirt) to mediate this relationship, the reader's experience mirrors the playwright's own creative process, since the reader relies solely on the text to imagine an entire visual, aural, and emotional landscape. In other words, this activity demands that the reader become the director, designer, and actor of the event in his or her mind, which is precisely how the playwright began writing the play.

So here are twenty-five plays to direct, design, and perform for the theatre in your head. Your imagination will get a good workout, but isn't that the point?

Michael Bigelow Dixon & Amy Wegener

Humana Festival '99
The Complete Plays

Cabin Pressure
Created by the SITI Company
Conceived by Anne Bogart

BIOGRAPHY

Anne Bogart is artistic director of the SITI Company, which she founded in 1992 with Japanese director Tadashi Suzuki. She is also an Associate Professor at Columbia University. Previous productions at ATL: *In the Eye of the Hurricane*; *Picnic*; *The Adding Machine*; *Going, Going, Gone*; *Small Lives/Big Dreams*; *The Medium*; *Miss Julie* and *Private Lives*. Recent works with the SITI Company include *Alice's Adventures*, *Culture of Desire*, *Bob* and *Seven Deadly Sins*.

HUMANA FESTIVAL PRODUCTION

Cabin Pressure premiered at the Humana Festival of New American Plays in March 1999. It was directed by Anne Bogart with the following cast:

Will Bond
Ellen Lauren
Kelly Maurer
Barney O'Hanlon
Stephen Webber

and the following production staff:

Scenic Designer . . . . Paul Owen
Costume Designer . . . . Walt Spangler
Lighting Designer . . . . Mimi Jordan Sherin
Sound Designer . . . . Darron L. West
Properties Designer . . . . Ben Hohman
Stage Manager . . . . Megan Wanlass
Dramaturgs . . . . Adrien-Alice Hansel, Kae Koger

Stephen Webber, Ellen Lauren and Barney O'Hanlon
in *Cabin Pressure*, created by the SITI Company,
conceived by Anne Bogart

23rd Annual Humana Festival of New American Plays
Actors Theatre of Louisville, 1999
photo by Richard Trigg

Notes on *Cabin Pressure*
by Anne Bogart

A friend once described to me an incident in a crowded bus in San Francisco. She noticed two distinctly disparate individuals pushed up against one another on a narrow seat across from her: one, an outwardly fragile elderly lady, and the second, a flashy transvestite.

Suddenly the bus lurched and the elderly lady's hair-net caught onto a ring on the transvestite's hand.

When I heard this story I jumped. The story embodies an unmistakable lesson about what is possible between actors on stage and between actors and audience in a theater.

The moment the elderly lady's hair-net caught onto the transvestite's ring, the two were caught up in an exquisite mutual crisis outside of their day-to-day lives. Forced by circumstances to deal with one another, the boundaries that normally defined and separated them dissolved instantly. Suddenly the potential for something new and fresh sprang into being. Perhaps one might express outrage, or possibly they would both burst out laughing. The boundaries evaporated and they found themselves without the cushion of definitions that had formerly sufficed to keep them separate.

The Japanese have a word to describe the quality of space between two people: *m'ai*. In the martial arts, the *m'ai* is vital because of the peril of weaponry and attack. The danger invokes hyper-awareness of the space between people. On the stage, the space between actors and the space between actor and audience must continually be endowed with quality, attention and potential danger. The tension of the *m'ai* must be respected and tended.

As a director in the theater, I am acutely aware of the tension, the exquisite pressure, or the lack of pressure, this *m'ai*, between the audience and actors on the stage. The dynamics between an actor and audience constitute a creative relationship very different from daily life. The theater is what happens in the space between spectator and actor. It is an art form completely dependent upon the creative potential of each audience member in relation to the events on stage. Without a receiver, there is no experience. The receiver completes the circle with his/her own experience, imagination, and creativity. Sometimes the relationship functions and, at times, it does not.

I decided to create a play with the SITI Company about this vital relationship. The title of the play, *Cabin Pressure*, is a metaphor for our investigation.

•

> *The public sometimes thinks an artist is a television set— something comes out, nothing goes back. They don't realize that if they can hear me, then I can hear them—their coughs, the electronic beeps from their wristwatches, the squeaking of their shoes.*

These words were spoken during an interview with the great pianist Alfred Brendel. He continues,

> *The art of performance depends on the relationship between the musician and the audience. In the concert hall, each motionless listener is part of the performance. The concentration of the player charges the electric tension in the auditorium and returns to him magnified…. The audience grows together and becomes a group. There's the impression of a journey undertaken together and a goal achieved.*

Occasionally, in preparation for a concert, Alfred Brendel invited his neighbor and friend A. Alvarez to his home in London to listen. The first time Alvarez accepted the invitation, he worried that Brendel expected criticism or feedback but soon he understood the invitation. Alvarez would arrive in Brendel's home to find a chair sitting next to the piano. "What I assume," writes Alvarez, "is that he wants a sympathetic and attentive presence in the room, simply to complete the artistic circle."

With *Cabin Pressure* I wanted to create a new play which would address the issues of this "artistic circle." What is the creative role of the audience in the theater? What is the audience's responsibility to the actor? What is the actor's responsibility to the audience? What is an audience? What is an actor doing?

These are some of the issues I presented to the SITI Company actors in early rehearsal for this new collaboratively-created play. I wanted us to start with no preconceived notions or assumptions about the answers to these questions, but rather to experiment freely and play with possible variations on the theme. The result of these explorations is *Cabin Pressure*, which premiered at the Humana Festival of New American Plays.

In any production, once the director, the playwright and the designers have gone, the actor is left with a very particular daily dilemma: How to adjust to each new audience. A performance has a fluid rhythm that changes with each audience it touches. An actor can feel an audience no less palpably than the audience can feel the actors. The actor stands backstage and listens to the audience before making an entrance. The reception is palpable. Listening to the listening, the actor adjusts the speed of an entrance, the intensity of the first line spoken or the length of a pause. An actor learns when to hold back and when to open up based on the agility and responsiveness of the audience.

•

The realization of *Cabin Pressure* was a two-year process made possible by the National Theatre Artist Residency Program, administered by Theatre Communications Group and funded by The Pew Charitable Trusts. Over the course of two years I worked closely with the staff of Actors Theatre of Louisville (ATL) and the SITI Company in intensive collaboration with Michael Dixon and Adrien-Alice Hansel at Actors Theatre. We chose forty-seven Louisville "civilians" from different age groups, different religions and diverse theatergoing experiences to take part in the first stages of what we called the Audience Project.

The first year encompassed work on Noel Coward's *Private Lives*, which I directed at ATL with members of the SITI Company. During this period of development and performance of *Private Lives*, each of the Audience Project participants agreed to attend a minimum of two rehearsals, one technical rehearsal, one performance and to take part in post-show discussions, from the stage, with the audiences for *Private Lives*. During first year of the residency, I took as much opportunity as time allowed to conduct ongoing discussions with the members of the Audience Project. It was important to fully describe the project and share my thoughts and questions about the creative role of the audience. I wanted to familiarize everyone with the terrain, pose the central questions of the project, and make clear what was expected. These sessions were always taped and transcribed for future use.

At first it was disorienting to have the Audience Project in the room with us in rehearsal as we struggled to find our way through *Private Lives*. Early on, the actors complained about the discomfort of the situation. They took me aside and pointed out that a rehearsal, for them, is a vulnerable period and they felt that they should be able to make mistakes freely without civilians watching. They asked what their responsibility to the visitors was supposed to be and wondered how they should relate to them. This, for me, was the first insight into the relationship between audience and actor: the director is the very first audience and the only person that the actors should have a relationship with until the production is ready. In order to continue with this project, I told the actors that they were responsible only to the line between them and me. They had absolutely no responsibility to the visitors. At a certain point, the director can turn the actors over to a wider audience.

During the run of *Private Lives*, certain performances featured post-show discussions with members of the Audience Project and me, from the stage, for audiences who had just seen the show. These sessions were also taped and transcribed for use in the development of *Cabin Pressure*.

At the end of the *Private Lives* phase of the project, I conducted individual interviews with all Audience Project participants. Each interview lasted about a half hour and was also taped and transcribed.

In the interviews, I asked the Audience Project members about their experiences in rehearsal. I wanted to know what had intrigued them and how being in rehearsal had changed their experience of the production in front of a regular audience. I asked them other questions about what they remembered most vividly from the rehearsal process. I asked them to formulate questions they would have wanted to ask the actors. I asked why they went to the theater and how going to the theater affected their lives. I asked if they preferred going to the theater alone or with other people.

Some of the text from these interviews as well as transcriptions of the talk-back sessions eventually became dialogue in our new play *Cabin Pressure*.

The rest of the text in *Cabin Pressure* was sampled freely from various theoretical writings about the actor/audience relationship as well as excerpts from existing plays, including *Private Lives* and Edward Albee's *Who's Afraid of Virginia Woolf.*

All of the actors in *Cabin Pressure*—SITI Company members Ellen Lauren, Kelley Maurer, Stephen Webber, Barney O'Hanlon and Will Bond—had performed extensively on the ATL stages and were well known to Louisville audiences. They read all of the interviews and the collected theoretical writings and plays culled by the literary staff at ATL, and from this material we fashioned a play. The process of writing the play was one of intense collaboration among the actors, sound designer Darron West, stage manager Megan Wanlass, and myself. In any moment we were willing to follow the lead of whoever in the room was onto something. We never knew ahead of time what would develop or who would lead. We tried to listen to one another and to the work that was manifesting itself.

Within the structure of *Cabin Pressure*, we explored the different qualities of *m'ai* found in the history of theatergoing. We achieved this by dramatizations of the many actor/audience relationships found throughout the history of theater, such as: spectacle, ritual, confession, participation and the "fourth wall."

Perhaps because we had no idea what we were hatching, the performances of *Cabin Pressure* at the Humana Festival were revelatory. Suddenly we were performing a play about the people in the room and the response of those very people was palpable. There were wonderful moments when we sensed that the audience was aware of themselves in the room, aware of their participation in the creation of an event. We were all together, breathing common air.

I hope that *Cabin Pressure* will continue in forthcoming performances to be a celebration of the potential humanity of the audience/actor relationship in the theater. In a time when computers, television, film and mega-malls dominate and mediate our relationships with others, the theater is a place to strengthen and heighten our direct connection with one another.

Excerpts from the Text

Some of this material has been sampled from published sources, which are noted. The remaining material is drawn from statements made by Anne Bogart and members of the Actors Theatre of Louisville Audience Project.

Q and A II

YOSHI: [I can say] "manipulation." "Style." With a capital "S." Um—"acrobatics." Uh—silence, whistling, sighing, faster pulse, heavier breathing, tension in the pit of the stomach, sexual arousal, and—I guess misguided passion.

ROZANNE: It's—it's just pretty.

EDDIE: What did you think?

VANESSA: I liked it.

BERT: Hmmm….

EDDIE: Did you learn anything? *(Silence.)* What was your experience?

ROZANNE: It was fun.

BERT/VANESSA: Uh….

BERT: I was very embarrassed most of the time.

VANESSA: I was uncomfortable.

EDDIE: What is it that makes an actor interesting?

ROZANNE: Teeth. Like her front teeth look like her smile went back to her ears. And her front teeth were like this big and I really liked it. And uh—um—she—her eyes looked really huge and like they were pointing upwards. Her role reminded me of a Dr. Seuss character. Because the way she smiled and like her teeth were really huge and I'm nearsighted and so um—I think that helps my creativity, I guess. Because, uh, otherwise, everything is so—you know.

EDDIE: Where were you sitting?

ROZANNE: In the balcony.

YOSHI: I was so far away I couldn't hear anything that was going on except for an occasional line. And I wanted to get up and come over just to listen, you know. Uh—so I missed that a lot. And I was uncomfortable physically. I was chilly and the—the chair got harder and harder. And I was desperate for a cup of coffee.

VANESSA: I really do like sitting down front. On the stage if you let me. The closer the better. I wanna feel the vibes. I wanna feel the heat off the actors. It's like being close to the drums. You know how—when you can feel the vibe. You can feel that off an actor.

EDDIE: What were your expectations? *(Silence.)* Was there anything you really liked?

BERT: I love the magic. It's just magic because it's—it's lights and it's—it's movement and it's—it's—in another time and space than I am. I mean I'm there but—you know, it's sort of watching fantasy ge[t]—happen in front of your eyes or—or unfold—um—and the bigger—I mean, the bigger the show, the bolder the show, the brighter the show, the more I love it. Um—cause, I just—I like everything really big.

EDDIE: Who is the audience? *(Silence.)* What do you feel when you are sitting in an audience?

ROZANNE: You're in—number one, you're—it's a live performance. Number two, in a room full of people. And three, you don't know half of them. Most of them. So—you know, you're already in clothes you might not like, wear on a normal basis. Might feel constricted. It's the end of the day. It was the end of the d[ay]—a long day for me. I had my husband with me so I had to entertain his—whatever—was going on with him. And the cigarette smoke was the last thing I could handle.

EDDIE: What is the actor doing? *(Silence.)* If you could ask an actor anything, what would it be?

YOSHI: Well, do—do they mi[nd]—do they mind doing the—you know, over and over again?

BERT: Well, do—do they mi[nd]—do they mind doing the—you know, over and over again?

VANESSA: Well, do—do they mi[nd]—do they mind doing the—you know, over and over again?

ROZANNE: Well, do—do they mi[nd]—do they mind doing the—you know, over and over again?

EDDIE: Who is the actor secretly addressing?[i] Audiences clearly play a role but what kind of role? And what kind of audience?[ii] Is the audience a group of individual specters each dreaming the action in a dark room? Is the audience a number of people who are each potential rescuers to the drowning of a civilization? Or is the audience a group of people wanting the relaxation of an entertainment—to be comfortably purged, fascinated, amused? Must the audience, like the actor, be an active participant in the performance? The baffling question for the actor is "who is the audience?" To whom does the actor personally dedicate his or her performance?[iii] Who is the actor secretly addressing?[iv]

Q and A IV

EDDIE: Which brings me to my next question. When does it begin?

YOSHI: Yeah, it's like a snowball. Is that, you know, all of us know that what we have to is, you know, you can start with anything. You put something on the stage—you start with an idea. But then you start to intensify it. Like…storing chemicals or something. Something starts to happen in the room. The wonderful thing is it's about the presence "in the room." And the play doesn't make sense unless it's actually happening. There's something happening. All the good ideas in the world, uh, don't, don't mean anything unless there's something, some quality, that's generated. And I have a theory that's never been proved but I think you cannot disguise the rehearsal process, uh, from the performance. What I mean is: something that one feels in performance; the politics in the room; the values; how, how people are, uh, interacting; the quality of relationships; the quality of attention in the room, uh, is evident on the stage in performance. You can't hide behind any, you can't hide behind a bad rehearsal process. So that in a way, everybody's responsibility comes to create a, a, a beautiful quality of concentration and, dare I use the word, artfulness, in the room. And I think one thing that I learned by being in the room is that it was very important that I contributed as well and that my presence was, was felt. Immensely. Um.

EDDIE: What is the actor doing?

Q and A VII: The Confession

EDDIE: I've become extremely interested in the relationship between the audience and the actors on the stage. You can look at it historically, the history of audiences in the history of the world, you can look at it in terms of this country: what is the role of the audience in this country at the turn of this century?

I believe theater is a form of active culture. That participating in the theater is an act of leaning forward as opposed to leaning back. For me, the most thrilling experiences in the theater have always been ones where I've felt like I've had a role to play in this room, where something is asked of me as an audience member and I have to meet the actors halfway. Because it's about that, being in the room together, this notion of breathing common air, and that the relationship between the audience and the actor is a circular one.

Theater is not a descriptive art form, it is a poetic medium where you do the least on stage so that the imagination is released in the audience. So just hints are given and and what that does is that asks something of an audience; it asks you to participate emotionally, intellectually, spiritually in every way.

So that every beeper that goes off, or every cough or shuffling, every, uh, anything becomes part of the experience, and the generosity of the audience will allow the actors to do more.

And that, the vital link between the actor and the audience is something which is now, in our culture, suffering. So I decided to create a project in which we really together investigated this vital and creative link in an attempt to strengthen the lifeblood between the actors and the audience, starting with the notion that being an audience is a creative act...

The Interview

EDDIE: Why do you go?

VANESSA: I go to the theater because for me, it's the sense that anything can happen. Anything can happen.

ROZANNE: I've been going to the theater alone since I was a little girl. My family didn't like the theater. But they always made sure I had a ticket.

YOSHI: I believe theater is another way to exist.

BERT: I go because life is unbearable.

EDDIE: I go because it's otherworldly and it's festive and I like the way people smell, and I like what they wear and it's a lot better than seeing a play on television.

VANESSA: Just the being still or the, or the quiet movement or whatever or just the listening of the audience not knowing exactly what was going to happen, and you're sitting there, because it's so real.

YOSHI: So, theater is, uh, I go, really, to be entertained to, uh, lose what I do the rest of my time and to smile, or to gasp, or uh, to kind of vicariously live a different life.

ROZANNE: As I've gotten older—I look at life a lot differently and maybe it's a little more fragile now. So I look for the touch of emotion. I don't want to go to the theater and have it be heavy. I don't want to be transcended into deep thought. I basically want to be entertained. I want to sit there and eat the icing off the cake. But I don't really want the cake.

BERT: Oh, that's almost intangible—that's again, something deep in me that it answers. I think probably I like getting away from reality. A little. I grew up Bohemian and reading and getting away, being a loner, which I've always been. I think maybe I gravitated to the theater as a way of getting out of myself.

EDDIE: I've always liked the mystery. I was one of the fortunate ones. Now most theaters don't have curtains. But when we went fifty years ago, they all had curtains, so you never knew what was behind until the curtain went up. So you really got a feeling of mystery.

VANESSA: My parents gave us a subscription. My wife really likes the theater and it's a planned entertainment. It's not an off-the-cuff thing to do. It's nice.

ROZANNE: The art of theater is an art of feeling. The subject matter of the theater is the beating of the human heart. And the human heart is very old.[v]

BERT: Think of this moment. All that has ever been is in this moment; all that will ever be is in this moment. This is drama; this is theater—to be aware of the Now.[vi]

YOSHI: It's always been important to go on the stage. The stage is something special. The way you behave must be different. Theater is not a private place, it's a special place and it's a forum. What's important once in this forum is to ask a question.[vii]

EDDIE: But as I see it, our theater is in a rut, it's so damn conventional. The modern stage is nothing but an old prejudice, nothing but a sad and dreary routine.[viii]

VANESSA: The theater remains the form most dependent upon, fascinated with, drawn, quartered by and fixated upon the body, its vulnerabilities, pain and disappearance.[ix]

[i] Chaikin, Joseph. *The Presence of the Actor.*

[ii] Bennett, Susan. *Theatre Audiences.*

[iii] Mamet, David. *True and False.*

[iv] Chaikin, Joseph. *The Presence of the Actor.*

[v] Edmond Jones, Robert. *Towards a New Theatre.*

[vi] Edmond Jones, Robert. *Towards a New Theatre.*

[vii] Wilson, Robert. *Interviews.*

[viii] Chekhov, Anton. *The Seagull.*

[ix] Blau, Herbert. *Distance in Theatre.*

Aloha, Say the Pretty Girls
by Naomi Iizuka

BIOGRAPHY

Naomi Iizuka made her ATL debut in 1997 with *Polaroid Stories*, which was originally commissioned by En Garde Arts and received the 1998 PEN Center USA West Award for Drama. Other plays include *Scheherazade, Skin, Marlowe's Eye* and *Tattoo Girl*. Her work has been produced at the Dallas Theatre Center, SoHo Rep, Sledgehammer Theatre in San Diego, Printer's Devil and Annex in Seattle, and Campo Santo and the Magic Theatre in San Francisco. Her plays have also been workshopped at Midwest PlayLabs, A.S.K. Theater Projects, the Public Theater and New York Theatre Workshop. *Aloha, Say the Pretty Girls* was workshopped at San Francisco's Brava, A Contemporary Theatre in Seattle and the Bay Area Playwrights Festival. Ms. Iizuka is the recipient of a TCG Artist-in-Residence grant, Princeton University's Hodder Fellowship, a McKnight Advancement Grant and a Jerome Playwriting Fellowship. She received her BA from Yale University and her MFA from the University of California–San Diego.

HUMANA FESTIVAL PRODUCTION

Aloha, Say the Pretty Girls premiered at the Humana Festival of New American Plays in February 1999. It was directed by Jon Jory with the following cast:

Will/Derek	Bruce McKenzie
Vivian	Carla Harting
Joy/Lee	Peter Pamela Rose
Myrna/Richard	Nick Garrison
Efran/Jed	Todd Cerveris
Wendy	Caitlin Miller
Jason	Derek Cecil

and the following production staff:

Scenic Designer	Paul Owen
Costume Designer	Jack Taggart
Lighting Designer	Pip Gordon
Sound Designer	Malcolm Nicholls
Properties Designer	Mark Walston
Production Stage Manager	Debra Acquavella
Assistant Stage Manager	Jennifer Wills
Dramaturg	Amy Wegener
Assistant Dramaturg	Ilana M. Brownstein
Casting	Laura Richin Casting

CHARACTERS

WILL/DEREK

VIVIAN

JOY/LEE

MYRNA/RICHARD

EFRAN/JED

WENDY

JASON

TIME & PLACE

ACT 1: new york. the not-too-distant-past.

ACT 2: hawaii, alaska, and other exotic locales. the not-too-distant-future.

Peter Pamela Rose, Caitlin Miller, Bruce McKenzie and Carla Harting
in *Aloha, Say the Pretty Girls* by Naomi Iizuka

23rd Annual Humana Festival of New American Plays
Actors Theatre of Louisville, 1999
photo by Richard Trigg

Aloha, Say the Pretty Girls

ACT ONE

1.

in darkness, will is a tiny figure standing on the edge.

WILL: bye, good-bye, ciao, catch you later, catch you on the rebound, gotta jet, gotta dash, outta here, i'm outta here, i'm history, till we meet again, adieu, farewell, aloha. aloha means good-bye—
(a light goes on within.)

2.

a miniscule apartment in the city. a large plant. vivian is making a piñata with papier-mâché and wire. it's a large, indeterminate animal.

VIVIAN: will? will, is that you?
(enter will.)
VIVIAN: hi.
WILL: hi.
VIVIAN: *(holding up her creation.)* how does it look?
WILL: nice, really nice.
VIVIAN: it's a piñata for myrna's class. isn't that neat?
WILL: yes, very, vivian—?
VIVIAN: it's a komodo dragon. a komodo dragon is like a living dinosaur, that's what myrna says. to look at a komodo dragon is to look at something pre-historic and strange. i hope the kids like it, i hope they can tell what it is, they'll have to use their imaginations, and that's ok, because kids are really

imaginative, don't you think? god, i love kids, kids are great, they really are, they're what it's all about. don't you think? will?

WILL: i don't love you anymore.

VIVIAN: what?

WILL: i love joy.

VIVIAN: what?

WILL: her name is joy, you don't know her, she's no one you know, she's nothing like you, we're deeply and profoundly in love, don't ask me why, i don't know why, i don't know how it happened, it all just kind of snuck up on me. i finally know what people mean when they say they're in love. say something, vivvie, please.

VIVIAN: wow. i mean, wow.

WILL: say something else.

VIVIAN: uh, weren't we, you know, like, in love? i mean, i thought we were, i thought we had been for a while now, and now you're saying you stopped, you just kinda stopped, and doesn't that seem a little random and arbitrary and strange, i mean doesn't that seem a little strange to you? will?

WILL: ok, look, vivian, i know this is hard, but these things happen to people, they happen all the time, and people live, they go on, they do ok, they survive. say something else.

VIVIAN: i think i'm going to be sick.

WILL: say something else.

VIVIAN: ok. i wish you and joy nothing but the best.

WILL: no hard feelings.

VIVIAN: no, none, none whatsoever. really.

WILL: great. ok, all right then. i'll see you, vivvie, i'll see you around.

(the sound of chaos in the jungle. will exits. vivian grabs the plant and exits. myrna enters, picks up the komodo dragon, and exits. darkness. the sound of unseen animals skittering in the shadows. joy appears in a bubble of light.)

JOY: will?

(enter will.)

WILL: joy?

JOY: will

WILL: joy

(the jungle sounds grow.)

the jungle sounds turn into the chatter and laughing of antic children. myrna appears holding the komodo dragon. she addresses the children.

MYRNA: all right, children, that's enough. this is a komodo dragon. a komodo dragon is a kind of lizard. it lives in the jungles of inner borneo. the komodo dragon is like a living dinosaur. this is what we used to look like, we all used to look like this, and then things changed, and we changed, and the only thing that didn't change was the komodo dragon which stayed exactly the same. animals don't look like this anymore, they all died out, except for the komodo dragon which lives on, we know not why, it's a mystery. this is also a piñata. it's a komodo dragon and a piñata. komodo dragon, piñata. piñatas come from mexico which is nowhere near borneo, and that's ok, the world is full of contradictions such as these, life goes on. piñatas are made of papier-mâché and wire, and are filled with all kinds of sweet-tasting surprises. in mexico, little children put on blindfolds, and take the piñata, and smash it with sticks. it's a tradition. i don't have a stick so i'm just going to use my hands. one, two, three. hoopa.

(myrna destroys the piñata and exits. the sound of frenzied animals in the jungle. and then silence. will and joy live in a bubble of bright, happy light.)

JOY: will

WILL: joy

JOY: will

WILL: joy

JOY: will

WILL: joy

(vivian appears with plant.)

VIVIAN: will?

(the scream of siamangs. jungle sounds grow louder. the bubble of light bursts.)

a bell. light. a miniscule pet store. no animals in sight. efran gazes into a giant, densely foliaged terrarium. enter wendy.

EFRAN: hi there. can i help you?

WENDY: i'm from the temp agency, some girl quit like out of the blue, i got a call. o my god, i'm going to love this job. i love animals, i love them so much, their musky smell, their mute animalistic heat. right now, i'm like an actress, i'm like laura in glass menagerie, tennessee williams' glass menagerie, which is kinda like a zoo, and laura, she's kinda like the zookeeper, but the animals aren't real, they're made of glass, and at the end they break, and it's really intense. so, uh, where are they? the pets. this is a pet store, and yet i see no pets.

EFRAN: well, the turtles are over there, and we just got some hermit crabs in yesterday, little baby hermit crabs. they're over there. by the turtles.

WENDY: no no no, i'm talking about mammals: kitties and puppies, elephants, giraffes.

EFRAN: o, we don't stock mammals here. they're really high-maintenance, mammals are super-high maintenance, and the owner's like: it's just not worth the hassle. it's store policy. if it was up to me, we'd have mammals. i like mammals. mammals are swell.

WENDY: are you kidding? mammals are great. we, we are mammals. first and foremost, when you strip it all away, that's what we are: mammals. don't you ever think about these things?

EFRAN: no, i guess not.

WENDY: well like what do you think about?

EFRAN: i don't know. stuff.

WENDY: what kinda stuff?

EFRAN: i don't know. you know. stuff.

WENDY: well like what are you thinking about right this second?

EFRAN: nothing.

WENDY: i don't believe you. tell the truth.

EFRAN: really, honestly, my mind is a blank, it's just a total blank.

WENDY: you're kinda mysterious, aren't you? you're a very mysterious person.

EFRAN: no, not really, no.

WENDY: where are you going?

EFRAN: i need to, uh, feed the turtles.

WENDY: right this second?

EFRAN: uh huh. i hear them calling.

WENDY: i'll help.

EFRAN: that's ok, really, i think i got it covered.

(efran flees. wendy pursues. a ruckus in the jungle. the sound of growling.)

5.

a miniscule apartment in the city. a large kennel. jason crouches at the entrance of the kennel. from inside the kennel, the deep, sonorous growl of a full-grown, dominant male.

JASON: hey, otis, it's me, buddy. what's going on, what's going on, big guy?

DEREK: *(off.)* shit shit shit.

(enter derek holding shit-spattered pages of his work-in-progress.)

DEREK: i'm going to kill that dog. do you know what this is, jason, do you?

JASON: uh, it looks like the written word.

DEREK: yes, uh huh, that's right, writing, yes, it's my novel, my work-in-progress, and right now, see, it's covered in shit, dog shit, otis shit.

JASON: wow. drag. you know, i think something's up with otis. i think he's like depressed.

DEREK: depressed, you say?

JASON: that's my take on it.

DEREK: he's shitting on my stuff, jason.

JASON: i don't know what to tell you, dude. the way otis' mind works, it's like a mystery. like when he's sleeping, you know, and his eyes roll back in his head and he makes these little "oof oof oof" noises, and i think he's maybe dreaming some weird dog dream, but there's no way i'll ever know for sure, 'cause he can't tell me, that's the deal with dogs, they keep you guessing.

DEREK: otis hates me.

JASON: no, derek, no. see, dogs don't hate. dogs love. dogs are all about love.

DEREK: are you high? i see how he looks at me. he's got a plan. he's got a plan and he's big. do you see how big he's getting? he's too big. nobody should have a dog this big in the city. something bad could happen, something very very bad.

JASON: dude, you need to relax. nothing bad's going to happen. i mean, what could happen?

DEREK: all kinds of things.

JASON: derek, you gotta get out more, get out of your head. you're tense. you're so tense. you gotta relax. just relax—o wait, wait, ssh. he's sleeping. i'm gonna go out, get some air, you wanna maybe come with?

DEREK: i think i'll pass.

JASON: need anything?

DEREK: all set.

JASON: ok, dude, i'll be back. watch otis for me, will ya?

DEREK: sure. sure thing.

JASON: thanks, derek.

DEREK: you bet.

>*(jason exits. derek approaches otis' kennel with murder in his heart. the growling begins. derek skulks away, otis' kennel in tow. he clutches his shitty manuscript.)*

6.

>*the roar of a subway. a deserted subway platform. lee and vivian are waiting. vivian holds the plant.*

LEE: give me the plant.

VIVIAN: what?

LEE: give me the plant.

VIVIAN: i don't think i'm understanding you.

LEE: *(pulling out a gun.)* give me the plant or i'm gonna blow your head off.

VIVIAN: ok, you know what? i don't think i can help you.

LEE: i got a gun.

VIVIAN: ok, wow, you're not really listening to me, or maybe i'm just not making myself clear: i'm having a really weird and crummy day, which happens to be just one in a string of weird and crummy days that i've been having recently, for reasons which i don't even want to get into with you, because frankly it's personal and none of your business, and i don't know if it's this city or if it's me, but right now, i'm telling you, i really don't need this nonsense.

LEE: are you retarded or what? i got a gun.

VIVIAN: we're not communicating very well, are we?

LEE: give me that goddamn plant or i swear to god i'm gonna do something.

VIVIAN: you're going to do something? that's so open-ended. what does that mean: "you're going to do something?" maybe i'm going to do something. what do you think of that?

>*(lee and vivian struggle. lee pries away vivian's plant. she falls.)*

VIVIAN: ow.

LEE: shit.

>*(the sound of growling. exit lee. exit vivian. the roar of an airplane.)*

7.

the hum of an airplane. jed is a tiny figure in the darkness. he wears an air steward's uniform and an inflatable vest. he gestures towards the exits.

JED: dear dehmee, dehmay, dehmee, dear deemeedeemeedeemee, dear ms. moore: i have been an admirer of your work since st. elmo's fire which I liked a lot, in particular your character who was beautiful and glamorous and drank like a fish because she felt lost and unloved in the world, and i could really relate to that, having myself had a small drinking problem once from which i have since totally and completely recovered. i became a true fan, however, upon seeing the movie ghost, which i loved, and in particular was touched by the fantastical sequence in which you dance with whoopi goldberg who miraculously transforms during the dance into patrick swayze, your late husband, because i, like many others, have come to believe in channeling, soothsaying and other paranormal activities, and had no trouble whatsoever buying that whoopi could embody the ghost of patrick. also, and most important, i believe you were truly sad in that movie, and because i am someone who has known sadness in my own life, i felt deeply connected to you from then on, and wished i could have coffee with you and talk about stuff, because i can't help feeling we have this special bond, and that we could be best friends, and that i could be your personal assistant or something, because i'm a really fun and efficient person, and a good listener, and i need another job, and more than that, i need a calling, which being your right-hand man would, in some senses, be, because the idea of being aimless and without direction, treading psychic water for the rest of my life, however long the rest of my life may be, makes me want to stick my head in an oven or something, if you know what i'm saying, if you know what i mean. write me or call. yours forever, jed.
(the roar of a low-flying airplane. jed is engulfed by darkness.)

8.

a tiny plane hurtles by overhead. will and joy are happy, young lovers. they live in a bubble of bright, happy light. enter vivian, bruised and muddied. she darts behind a small shrub.

JOY: will
WILL: joy

JOY: will

WILL: joy

JOY: will

WILL: joy

JOY: will

WILL: i love you

JOY: i love you, too

WILL: will you marry me joy?

JOY: o will—sure, yes, i mean, yes.

(will and joy exit. enter richard. he passes vivian.)

RICHARD: vivian? vivian, is that you?

VIVIAN: hi, richard.

RICHARD: girl, i haven't seen you in a million years. how are you?

VIVIAN: o you know.

RICHARD: how's will?

VIVIAN: o well, will and i broke up. i actually just ran into him and his new fiancée, joy, i run into them everywhere i go, they didn't see me, they were too busy being in love, it's like they're really in love, it's like they're really truly happy, it's like they're the happiest people in the whole wide world, isn't that weird, don't you think that's weird?

RICHARD: vivvie, honey, you're babbling. here, you have twigs in your hair.

VIVIAN: thanks. you look great, richard.

RICHARD: o my god, i feel great. i just got the greatest job in the whole universe. it's like the most amazing thing. i'm like the personal assistant to somebody very, very famous. i bet you'll never guess who. guess, go on, guess.

VIVIAN: you know, richard, i'm not really in the mood.

RICHARD: demi.

VIVIAN: who?

RICHARD: demi moore. isn't that amazing?

VIVIAN: that's wonderful, richard. congratulations.

RICHARD: she's so beautiful and glamorous, but she's totally down to earth. all that stuff that people say about her being temperamental, don't you believe it. she's just assertive, and strong, she's really really strong. people are threatened by a strong woman, but you know, you just have to ignore all that stuff because in the end, it's the art that matters, that's all that matters. we talk about it, demi and me.

VIVIAN: richard, my life is not as it should be.

RICHARD: demi feels that way sometimes. she has her bad days. demi and me, we talk about it. we talk about a lot of things. it's the best.

VIVIAN: i don't know what's happening. i don't know what to do.

RICHARD: life is complicated. demi's life is unbelievably complicated. i plan her day, i know. i screen her calls, i answer her mail, i listen to her rant and rave, i'm her ear, i tell her what i really think about things. she respects that about me a lot.

VIVIAN: ok, richard, i think i'm going now.

RICHARD: already?

VIVIAN: yeah, i'm afraid so.

RICHARD: vivvie, honey, are you ok?

VIVIAN: no, no, i'm not.

RICHARD: listen, vivvie, why don't you come to la? a little change of scenery, a little change of pace, shake things up. why not? i'll hook you up. new place, new life, new you. la: think about it.

(the sound of a jungle. exit richard. exit vivian. somewhere else, derek walks by furtively pulling a cart on which sits otis' kennel. he clutches his shitty manuscript.)

9.

a pet store. a giant, densely foliaged terrarium. efran gazes into the terrarium. a bell. enter jason.

EFRAN: hi there, can i help you?

JASON: yeah, i want to buy a toy, for my dog.

EFRAN: does he fetch?

JASON: no.

EFRAN: does he play tug-o-war?

JASON: no.

EFRAN: is he in any way playful?

JASON: he likes to chew. he likes to sit around and chew. right now i think he's kinda depressed.

EFRAN: *(retrieving a ball.)* here. indestructible, easy to clean, and it bounces.

JASON: wow. cool. thanks.

(jason exits with ball. a bell. enter lee with vivian's plant.)

EFRAN: hi there, can i help you?

LEE: this plant is dying. i don't want to be around that. who wants to be around that?

EFRAN: this is a pet store. we don't do plants.

LEE: *(chucking the plant into oblivion.)* i'm thinking i want a dog, i'm thinking i want a big dog. they say a dog is man's best friend.

EFRAN: so i've heard. sadly, we don't carry dogs here. we don't carry dogs or cats or mammals of any kind. can i interest you in a turtle?

LEE: i don't want a turtle.

EFRAN: how about a frog?

LEE: i don't want a frog. frogs suck.

> *(lee spots the terrarium.)*

LEE: what's in there?

EFRAN: that's a giant python. sixteen feet long. this guy can eat a small pig for lunch.

LEE: yeah, how much?

EFRAN: o no, see, the snake belongs to the owner. he's not for sale.

LEE: screw that. i want that snake. that snake is mine.

EFRAN: sorry, buddy, you're out of luck.

LEE: *(pulling out a gun.)* i don't think so, pet shop boy.

EFRAN: o god don't shoot.

LEE: hands in the air, now. *(gazing into the terrarium.)* where is he?

EFRAN: he's hiding. he's shy.

LEE: i want the terrarium. the terrarium comes with.

EFRAN: take it, take it all, it's yours, it's all yours.

LEE: yeah? ok great.

> *(lee exits, taking the terrarium with. strange birds call out. water dripping and the swoosh of creatures moving through the undergrowth. the sound of a jungle. wendy appears. she takes a bite of apple. exit efran.)*

10.

> *the roar of a subway. a deserted subway platform. derek and wendy are waiting. wendy is eating an apple. derek clutches his shitty manuscript.*

WENDY: whatcha thinking, stranger?

DEREK: nothing.

WENDY: what's that?

DEREK: nothing.

WENDY: can i see?

DEREK: no.

WENDY: it's kinda stinky.

DEREK: do you mind.

WENDY: you know, you seem really wound up. i can tell. i'm like a very intuitive person. i'm an actress. i act. well, actually i temp, i'm a temp, but the thing about temping is that it's temporary, and doesn't always work out, and anyway it's not what i really am, because what i really am is an actress. what's wrong?

DEREK: nothing.

WENDY: i think you're lying.

DEREK: i think you're weird.

WENDY: ok, but this is the thing, when you lie, your soul shrivels up little by little until it looks like one of those little, shrunken heads you see in photographs, they look like little, dried kumquats, do you know what i'm talking about, do you know what i mean?

DEREK: all right look, maybe it's none of your business, ok? maybe there's something called appropriate distance. maybe i don't feel like baring my soul to some stranger i don't even know.

WENDY: i get you. no problem. it's cool. the thing is i like true stories. i like them a lot. i think they're kinda sexy.

DEREK: o?

WENDY: uh huh. the truth is sexy, it's very, very sexy. i think of the truth as a kinda mating call in the wild.

DEREK: you know, you have a very small mouth, and yet you talk so much with it.

WENDY: i'm very, very verbal.

DEREK: yes, yes, you are.

WENDY: *(offering some apple.)* last bite. want some?

(derek eats some apple. the roar of the subway. darkness. the sound of a jungle.)

11.

the sound of an airplane. jed is a tiny figure on the ground. he wears an air steward's uniform.

JED: dear ms. moore, last night, i saw your mother interviewed on tv, and i have to say, as your future friend and personal assistant, i was completely mortified on your behalf. i mean, no offense to your mother, because no matter what, i realize she is your mother, but can i just say, what a lush, what a shrew. no wonder you cut her off without a dime, and won't take any of her phone calls. i sympathize with your plight completely as my mother, too, is all of the above, and when i am successful and famous enough to have somebody to screen my calls, i, too, will shun my mother. as to the photos of you naked and pregnant on the cover of vanity fair, i have to say i am torn. though you are always beautiful and glamorous and a star, seeing you naked and pregnant on the cover of a national magazine was somehow strange and upsetting to me. i would also like to express my deep reservations about gi jane. i don't really know what to think about gi jane. she seems really unpleasant and kinda scary to me, but that's a whole other can of worms i would just rather not open at this time. i wonder where you are right this second. i wonder what you're doing and what you're thinking about. though i feel so close to you, sometimes you are a complete mystery to me. yours forever, jed.

(incipient turbulence. the roar of an airplane. jed flees. somewhere else, myrna watches a plane fly overhead. myrna spots vivian's plant in the trash. she picks it up and goes.)

12.

a miniscule apartment. enter myrna with plant. vivian lights up a bong with difficulty. myrna sets down the plant, and begins to pack. the intermittent sound of burbling bong water.

VIVIAN: bad things are happening to me, myrna. is there a reason? is this a test, am i being tested?

MYRNA: vivian, you are the architect of your own destiny.

VIVIAN: i don't know what that means. what does that mean?

MYRNA: you are the the lone wildebeest at the edge of the herd.

VIVIAN: wow. where is my herd? i think my herd is hiding. i have a brother, but i think he's maybe in a different herd.

MYRNA: face it, honey: you have no herd. you're herdless. people sense this. they smell it off your skin like a pheromone. you know, pheromone. a glandular scent, a distinctive musk that signals fertility, sexual readiness, and on occasion, fear.

VIVIAN: i'm not afraid, just deeply deeply depressed.

MYRNA: depression is anger turned inward.

VIVIAN: you know, i don't know what to do with that information.

MYRNA: be decisive. take action. bust some balls.

VIVIAN: are you going somewhere, myrna?

MYRNA: i am, honey, i am. myrna's moving on. i've done all i can here. there's so much to do in a global sense. can you fill in for me at school tomorrow by any chance?

VIVIAN: sure, no problem. i love children. i love them so much.

MYRNA: what's going on, vivian? something's up, something is different, i can't quite put my finger on it. what is happening to your posture? here, don't be such a limp noodle, sit up, up. you know, vivian, you should smoke less pot. pot dulls your senses.

VIVIAN: uh huh.

MYRNA: it makes you silly. pot makes you silly. did you know that men who smoke pot grow breasts? do you want to be a man with breasts? is that what you want out of life, to be a man with breasts?

(vivian falls asleep. myrna exits with suitcase.)

13.

will and joy appear in a bubble of light. a tiny bed. joy wears a nightgown. will wears pajamas. he reads. joy watches him read.

WILL: do I want to be a man with breasts? the ancient soothsayer tiresias was a wise man who could predict the future. but he was also a blind man with breasts. i think the moral of the story is tit for tat. something's got to give. so then the question is: if i could predict the future and be very, very wise would i trade in who i am now to become a blind man with breasts?

JOY: wow, will, i don't know. that's a biggie.

WILL: what am i willing to sacrifice? my eyeball? my thumb? would i be willing to chop off my thumb? would it be worth it?

JOY: will, that is so deep.

WILL: thanks, joy.

JOY: you are so brilliant.

WILL: thanks, joy.

JOY: what am i, will?

WILL: what do you mean?

JOY: well, i mean, if you're brilliant, what am i?

WILL: i don't know, joy. you're nice. you're really really nice. you're the nicest girl i know. i love you, joy. i love you. joy?

(the sound of growling.)
JOY: what was that?
WILL: i don't know.
JOY: go look.
WILL: i don't think that's necessary.
JOY: please just go and look.
WILL: it's nothing, joy. trust me.
   (the sound of growling.)
JOY: something's happening, something's out there. i want you to go look. for chrissakes, will, you're the man.
WILL: what is that supposed to mean?
JOY: i don't know. just make sure everything's ok, please. just go. here.
   (joy gives will a penlight. will disappears into the darkness with only a tiny beam of light to guide him.)

14.

   the sound of chaos in the jungle. myrna appears with suitcase and piñatas.

MYRNA: this is a baboon, this is a sea turtle, this is a salamander, this is a fruit bat, this is an amoeba, it's hard to see, it's very small. these are all fossils. these are also piñatas. remember piñatas? fossil, piñata. fossil, piñata. this is a mummy. a mummy is kinda like a fossil. it, too, is a piñata. mummy, piñata. mummy, piñata. this young lady was ritually sacrificed and buried at the lip of an active volcano the incans called ampato. there she lay under the permafrost for centuries, wearing only festive, native textiles and a headdress made of brightly colored macaw feathers. german tourists stumbled across her shrunken body while hiking in a remote region of the andes. they named the mummy edelweiss after a pretty, alpine flower.
   (a burst of simian activity. chaos in the jungle.)

15.

   vivian hears a noise and wakes up. she's wearing brightly colored feathers in her hair. will enters. he wears prosthetic breasts.

VIVIAN: who's there? will?

WILL: i don't love you anymore, i don't want to be your friend, i don't want to keep in touch, i don't want to get together for coffee. frankly, vivian, i wish you'd just disappear off the face of the earth, so i wouldn't keep running into you.

VIVIAN: will?

WILL: what?

VIVIAN: why do you have breasts?

WILL: i don't. these are not real breasts, they're a projection, a crisis of identity, a grappling with the other—i don't know why i have breasts, vivian, don't change the subject. why is it that i see you everywhere i go? what is that all about?

VIVIAN: o please, will, it's not like i'm following you. don't flatter yourself.

WILL: because either you're following me or i'm losing my mind. i don't know what's happening, i don't know what's going on, i'm ambivalent, i'm in denial, i don't know what i am—do you have something you want to tell me, vivian? i sense you're keeping something from me, some little secret, some piece of unfinished business.

VIVIAN: what does this have to do with your breasts, will?

WILL: i don't know what it has to do with my breasts, i don't know what these breasts have to do with anything, i'm stupefied.

VIVIAN: i have nothing i want to say to you.

WILL: god, you always do that, you always make things so difficult, everything's got to be this complicated production with you, only this time i'm not going to play. i refuse.

VIVIAN: ok, will. whatever.

WILL: don't say that, i hate when you say that. "whatever." it's so high school.

VIVIAN: whatever.

WILL: god, what did i ever see in you?

VIVIAN: what did i ever see in you?

WILL: what did i ever see to love?

VIVIAN: what did i ever see to love?

WILL: is this a dream? is life a dream?

VIVIAN: "is life a dream?" wow, will, that's really profound.

WILL: o just go away.

VIVIAN: you go away. this is my place, you idiot. you're the intruder, not me. you're the one who messed it up, will, not me. you, you did. never mind. fine. i'll go. i don't care. it'll be refreshing not to be left for a change.

WILL: don't you try to guilt me out. i refuse.

(vivian exits with the plant. the sound of growling.)

WILL: i refuse to feel guilty. the heart wants what the heart wants. and right now it wants to go. i'm going. i'm going now—vivian?

(the sound of growling grows. will disappears into the darkness.)

16.

the sound of unseen animals prowling in the dark. panic in the jungle. joy appears.

JOY: will?

(jason appears, holding the ball.)

JOY: o.

JASON: i'm looking for my dog. his name is otis. have you seen him? i think he ran away. i've been looking all over for him.

JOY: i don't think so. i'm sorry.

JASON: he's big, he's really really big. he's kinda hard to miss.

JOY: i'm sorry. i'm sorry.

JASON: don't be sorry. i mean, the only reason to be sorry is if you did something wrong. did you do something wrong? did you like run over my dog or something?

JOY: i didn't run over your dog. i'm on foot. please just leave me alone.

JASON: what's going on with your face?

JOY: nothing.

JASON: it's doing funny things.

JOY: it's a twitch, my face, it twitches.

JASON: why?

JOY: i don't know why, it just does that, it does that sometimes, it's a twitch, it's nothing.

JASON: are you ok?

JOY: i'm fine.

JASON: are you sure?

JOY: yes, i'm fine, i'm fine. everything is fine, it's all just fine, really, fine.

(in the night sky overhead, the roar of an airplane. a whistling descent. and then the sound of the jungle. jed is a tiny figure in the darkness, typing in time, destinations, travel plans at an airport terminal. somewhere else, richard is reading a letter.)

JED: dear ms. moore, why don't you answer any of my letters? i know you are a busy person, but even a postcard would be greatly appreciated. the thing is, i'm wondering if any of my letters have even gotten to you. let me not mince words. i'm wondering if maybe some evil toad is intercepting them before you even see them. i know because you are a big star, you are surrounded by an army of vile parasites who monitor your every move and tell you all kinds of horrible lies to keep you in the dark because they have no lives and live to feed off you like the hoard of no-talent, dysfunctional bloodsuckers they are. because i have come to see the light, having realized that letters are fragile and ephemeral things, and can be burned or shredded or thrown away—let's just say, waylaid, if you will, by the malevolent, prying fingers of anonymous no-goodniks, which is a federal crime and will be prosecuted to the full extent of the law. so for all the toads who may be intercepting and reading this private correspondence, be so forewarned. yours forever, jed.

(somewhere else, richard crumples up a letter. jed and richard are engulfed by darkness. the shriek of primates in the trees.)

17.

panic in the jungle. derek and joy appear in two bubbles of light, separate, alone, suspended in the darkness like distant stars in far-off galaxies.

DEREK: ok, all right, this is the thing, my roommate, he has this dog, his name is otis

JOY: i just got engaged to this guy, his name is will

DEREK: and the thing about otis, he's big, he's really really big

JOY: he's smart, he's handsome, he's nice

DEREK: he scares me, otis he really scares me

JOY: something, i don't know what, has begun to scare me, really scare me

DEREK: i started having these dreams, these really weird dreams

JOY: i'm going to get married to a man i love, his name is will, will's the man i love

DEREK: i dreamed of teeth and meat, and i was the meat

JOY: but this is the thing

DEREK: this is the thing

JOY: my face hurts from smiling and if i hear myself say "i love you" one more time, i swear i'm going to barf

DEREK: otis or me, survival of the fittest, i saw the writing on the wall

JOY: because i don't love will, i don't want to spend the rest of my life with will, the thought of spending the rest of my life with will makes me want to hyperventilate

DEREK: because in my heart of hearts, i knew that dog was smarter, and stronger, and more highly evolved than i will ever hope to be, and that just sucks, because i'm a human being, i'm a homo-sapien for chrissakes, i should be king of the hill, i should rule.

(the jungle sounds stop. silence.)

JOY: because i don't love will, not in the way that love should be, and there's a way it should be, i know it, like i know there are strange see-through fish at the bottom of the sea, and i know i should just count my blessings and be happy, but i'm not, because i'm not happy, because maybe i don't know how to be happy.

(a sound like a sound heard in the heart of darkness, in the deepest darkest jungle. a bird call, a breathing.)

JOY: will? will, is that you?

(the sound of growling grows. the shrieks of unseen animals. the sound of jungle mayhem. bones crunching, flesh ripping, feathers flapping. and then it stops.)

18.

darkness. a bubble of light. wendy and derek. a tiny bed. a shitty manuscript.

WENDY: o my god. did you kill that dog?

DEREK: no. what? what, i didn't kill him. i just sedated him and dumped him somewhere in brooklyn—look, i tried to go back, i tried to find him, but he wasn't where i left him, or maybe he moved, either way he was gone. i don't know what happened to him. what did i do? oh my god, i can't believe what i did. do you think what i did was evil?

WENDY: o yeah totally.

DEREK: great, just what i needed to hear.

WENDY: i mean, poor otis, and your roommate, poor guy, he must be going nuts. i mean, in a karmic sense, your ass is gonna fry.

DEREK: what am i going to do? i feel so guilty.

WENDY: no, don't do that. guilt is bad, it's toxic, it'll clog you up, and your soul will become just like a little la brea tar pit. have you ever been to the la brea tar pits? o you gotta go. they're the most amazing thing. they're these pits in the middle of la, and they're filled with tar, and back in the day, these animals, they'd think it was like a watering hole or something, and they'd wade in for what they thought was going to be a nice, refreshing drink, and then they'd realize that it wasn't water, but tar, but by then it'd be too late, and they'd get stuck in all this hot, burbling goo, and they'd die this slow, horrible death.

DEREK: i can't believe we just had sex.

WENDY: i know, but the thing is, for me, i try to have sex in a really casual, sort of low-key way with guys i don't know that well or guys i don't like that much, because with most guys, i find, it's better that way. like you. i'd never in a million years want to be involved with someone like you. i mean, it's not like you're repulsive or anything, but the more i get to know you, the more i realize you're kind of insecure, and i think you have a lot of anger, and the whole thing with the dog, that really gives me pause.

DEREK: you're the one who wanted the truth, miss i-love-true-stories.

WENDY: yeah, well, what do you want? a medal? jeez.

DEREK: i don't believe this. you know what? i may have a lot of anger, and i may be just a wee bit insecure, but you know what you are, you're a fruit-cake. you're a kook. and another thing, i don't know if anybody's ever said this to you before, but you talk way too much, you're a goddamn motormouth, and it's not like every word out of your mouth is exactly what i'd call a pearl, so maybe in the future, you should consider giving your jaw muscles a little rest.

WENDY: wow, that was kinda hostile.

DEREK: you're right, you're totally one hundred percent right. god, what am i doing here? i don't even know what i'm doing here. look, i gotta go, i gotta get out of here, i'm sorry, forget what i said, forget everything, forget tonight, forget you ever met me.

WENDY: ok. vaya con dios. that means, go with god, in spanish.

DEREK: yeah, i know what it means. you, too. vaya con dios.

(wendy exits with the tiny bed. derek exits with his shitty manuscript.)

19.

light. a tiny park bench. the chirping of birds in invisible trees. joy is sitting, holding a small, cardboard box. enter vivian with the plant.

VIVIAN: hi. i'm vivian. you don't know who i am, do you?

JOY: i don't think so.

VIVIAN: will never mentioned me, i guess. no need to introduce yourself. i know your name is joy. will told me all about you. in fact, i ran into the two of you just the other day. you were kissing in the street. i was behind a shrub. it was one of those weird coincidences. i wasn't following you, i don't care what will thinks. i remember looking at the back of your head and thinking you had really nice hair.

JOY: thanks.

VIVIAN: this is will's plant. he left it at my place. i think it has root rot. where is he? will? in there? o my god. you cremated him, and i didn't even know he was dead.

JOY: no, no, you don't understand. it's not actually will inside. i mean, we never found will. his body, i mean.

VIVIAN: so, uh, what's in the box?

JOY: air.

VIVIAN: air? in other words, it's empty.

JOY: you know, i don't think of it that way. for me, it's a symbol of will, who will was once.

VIVIAN: you know, joy, this all seems very strange to me. are you sure he's, you know, passed on?

JOY: i'm not sure, i'm not sure about anything anymore. i mean, i heard this noise, and then i saw this thing, and it was big, it was really big, and then it was gone, and will, he was gone, too.

VIVIAN: wow. maybe he was abducted by aliens.

JOY: i really don't think so.

VIVIAN: o? you think that's far-fetched, joy?

JOY: yeah, vivian, i'm afraid i do.

VIVIAN: well, how do you know, joy? you don't know. you don't have a handle on what happened, you don't have a handle on anything. you just have a cardboard box.

(vivian snatches the box.)

JOY: please, ok, this whole thing has been kinda hard for me.

VIVIAN: i'm sorry. i had a dream last night. at least i think it was a dream. will was in it. we had a fight. he had breasts.

JOY: i don't think i need to be hearing this, vivian.

VIVIAN: you're right, you're right. i'm sorry. he loved you, he really did. i think he used to love me. i mean, i think we used to love each other, but then one day, i don't know when exactly, we just kinda stopped.

JOY: you know, i don't think it was meant to be, this thing with will and me, but still i think i'm having trouble with how people enter and leave each other's lives, how suddenly they're just out of your life, there's no warning, they're just gone, and everything's different, and all you can think is how exactly did i get here. do you notice that ever?

VIVIAN: yeah. yeah, i do. listen, i should go. i'm leaving town, i'm actually moving, it's kinda crazy, i mean, it's been kinda crazy, i never knew everything could get so crazy. it was nice meeting you, and maybe we'll run into each other sometime, in some other life, in some other incarnation, i somehow doubt it, but who knows, truth is weirder than fiction. so goodbye, good luck, and that's about all, i guess.

JOY: vivian? you, too. good luck.

(vivian exits with plant. joy exits with box. the roar of an airplane.)

20.

an airport. the intermittent announcements of flights arriving and departing. muzak. a soothing, female voice ticks off flight numbers, gate numbers, random destinations. jed wears an air steward's uniform. enter richard with a suitcase and a big bag.

RICHARD: o my lord, help, help me. i need to be on that plane, i need to be on it right now.

JED: uh, i think they're about to close the doors.

RICHARD: o god no. hurry, hurry, it's an emergency. i work for demi moore.

JED: what?

RICHARD: i work for demi moore, i'm her personal assistant.

JED: really. neat.

RICHARD: look, i'm kind of in a rush, ok, time is of the essence, i need to be in la, i need to be in la right now, i'm already late, i'm very, very late, o my god, she's gonna kill me.

JED: bags to check?

RICHARD: this? no, this is just garbage, all these letters, you have no idea, tons of letters, "dear ms. moore, blah, blah, blah." i mean, who are these people? have they no lives? have they no shame? like she cares, like she gives a good goddamn. what's the matter? are you ok?

JED: fine. window or aisle?

(enter derek with shitty manuscript and suitcase.)

RICHARD: window, no, aisle, no, window, no, aisle, o i don't care. look, can i just leave this here with you, would you mind? thank you, thanks.

(exit richard. exit jed with the bag of letters. enter jason with suitcase and surfboard. exit jason. exit derek. enter lee pulling a cart on which sits the giant terrarium.)

JASON: hey. do you like work here?

LEE: nah, i'm just passing through.

JASON: what's in there?

LEE: there's supposed to be this snake, but i think it's empty.

JASON: wow, it looks nice in there. it's so lush. o man, is that a little baby waterfall i'm seeing? that's incredible. wouldn't it be like great if you could just shrink yourself down, and crawl inside and live in there, just like live in the lushness?

LEE: yeah, i guess. you have any pets?

JASON: i used to have this dog, but he ran away. he was big, i mean, he was really kinda big, and my world, you know, my world, it was just kinda, small. i think i gotta get a bigger life, you know, a whole like bigger way of being.

LEE: wait a second, wait a second, did you see that? i think something moved in there.

JASON: i missed it.

LEE: i'm going in, see what's up. you wanna give me a hand?

JASON: sure.

LEE: thanks, man. watch my back.

JASON: yeah, you bet.

(jason gives lee a leg up into the terrarium. exit jason. enter wendy with a suitcase. re-enter derek. re-exit derek. enter efran with a suitcase. he sees the terrarium. he sees wendy.)

WENDY: hi.

EFRAN: hi.

WENDY: weird.

EFRAN: uh huh.

WENDY: did you bring this with?

EFRAN: no.

WENDY: how did it get here?

EFRAN: i have no idea.

WENDY: i no longer temp.

EFRAN: o?

WENDY: it's not for me. lots of things are not for me. i think i'm about to turn over a new leaf, many new leaves, a whole big tree. why aren't you tending the pets?

EFRAN: no more pets. it was too much for me. everything's been a little too much for me, pets, people, people, pets.

WENDY: you know, i kinda liked you.

EFRAN: uh huh.

WENDY: i kinda liked the pet store. i could have seen that. me. you. the pet store.

EFRAN: i think i need to go now.

WENDY: why?

EFRAN: because you're scary, because you're weird and scary, because everything is just a little too weird and scary.

WENDY: bye.

EFRAN: see ya.

(exit efran. exit wendy. enter myrna with a suitcase. re-enter derek.)

DEREK: if i don't get out of this city now, my head is gonna explode.

MYRNA: you know, airports can be very stressful. all that coming and going. it brings out the worst in people, a kind of shrill panic, an impending sense of doom. gum? mint? towlette?

DEREK: no. don't you get it? i'm not happy.

MYRNA: i'm sure you'll live.

DEREK: but, see i don't want to just live. i want to be happy. when i was a little boy, i was happy. i want to find that happiness i had as a child.

MYRNA: ok look, buddy, i used to be a schoolteacher, and the whole happy childhood thing, that's just a big fat myth. take it from me, children are not happy. if they're not cruel little power mongers, they're anxious and unhappy loners, i see them everyday, chewing their cuticles and roaming the jungle gyms in search of a friendly face.

DEREK: who are you?

MYRNA: honey, i'm the grownup in the room. now if you'll excuse me, i have a plane to catch.

(exit myrna. exit derek. enter jed with bag of letters and a bottle of duty-free. enter joy with a suitcase. she wears a wedding veil.)

JOY: excuse me, i don't know where i'm supposed to go. i'm on standby. i mean, we're on standby, me and my husband. i just got married. it's a little strange. i was supposed to get married to this one person, but i ended up getting married to somebody else. i guess i'm just sort of in marriage mode. we're going on our honeymoon now. he went to get me a snack. i'm not sure i need a snack. i'm not sure what i need. have a nice trip.

(exit joy. jed approaches the terrarium and hoists himself inside. the roar of an airplane. a tiny airplane in a tiny sky. silence.)

21.

vivian clutches a suitcase, the plant, and a large, laminated map of the united states. she can't carry everything. she puts down the suitcase and the plant.

VIVIAN: hello. i'm vivian, i'm your substitute teacher, sort of. your real teacher, myrna, she's gone away for a little while, so she asked me to cover for her even though i'm not sure it's legal, because i'm not technically a teacher, and i don't know what i'm supposed to be doing exactly, which is how i feel often these days, not just here. anyway i can't stay that long. i didn't know what to say to you guys, so i brought this map. this is a map of the continental united states. right now, we're here. this is new york. i'm leaving new york. i'm flying all the way across all these states, and i'm ending up here in los angeles, and after los angeles, there's nothing but ocean as far as the eye can see, and then the next real land mass you get to is hawaii, i guess, which really, if you think about it, is just a few tiny islands in the middle of this huge, enormous ocean, in the middle of nowhere, so tiny you can barely see them, and they're so far away. i mean, it's a whole different map that i didn't happen to bring with me today, maybe not even a map, maybe more of a globe, which i don't have, i have no globe, and anyway, it's not like i'm even going to hawaii, so i don't even know why i brought it up, so never mind hawaii, forget hawaii, because where i'm going is here: los angeles. i wasn't really planning on going to los angeles, but i have this friend there, i don't know if friend is the right word, he's kind of a friend, i mean, he was a friend once, but we haven't really seen each other in a long time, and to be honest, i don't know exactly how i feel about him, because i think we're actually very different people, and i'm not sure we communicate very well, and i'm not sure we have all that much in common anymore, but friend, i guess, is the only word there really is out there, and so my friend, he works for this really big movie star, and what he did, which was really a very kind thing and something that a friend would, in fact, do, he got me a job doing something, i'm not sure what, for this really big movie star, but it doesn't even really matter, because it's a job, and it's a whole new beginning for me, and that sounds really good right this second, because the thing is, i really need something like that in my life right now, because i'm finding i have this need lately to feel settled and safe and sane, which it feels more and more like i never am here, i'm not sure why, because the thing is, i just found out a little while ago that i'm going to have a baby. wow. that was weird. that just came out. you're the first people i've told. i was going to tell will, but then things got strange, and one thing led to another, and anyway, you don't know will, i'm not sure i know will. i don't know why i'm telling you all this. i don't know you, and maybe it's not appropriate to talk about this kind of stuff with small children, but for some reason, i don't know why, i feel really at ease with you. you all seem very wise for your years. i'm not ready for all of this, but it's not really about me anymore, because the thing is it's not just me floating around in space now. it's also this little person inside of me, who's also kinda floating around in space, and who probably looks kinda like a little fishy right about now, and that is so scary to me, but it's also kind of amazing. you were all little fishies once. and all of you have mommies and daddies, too. well, my baby doesn't have a daddy which is a little complicated and strange and not how i wanted it to be or thought it would be, but you know what? it's ok. i mean, there was a daddy once, but he fell in love with somebody else, and then after that, he kinda disappeared. we think he maybe got eaten by a giant animal or maybe he was abducted by aliens. nobody knows for sure. it's a mystery. this all happened here in new york, in brooklyn actually, which is right about here. i like maps so much. i like how everything is pink and orange and aquamarine, and all the countries and states look like little, funny-shaped candies. i like how all the names of the places are written in these perfect, block letters. i like that. but the thing about a map, the best thing of all, you look at it, and places that are really big and faraway, don't seem so big and faraway. a whole continent is the distance from your thumb to your fingertip. a whole entire ocean is as big as the palm of your hand. magic. truly. well, i guess that's all i have to say for now. it was very nice being your substitute teacher. you were very good today, and i hope you all eventually grow up to be happy and productive people in the world. i guess it's recess now. good-bye.

(a bell rings. voices, laughter, the sound of chairs scraping against the floor. the sound of happy children running into the sunshine. the sounds of the jungle, the joyous caterwauling of monkeys and birds in the trees, the call of one lone elephant to his herd. vivian puts down the map, picks up her suitcase and her plant, and goes. the roar of an airplane. darkness. end of act one.)

ACT TWO

the sound of the surf. a beach in hawaii. a bright, blank place. the sun is set-
ting. the sky is fuchsia and tangerine. efran is at the beach. efran has a six-
pack of cheap beer. he cracks open a can, and drinks. enter wendy.

EFRAN: hi.

WENDY: hi.

EFRAN: small world.

WENDY: yeah, i'll say.

EFRAN: i'm the lifeguard. and you are what exactly?

WENDY: i don't want to talk about it. can i get one of those? thanks.

    (wendy cracks open a beer and drinks. enter joy and richard.)

JOY: hi.

EFRAN: hi.

JOY: this is richard. richard almost drowned just now, but then i saved him. i
    pulled him back from the brink.

RICHARD: i thought i was going in for a little dip, and before i knew it, i was
    being sucked out to sea. i saw my whole life pass before my eyes. you
    saved my life. she saved my life.

WENDY: isn't that your job?

EFRAN: the beach is big.

WENDY: uh huh, the world is small, but the beach is big, that makes a lot of
    sense.

RICHARD: *(to efran.)* could i get one of those, do you mind?

EFRAN: you bet.

RICHARD: thanks.

JOY: wendy?

EFRAN: so what brings you to the aloha state?

JOY: wendy?

RICHARD: o my lord, where to begin? i was in new york on my way to la, i was
    in the middle of this airport, and i was late, i was beyond late, and the
    thing that slowly began to dawn on me was that i was so late i was never
    going to get to where i was supposed to be going, it just wasn't going to
    happen, and so i should've just given up, i should've just gone with the
    flow, but the thing is i don't know how to do that, because that's just not
    who i am, because i guess i haven't evolved, i haven't evolved to that
    point where i can look at my life imploding before my eyes and just say,

que sera sera, or whatever it is people say, because this is not just about missed connections, this is not just about air travel, because in a larger sense, i'm going to miss my flight, and then i'm going to be on standby, i'm just going to be standing by, or maybe i'll be bumped, i'll just be bumped, and that'll be it, i'll be stuck in this airport for the rest of all eternity like some suitcase nobody ever claims, one of those sorry, old samsonites that just keeps going round and round on the carousel, all battered and dented and coming apart at the seams, and the clothes are are coming out every which way, and there's some duct tape maybe wrapped around the middle, and maybe a little string, and the bag is a mess, it's just a total mess, and all you can think is: how did this bag get to be this way? whose bag is this, and where is this person now? what happened to them? did something bad happen to them? or did they maybe just get lost along the way?

EFRAN: basically, i think, we're all just polynesian.

RICHARD: excuse me?

EFRAN: i mean, i think we're all polynesians, you know, in a larger sense. the polynesians were the first real hawaiians. they rowed over from polynesia in these big double canoes. they had no clue. they rowed for a really long time. they thought they were going to fiji, but then they got into open sea, and they got waylaid. people, you know, not just polynesians, get waylaid. that's like the human deal.

WENDY: that's what happens to me, i get waylaid all the time, in parties as in life, it's like a recurring theme for me. it's like i'm on my way to get some chips or some punch or something, it doesn't matter what, and always, it never fails, i always get waylaid by some person from my past, some walking reminder of some past weirdness i'd just as soon put behind me, and it's gotta be like the last person in the world i want to see, and it's gotta be like this totally awkward thing, and i have to be nice, but i'm not that nice, i'm just not a nice person.

(joy sighs.)

EFRAN: you want another beer?

WENDY: uh, no.

EFRAN: you?

JOY: ok.

RICHARD: can i have another?

EFRAN: you bet.

RICHARD: thanks.

(jason passes by.)

RICHARD: surfer.

WENDY: i think i've seen him before. *(to joy.)* honey, you're twitching.

JOY: i am?

WENDY: what is wrong with you? relax, just relax.

JOY: ok.

WENDY: you don't look relaxed.

JOY: i'm a little tense.

RICHARD: you know, i would love to go to a party. i haven't been to a party in like a million years.

EFRAN: this is kinda like a party.

RICHARD: i mean, a real party. i want to go to a real party. i want to be festive. i want to get drunk and do stupid things, but in a festive setting.

EFRAN: i think i want to do that, too, but in a larger sense.

WENDY: i wouldn't mind a party, a little shindig.

JOY: *(to wendy.)* you go to luaus all the time.

WENDY: luaus don't count. that's work. i want to go to a party where i don't have to wear a grass skirt and hula all night long.

RICHARD: hula is a beautiful thing. i saw a brochure in my hotel room: luau. hula. it sounded so nice.

JOY: i would love to go to a luau. i would love to eat some roast pig somebody roasted in the ground, a big pig, and poi. i would love to eat some poi. but most of all i would love to watch you hula. i love to watch you hula.

EFRAN: *(to wendy.)* i take it you're a hula dancer.

JOY: she's a wonderful hula dancer. she can hula like you wouldn't believe.

WENDY: look, i'm not a hula dancer, ok? i'm an actress. i act. the hula thing is temporary. it's like a job. it's not who i really am.

RICHARD: what i really am is a tourist. i'm a tourist.

JOY: i was a tourist, but then i stayed. i guess i'm no longer a tourist. i'm a local i guess is what i am.

EFRAN: i don't know who i really am.

WENDY: you're a lifeguard. you're a guarder of lives.

EFRAN: i mean it like in a larger sense.

WENDY: you know, i think you spend way too much time thinking about stuff in a larger sense. just think small. what's for lunch? what am i going to do with my hair?

EFRAN: where's the rest of the beer?

WENDY: that's the idea.

EFRAN: no, i mean: where is the rest of the beer? i had all this beer, and now it's gone.

RICHARD: i think we drank it. i think we drank it all. here's some cash. it's a little damp.

(efran exits.)

WENDY: he's a very bad lifeguard. he's all about the beer. isn't that illegal? i mean, the guy's the lifeguard for chrissakes. i mean, who's in charge here, you know what i'm saying? who's manning the store?

RICHARD: o my god, nobody. we're all alone, we're on our own.

JOY: he seems nice, the lifeguard.

WENDY: niceness doesn't save lives, joy.

JOY: maybe he's just kinda mellow.

RICHARD: i would like to be more mellow.

WENDY: the guy is a lifeguard. he's not suppposed to be mellow. he's supposed to be vigilant. and he's not. he's not vigilant. he's like drunk. he's drunk and he's dumb, i think he's kinda dumb. jeez, i can't believe i had a thing with that guy.

JOY: you had a "thing" with the lifeguard guy? what kinda "thing?"

WENDY: you know, i don't want to talk about it.

RICHARD: ok, look, something i'm noticing here is that the sand is black.

WENDY: volcanic ash.

RICHARD: really?

WENDY: these islands, they're volcanoes. right now, we're all sitting on top of a volcano. any second, it could blow, and that'd be it. we'd all be dead meat.

JOY: god, you're being so negative. why are you being so negative?

WENDY: i'm not being negative. i'm just explaining something about our environment.

JOY: *(to richard.)* don't worry. you have nothing to worry about.

WENDY: that's so not true. personally, i think he's got plenty to worry about. the guy could be dead within the hour. he could go for a swim, and drown. a volcano could erupt, and he could be entombed in hot, molten lava before he even knew what hit him.

RICHARD: i came to hawaii to relax. i thought it was supposed to be a relaxing place.

WENDY: it's not.

JOY: ok, you want to know why i'm tense? i'm tense because of you. you make me tense. you're so dramatic. why do you have to be so dramatic?

WENDY: because i'm a dramatic person by nature. that's who i am.

JOY: when exactly did you have your "thing" with the lifeguard?

WENDY: i don't remember. it was another place, another time, another time zone.

(derek passes by with shitty manuscript.)

WENDY: ok, is it me or is the world just like shrinking?

JOY: what? do you know that guy?

WENDY: i wouldn't say i know him. i mean, "knowing": what does that mean, joy? i mean, do any of us really know each other?

JOY: you had a "thing" with him, too. you did, didn't you? have you like had a "thing" with everybody?

WENDY: i've had a few "things."

JOY: you've had a lot "things," wendy. you know, sometimes i have no idea who you are. i mean, i think i know who you are, but i don't, i really don't. i mean, who are you? who are you?

RICHARD: she's wendy, you're joy, and maybe we should just not discuss who we used to have sex with, maybe we should just not do that. i think it's a very bad idea. it's all just water under the bridge. lots of water. a bridge.

JOY: fine.

WENDY: fine.

RICHARD: fine.

(exit joy, wendy and richard in different directions. somewhere else, vivian is very pregnant. a room in alaska. enter jed, carrying plants. he carries too many plants. he lists.)

JED: hi.

VIVIAN: hi.

JED: i'm the plant guy.

VIVIAN: yes, yes, you are.

JED: where do you want these?

VIVIAN: o anywhere, anywhere's fine. great, great, o that's great, that's—o careful, careful, careful.

JED: so what's the deal with all the plants? are you just like a plant person or what?

VIVIAN: well, no, no, not really, no. i mean, i was supposed to move to la, i had this whole plan, but then it kinda fell apart, so here i am, in alaska, i just told the man at the airport: please choose a place for me, i have a map, and you can just pick and choose, it's gotta be very faraway, and also, it's gotta be a place where they speak english, because i think, you know, life is complicated enough, and so he picked alaska, it was kinda fluky, lots of things are kinda fluky, and now i'm here, and it's ok, it's a little cold and gray, and a little bit remote, and i think, you know, in a place like this, people really need plants, little green, leafy friends to brighten up their day, and so that's what i'm doing here now. plants.

JED: i think i need to sit.

(jed sits. he drinks from a bottle of duty-free.)

VIVIAN: are you ok?

JED: fine, i'm fine. you know, you're very pregnant. i find that kinda disturbing. you're very, very pregnant and i'm very, very drunk. right now, i'm very, very drunk. it's a miracle i got these plants in here. the ice, the snow, the fact that i can barely stand. so who do you think's going to buy all these plants?

VIVIAN: i don't know. people.

JED: i'm a person.

VIVIAN: yes. yes, you are.

JED: i am, i'm a person. and so what makes you think persons like myself are going to buy your plants? maybe persons like myself have all the plants we need. or maybe we're just not really plant persons. have you thought this through, have you thought this through at all? i think not. i mean, here you are, and you're very, very pregnant and you're stuck in alaska with a whole bunch of plants nobody's going to buy. nobody's going to buy these plants. i mean, who's going to want to buy these crummy plants? look, i'm just giving you my honest opinion. that's all. the truth hurts. it hurts like hell. you want some?

VIVIAN: no.

JED: all right. all right, look, that's a very nice shrub, and i would like to purchase it. *(taking out cash.)* here.

VIVIAN: you know, can you just go. i would just like for you to go now. just, please, go. go.

JED: ok. fine.

(jed rises with difficulty and starts to go.)

VIVIAN: o.

JED: o.

VIVIAN: o wow.

JED: o god.

VIVIAN: help.

JED: o you know, i don't know.

VIVIAN: i need you to help.

JED: o i don't know. i don't know, i don't know.

VIVIAN: o.

JED: o.

VIVIAN: o.

JED: o.

VIVIAN: ok, go. go. go. go. go. go. go.

(jed escorts vivian into the snow. somewhere else, wendy, joy, and richard together at the beach.)

RICHARD: people come. people go. the beach is big. the world is small.

JOY: i came to hawaii on my honeymoon, me and my ex-husband.

WENDY: ok, look, i've heard this story before.

JOY: it was very strange. he was very strange. one day he went for a swim, he said: i'm going for a swim. and then he went, and he never came back. i think maybe he was sucked out to sea, just like yourself. i don't know. i mean, i'll never know. it wasn't supposed to turn out this way. i mean, i came to hawaii on my honeymoon. it was a honeymoon package. it was all planned out. i used to have plans. i used to have all these plans.

WENDY: ok, listen up: we all had plans. i planned to be an actress. now i am a hula dancer, i hula, that's what i do, and you know what? it's ok. some of us are born to act. some of us are born to hula. that's the way it is. and another thing, before i forget: i am so sick of hearing about your ex-husband, you're always talking about your ex-husband. like i care, like i need that information, so just please, in the future, keep it to yourself, ok? can you do that, can you do that for me?

JOY: fine.

(joy exits.)

WENDY: fine, go, bye, see ya. god, she drives me up a wall.

RICHARD: for me, you know, the past is dead.

WENDY: i really try not to think about my past. it's just like too embarrassing.

RICHARD: like they say: this is the first day of the rest of your life.

WENDY: yeah, but what does that mean? i don't know exactly what that means. i mean, what does that mean?

RICHARD: you mean in a larger sense?

WENDY: in a larger sense, in a smaller sense, in any kind of sense.

(enter efran with beer and chips.)

EFRAN: beer?

RICHARD: o my god, bless you. oo chips. chip? *(to wendy:)* chip? have a chip.

WENDY: thanks.

(wendy, efran and richard eat and drink. a long silence as they eat and drink.)

WENDY: you know, there was a time in my life i used to fuck guys. i used to fuck a lot of guys.

EFRAN: uh huh.

RICHARD: celibate. i used to be celibate. i still am, i guess.

WENDY: and this is a choice?

RICHARD: not really, no.

WENDY: i know a lot of people who are choosing to be celibate.

RICHARD: oh, uh huh.

WENDY: it seems a lot less complicated.

RICHARD: yeah, uh huh, i guess i can see that.

EFRAN: i wouldn't mind having sex now and again.

RICHARD: yeah, you know, i have to say, too, i'm kinda with him.

WENDY: sex now and again is fine. the problem isn't the sex. the problem is everything around the sex. the problem is the i love yous, and the moo eyes, and the do you love me backs, and the neurotic late night phone calls. i wish it could just be like, you know, you have sex and it is what it is, and then it's like good-bye, see ya, and you move on to the next thing.

RICHARD: chip?

WENDY: thanks.

EFRAN: i would like to have sex, but i would also like to maybe fall in love. then maybe get married. i wouldn't mind getting married, having a baby.

WENDY: why does everybody want to get married and have babies, why is that?

RICHARD: i don't.

WENDY: yeah, but you're clearly a damaged individual. you don't count.

RICHARD: whatever you say, hula girl.

WENDY: just relax. i'm damaged, too. some of my best friends are damaged. it's not a big deal.

EFRAN: if you're damaged, does that mean you're never going to be happy, because thinking about it, i would have to say that i'm kinda damaged, too, i mean i think it would be fair to say that i'm a little bit damaged, but i want to be happy, i mean i really want to be happy, i want to be normal and happy, and so i'm wondering if that's even an option at this point.

RICHARD: probably not. i'm so sorry.

EFRAN: that's ok.

WENDY: all right, look, something i've noticed, something that's happening, is this thing, it's this whole thing, where all of a sudden everybody you know is getting married and having babies, and everything that comes

along with getting married and having babies, have you noticed this, have
you noticed this ever?

RICHARD: there's a little bit of that going on, uh huh.

WENDY: ok? and i don't know if it's this kinda instinct, this kinda lizard brain
instinct, like turtles or lemmings or moose in spring, or if it's just this
kinda sudden awareness that kicks in that you're not getting any younger,
and someday you're maybe gonna get sick and old and then maybe you're
gonna die, well not maybe, you are, i mean you are gonna die, we're all
gonna die, that's the deal, but whatever, maybe you're having trouble
with that concept, or maybe you just don't want to be doing all of that
stuff alone, and so anyway there you are, and i think you can think of this
in terms of musical chairs, i think it's actually a lot like musical chairs,
and so there you are, having spent most of your twenties playing this
game of musical chairs, and suddenly it's like you turn twenty-eight,
twenty-nine, and somebody turns the music off, and all of a sudden it's
like really quiet in the room, and you look around and you sort of scope
out the situation, and you see what's what, and the thing is, right, there's
just not enough chairs to go around, somebody's gonna be left chairless,
somebody's gonna get screwed, and before you know it, everybody's all
scrambling around, looking for a place to park their ass, and it's like a situation, i mean it's like a situation, people are getting knocked to the
ground, and there's shoving happening, and elbows in the eyes, and it's
ugly, ok, it's really ugly, but you're right in there, and so finally you get
yourself a chair, and you're happy because you're like seated, but then
before too long, you know, you turn to look at the people sitting next to
you, and it's like, who are you again? and what am i doing sitting next to
you? do i really want to be sitting next to you? and also, this chair, i'm not
so sure about this chair, i mean maybe i don't even want to be seated,
maybe i want to stand.

RICHARD: uh huh, the music, the chair, uh huh.

WENDY: right? ok? thank you. so now, ok, this is the thing: i used to fuck guys,
and now i fuck girls, and i'm personally very happy about that little
change of scenery, but you'd think, you know, that it's a different thing,
that this whole musical chair thing, it's a guy/girl thing, and now that i'm
doing this girl/girl thing, the whole musical chair thing, it's not going to
be the same thing, but it is, it's like the exact same thing, it's like musical
chairs only with different chairs.

(enter joy.)

JOY: i love you.

WENDY: o my god, stop.

JOY: i love you. and i was thinking: we could get married. we could have a baby. it would be a little untraditional, but i think that's fine. you would just have to be a lot nicer to me.

WENDY: ok joy, you know, it's like this: you've already been married once, and the guy was sucked out to sea. doesn't this tell you something? can't you take a hint?

RICHARD: can i have another beer?

EFRAN: you bet.

JOY: i didn't love him, not like i love you. i mean, you're a deeply damaged individual, and you're also kinda mean and slutty, but for some reason, i don't know why, i love you, i really love you.

WENDY: stop it, please. i hate when people say that. don't you hate when people say that? i mean, "i love you," god, people say it all the time, and what does it mean, what does it really mean, nobody knows what it really means, *(to richard.)* do you know what i mean?

RICHARD: uh-uh.

JOY: ok, i don't love you. i feel nothing for you. we're just sharing some oxygen here.

WENDY: just can you please not talk, can you do that for me?

JOY: human beings talk. that's part of being a human being. *(to efran.)* isn't that right?

EFRAN: uh huh.

WENDY: o please, talking is so overrated. *(to richard.)* is it not the most overrated thing?

RICHARD: uh huh.

WENDY: i used to talk a lot. i used to talk so much, it was exhausting to myself and to others. now i just want to be like one of those guys at the airport with the little flags, no talking, just little flags, waving my little flags.

JOY: i love you.

WENDY: o my god, are you retarded or what?

(joy exits.)

WENDY: fine, go, see ya. man, this chick is like an expert at leaving. she's always leaving, and then she's always coming back, she's got this whole boomerang thing going on, and i've about had it up to here.

RICHARD: you know, i think we maybe need to talk less and be a little nicer to each other.

WENDY: i'm plenty nice. i'm so nice, you have no idea. it's just that some people, you know, they're like these hothouse orchids, and that's what she is, she's a total orchid, and it's so exhausting, it just exhausts me.

RICHARD: i think i'm a rubber plant.

EFRAN: i think i'm maybe a fern. i think i'm kinda fern-like.

RICHARD: you are, you are kinda fern-like, i can see that.

WENDY: i don't want to talk about plants. i don't want to talk about love. i gotta go, i gotta go hula. i feel like kicking somebody in the head, but instead i'm gonna hula, i'm just gonna hula like there's no tomorrow.

RICHARD: aloha. aloha means good-bye.

(exit wendy. somewhere else, derek clutches his manuscript.)

DEREK: ok, aloha. i've been thinking about this. aloha means good-bye, but it also means hello. it actually means a lot of things. it's all about how you say it. you could say it as you're going, and the plane's about to take off, and you're waving, and you could just say: aloha, just let one fly instead of, say, adieu or ciao, which are both, in my opinion kinda pretentious ways of saying good-bye anyway, and if you were to say aloha like that, with the wave and everything else, i think everyone would be pretty clear about your meaning, but now here's the thing: let's say you're arriving somewhere, let's say you're arriving in a new locale like hawaii, which is after all where the word aloha is from, and the airplane lands, and the door opens, and suddenly you get a whiff of that air, do you know what i'm talking about? warm and moist and all smelling of plumeria, which is like a kind of orchid, i guess, or maybe it's not, it's its own thing, i don't know, i don't know what it is, and so anyway there you are, and you're making your way down the little metal staircase, and the light is so bright, it's blinding, and you're reeling from the smell of orchid, it's like the whole world is one big, bright orchid somebody just shoved in your face, and you are so overwhelmed, you don't even know what to do with yourself, and so what you do is you trip, you don't mean to, but you do, you just kinda fall, you fall down, and before you know it, you're flat on your back on the tarmac, and this pretty girl is standing over you, and maybe she's wearing a grass skirt, or maybe not, but it doesn't really matter 'cause the key detail, all right, is that around her neck, she's wearing all these leis, and before you know it, she's slipping one of her leis over your head, and all of a sudden you're overcome with this smell of orchid, and she's leaning real close, and whispering in your ear: aloha. she says, aloha. and i don't think it means good-bye in this situation. i think it means something else.

(somewhere else, enter joy holding a giant, stuffed fish. enter jason in a wet suit, with a duffel bag and a surfboard.)

JOY: hey.

JASON: hey. do i know you?

JOY: i don't think so.

JASON: what's up with the fish?

JOY: i'm not sure. i think somehow it got separated from its loved ones, and then somewhere along the line, it got stuffed and shellacked.

JASON: wow. i used to have this dog. he ran away from home. and then who knows what happened after that.

JOY: maybe he got stuffed and shellacked.

JASON: you know, i'd like to think that maybe some little kid found him and adopted him, and now he has this whole new adopted family, and maybe he thinks about me sometimes, but i'm just like this fuzzy face with hands, and basically it's all about this new family.

JOY: i would love to have a family.

JASON: family is cool. family is deep.

JOY: i would love to have a huge, enormous family where there's a lot of talking and laughing, and everybody is related and we all have nicknames and little traditions and all these family things we do together. what exactly do families do together?

JASON: you know, i don't really know. i'm still kinda figuring the family thing out. look, i gotta go. i got a plane to catch.

JOY: bye.

JASON: see ya.

(jason exits with surfboard. joy exits with fish. somewhere else, richard and efran are at the beach.)

RICHARD: i'm very drunk right now. is my face doing weird things? it feels like my face is doing weird things.

EFRAN: your face is fine. la, right?

RICHARD: excuse me?

EFRAN: that's where you're from?

RICHARD: no, no, no. la, god no. that was just a place i used to live. i used to be the personal assistant to a star, a very big star. i will not name names, i will not do that, but this woman, i'm telling you, this woman made my life a living hell, you have no idea. the rages, the abuse, the verbal abuse. i tried to hold it together, i did, the money was good, there were perks, i won't lie to you, there were all kinds of perks, but o my lord, at the end of the day, i'd rather suck sand and die than ever assist again. hawaii. wow. not much happens in hawaii. the sand is very black. the sun is very pink. the beer is very bad, this is very bad beer. do you think we're going to die?

EFRAN: yeah, eventually, yeah.

RICHARD: no, i mean like soon, are we going to die soon? are we all going to be entombed in hot, molten lava? is this something i should be worried about? are we just going to be covered up like those people in pompeii, remember pompeii, all those little people from pompeii just doing their thing, and then suddenly they're all shrivelled and gray and dead, that's the main thing, ok, they're dead? i don't want to die. i don't want to die in hawaii. hawaii would be a really bad place to die.

EFRAN: you know, i think most places would be a really bad place to die.

RICHARD: i don't want to die. if i die now, i will have led a really stupid and meaningless life, and i don't want to lead a stupid and meaningless life, i don't want to do that, and it's not like i want to be great or anything, i'm not talking about greatness, i'm just talking about a little meaning, a little meaning is a good thing. i think it's the least you can hope for. i think i'm having a panic attack.

EFRAN: breathe.

RICHARD: ok.

EFRAN: are you breathing?

RICHARD: i think so.

EFRAN: breathe.

RICHARD: breathing.

EFRAN: breathe.

RICHARD: i'm breathing, i'm still breathing.

(richard breathes. efran studies the ocean. richard, too, studies the ocean.)

RICHARD: wait a minute, wait a minute, what is that? did you just see that? there?

EFRAN: what?

RICHARD: here, wait, gimme those. *(taking the binoculars, and scanning the horizon.)* wow.

EFRAN: what? what is it?

RICHARD: i don't know. it looks like some kind of dog, some kind of really big dog. look, i think i'm gonna go in. i think i'm gonna get a closer look. i'll be back.

(exit richard. exit efran. somewhere else vivian and jason in vivian's room. the plants have grown. a small jungle. vivian holds a baby.)

JASON: "happy birthday to you, happy birthday to you, happy birthday, dear little baby person, happy birthday to you." i can't believe you're a mom, vivian. you're like a mom. that is so bizarre to me. weren't we just like recently kids ourselves? am i like remembering this wrong?

VIVIAN: i think we're grownups. i think we have been for a while now.

JASON: look at these weird little hands.

VIVIAN: do you have weird, little hands? you do, don't you, yes you do.

JASON: vivian? are we like the weirdest people in the universe?

VIVIAN: i think there are weirder people than ourselves, you know, in the universe, but i would have to say, compared to most people, yes, we are probably on the weird end of the dial.

JASON: are all families like us? i mean, you're my sister, vivvie, all right, you're like my sibling, and when i stop to think about it, i actually kinda like you, i mean, i think you're pretty cool, but i don't really know you at all, and i don't think you really know me, and we never see each other, even when we lived in the same city, we never saw each other, and we don't really talk, i mean, we never talk, and we're just not really part of each other's lives, because we're not close, we've never been close, i think you could even say we're strangers, i think it would be fair to say we're strangers, and we lead completely separate lives, and now you have a baby, and the whole thing is just kinda weird to me.

VIVIAN: what can i say? we are deeply fucked up individuals.

JASON: whoa, you just said the f word in front of your kid.

VIVIAN: i think it'll be ok. here, hold him, will you hold him for a sec. it's ok. you'll be fine, just careful of his neck. he's got a little spaghetti neck.

JASON: you know, in hawaii, like in traditional hawaiian culture, the maternal uncle is key, he's like really key. that's me, little buddy. i'm your maternal uncle. i'm thinking christmas. i'll fly back. i'll bring a ham. i mean, i'm not a big christmas person, but what the hey. a tree. we'll have a tree, tinsel. i like tinsel. do you like tinsel?

VIVIAN: i like tinsel. tinsel is nice.

(the baby begins to cry. vivian scoops him up.)

VIVIAN: o, o, o little baby. there, there, ssh. ssh.

(vivian coos to the baby. the baby grows quiet. jason checks out the plant life.)

JASON: these plants, these plants are like intense. man, it's so green in here. o wow, check it out.

(jason disappears into the foliage. enter wendy.)

WENDY: hi.

VIVIAN: hi.

WENDY: i'd like to buy a lei. you know, a lei.

VIVIAN: uh, we don't have any leis. what about a corsage?

WENDY: no, that's not going to work. it makes me think of prom night, and i just really don't want to be thinking about prom night at this stage of my life. what's that?

VIVIAN: that's a hibiscus. i don't know exactly how you'd wear it. it's a little big to wear.

WENDY: it's a gift for a friend. she doesn't have to wear it. she can just stick it in a corner. it'll be perfect.

(exit wendy with hibiscus. enter jed with a bundt cake. he falls down.)

VIVIAN: o god, are you ok?

JED: i'm fine, i'm fine. i'm sorry. i'm a little late for the party. i brought a cake. it's a little munched.

VIVIAN: thanks.

JED: i'm here. i'm all here. i made it.

VIVIAN: yes, you did.

JED: let me see the baby. he looks like a little alien. look at that head. what's going on with his head?

VIVIAN: i think that's just the way his head is.

JED: he's a very strange-looking baby. are all babies this strange-looking?

VIVIAN: i don't know. i think he's kinda cute.

JED: he's got room to grow. here, wait, i have a candle.

(jed retrieves the candle and plants it in the cake.)

VIVIAN: look at that.

JED: nice, huh? wait, wait, i also brought fire.

(jed retrieves a flame source. he lights the candle.)
make a wish.

VIVIAN: you know, i don't really know what to wish for. why don't you make a wish?

JED: me? o no, it's not my special day. i don't get any wishes. no wishes for me.

VIVIAN: i think we can make an exception. i don't think it's a problem.

JED: yeah? well, ok. ok. i have many wishes. i'm a man full of wishes.

VIVIAN: well, why don't you just pick one for now.

JED: ok. ok, i got it, i got it.

VIVIAN: good, that's good. ok, now you got to blow it out. quickly.

(jed blows out the candle. darkness. light on joy holding the stuffed fish. her face is twitching. light on derek clutching his ever-growing manuscript. they are suspended in the darkness like two stars from distant galaxies.)

DEREK: fate, you know, i think about fate, the concept of fate. and i think, what i think is that i don't believe in fate. i think, i think everything is kinda random, and also that the rules of time and space, which i think we often take for granted, are really kinda unreliable and strange. do i know you?

JOY: i'm not sure.

DEREK: i think i know you. i'm sure i know you. why is your face twitching?

JOY: it just does that sometimes.

DEREK: are you waiting for the tattoo guy?

JOY: uh huh.

DEREK: you know, hawaii is a wonderful place to get a tattoo. here, it's an ancient art form. it's part of the cultural fabric of the islands. they use ink-dipped wooden pegs and a little hammer. i just got one actually. you want to see?

(derek shows joy his tattoo. it is a very small tattoo.)

DEREK: what do you think?

JOY: it's small.

DEREK: it's not that small.

JOY: it's pretty small. i'm going for something bigger.

DEREK: tattoos are painful. i'm not sure you understand how painful it is. there was a lot of pain that went into this tattoo.

JOY: you know, i think i'm ok with pain. i think i have a lot of practice. in fact, i'm at a point in my life where i kinda welcome it. i really do. pain wakes you up. it gets you thinking. i want pain. i want lots and lots of pain. see this fish? this fish had pain. somewhere along the line, this fish had a lot of pain, and if he can handle it, so can i.

DEREK: that's the stupidest thing i've ever heard. that fish is dead. that's a dead fish.

JOY: ok, you know what, this fish may be dead, but you have a really bad tattoo, and every time someone looks at you from now on, all they'll be able to think is: there goes a man with a really bad tattoo. now if you'll excuse me.

(joy exits her light, carrying her fish with. light on wendy. she hulas. she is hulaing. she wears a grass skirt. she sings "edelweiss." she stops in the middle.)

DEREK: that song rings a bell.

WENDY: it rings a bell for everyone. it's like a classic. the sound of music is a classic. the von trapp family, they were like the ideal family. they wore matching lederhosen, and sang in harmony, and were very, very close. i think because i was a sad kid, i envy that closeness a lot. were you a sad kid? you look like you were one of those sad kids who had no friends and ate weird food and had weird hair. did you have weird hair?

DEREK: my hair was a little weird. look, i don't know what you're getting at. what are you getting at?

WENDY: some people are von trapps. some people are not. we are the not von trapps. we will never be von trapps. we will never be part of one big, happy family, because we were the kids with the weird hair, and nobody wants to have the kid with the weird hair in their pack or clan or tribe, unless of course they happen to be another kid with weird hair, and then it just becomes too weird. have you, by any chance, seen my girlfriend?

DEREK: i don't think so.

WENDY: i don't know what the hell she's up to. normally, what happens, right, we fight, and she takes off and eventually she comes back, and then we make up, and so it goes, only this time she's like gone, and i don't know if she's coming back, and it's kinda throwing me for a loop. is that a tattoo?

DEREK: uh huh.

WENDY: it's very small. it's a very small tattoo. in some cultures, men and women, their whole bodies are tattooed, head to foot, until they're just one big, walking tattoo with a face and some hair. it's a thing.

DEREK: i don't think that thing's for me.

WENDY: ok, but look, this is so wimpy. this is the tattoo of somebody who can't decide, somebody who can't commit, somebody who dithers. and you know what, we're just too old to be dithering. i mean it's one thing when you're a kid. you can dither all you want as a kid. but as you get older, dithering is just not cool.

DEREK: why is everyone all of a sudden attacking my tattoo?

WENDY: look, as far as i'm concerned, the tattoo is just the tip of the iceberg. (light off wendy. light on the beach. derek is examining his tattoo. next to him is his manuscript. efran is looking through binoculars. he's beginning to resemble a komodo dragon.)

EFRAN: have you seen a dog? a really big dog?

DEREK: no. why? why do you ask?

EFRAN: never mind. i think my vision is going or something. i don't know what the deal is. i mean, all this stuff could be happening out there, and i just wouldn't even know because i can't see, i can't see a damn thing. i don't know what's wrong with me. i'm feeling very prehistoric and strange. where did you come from?

DEREK: just up the beach a ways. i'm writing this thing, it's kinda autobiographical. i mean, it's about me. i mean, i didn't start out writing about me, and to be honest, you know, autobiography, it only works if you're willing to bare your soul, and i worry sometimes that i have a shitty little soul that i should just maybe keep covered up.

EFRAN: you want a beer?

DEREK: a beer would be swell.

EFRAN: you know, i'm a very bad lifeguard.

DEREK: i'm sure you're doing the best you can.

EFRAN: yeah, but what if that's just not good enough. i mean, i'm like the life guard. i'm the guarder of lives.

DEREK: don't beat yourself up, buddy. we're grownups. we can guard our own lives.

EFRAN: i used to have these hermit crabs. i gave them lettuce and water, and sometimes i'd take them out and they'd crawl up and down my arm. they lived a really long time. it was nice.

DEREK: you were like a god to those crabs, but people are not crabs. people are more like monkeys. when you get right down to it, we're all just basically a bunch of monkeys, running around, screeching and fucking, and throwing our shit up in the air. monkeys are out of control, they make a mess, so really you just gotta kinda let the monkeys do their thing, and stop worrying about it.

EFRAN: i have a tail.

DEREK: i wasn't going to say anything.

EFRAN: i think something strange is happening to me. my skin is kinda turning green, do you see what i'm saying, do you see what i'm talking about?

DEREK: there's a little bit of greenishness going on, uh huh.

EFRAN: also, i have a tail. i didn't used to have a tail.

DEREK: age.

EFRAN: you think?

DEREK: time passes. people change. we age. it's only natural.

EFRAN: what about the tail?

DEREK: the tail is weird, but who can say? we're strange and mysterious creatures. we move in mysterious ways. we change.

EFRAN: you know, i don't think i'm very good with change.

DEREK: change is hard. life is hard. come to think of it, lots of things, i guess, are hard.

EFRAN: easy for you to say. *(grabs derek's manuscript and throws it.)* you don't have a tail. you're not turning into a goddamn lizard. ok, i think i'm going now. i think it's time. i need to find some leafy greens, some shade.

DEREK: shit shit shit.

(derek chases down the sheets of paper as they fly away. light on myrna. myrna wears a santa hat.)

MYRNA: "jingle bells, jingle bells, jingle all the way, o what fun it is to ride in a one horse open sleigh, hey. jingle bells, jingle bells, jingle all the way, o what fun it is to ride in a one horse open sleigh. dashing through the snow, in a one horse open sleigh, through the fields we go, laughing all the way, ha ha ha, bells on bobtail ring, making spirits bright, what fun it is to laugh and sing this sleighing song tonight."

(light off myrna. somewhere else, vivian is decorating her foliage-filled room. lee emerges from the foliage.)

VIVIAN: merry christmas.

LEE: i hate christmas. christmas sucks.

VIVIAN: christmas is a happy time. it's a time when everybody is happy.

LEE: i don't buy it. i think lots of people are miserable at christmas. i think lots of people just want to shoot themselves in the face at christmas.

VIVIAN: okay, time for school.

LEE: can i get some drums for christmas? i really want some drums. and a tattoo. can i get a tattoo? i want to get a tattoo, a big tattoo like on my butt or maybe my face.

VIVIAN: tattoo, no. drums, maybe. you know, you have gotten very big. all of a sudden, you have gotten very, very big.

LEE: who am i? where do i come from? why am i here?

VIVIAN: those are really big questions. i don't know that i have answers to those questions.

LEE: is my hair weird?

VIVIAN: your hair is beautiful.

LEE: i have no friends. i'm a big fat loser.

VIVIAN: you have me.

LEE: you're like my mom. it doesn't count.

(enter jed with little, plastic christmas tree.)

JED: hi.

VIVIAN: hi.

LEE: what are you supposed to be?

JED: i'm the plant guy. i deliver the plants. i remember you when you were this big.

LEE: i don't care.

JED: you've gotten very big. all of a sudden, you've gotten very big.

LEE: why does everybody say that? i'm not big. i'm normal.

VIVIAN: you are. you're very normal. *(to jed.)* merry christmas.

JED: *(to vivian.)* merry christmas.

LEE: christmas sucks.

JED: you know, christmas can be problematic. parents, children, children, parents, family, family can be problematic.

LEE: what's up with the tree?

JED: it's a little baby christmas tree. it's plastic.

LEE: *(grabbing the tree.)* give me that. you call this a tree? this is like the stupidest tree i've ever seen. this tree sucks.

VIVIAN: ok, stop, ok. just stop. what is happening to you? you used to be so cute, you used to be so little and cute. and now i don't know what you are. you're something else. now please just give the man back his tree. do it. now.

LEE: *(giving jed back the tree.)* you suck. you both suck.
(lee exits.)

JED: time passes. kids grow. plants grow. your plants have grown a lot. here. *(giving vivian christmas tree.)* it's for you. it's kinda stupid.

VIVIAN: thanks, thank you. it's lovely, it is. am i a terrible mom? do i suck?

JED: you know, i'm not really the person to ask. i just deliver plants. that's all i really do. also, i was a drunk. for many years, i was a drunk. i have no memory. i fell down a lot.

VIVIAN: listen, i'm thinking of having a little christmas get-together, a little party. it'll be fun.

JED: uh huh.

VIVIAN: you're invited. i'm inviting you. that's what i'm doing right now, inviting you.

JED: i'm not very good in groups.

VIVIAN: you know, me neither. but it won't really be a group. who knows? it may just be me. me and your tree. i really, i like this tree. i'm making cookies. christmas cookies. maybe you'll come.

JED: we'll see.

VIVIAN: ok.

JED: i'll try.

VIVIAN: ok.

(exit jed and vivian in different directions. somewhere else, derek is looking out at the ocean with binoculars. his papers are scattered. he's been drinking. myrna washes up on shore with suitcase.)

MYRNA: merry christmas. what is this mess?

DEREK: is it christmas already? i think i'm a little bit confused about time. i think i'm also a little bit confused about space.

MYRNA: are you drunk?

DEREK: i would say i'm a little drunk, yes.

MYRNA: we drink too much, all of us, we all drink too much. it's decadent, and i don't like it.

DEREK: you know, i have all these friends now in aa. i see them sometimes, and these people they were just like wild in their twenties, they used to be fun, you know, they used to be really fun, and now they spend all their time in church basements, arranging chairs and drinking black coffee out of styrofoam cups.

MYRNA: eventually we grow up. we get out our ice picks, we get down to business. we just start hacking away.

DEREK: you have an ice pick?

MYRNA: i do. i also have a hammer. i had an axe, but i gave that away. i have a lot of things. i come prepared.

DEREK: i don't. i suck. i have nothing to show. i have accomplished nothing. what have i been doing all this time? what the hell have i been doing?

MYRNA: have you been a good boy?

DEREK: no, not really.

MYRNA: well, that's all right. i'm sure you meant well.

DEREK: no, i didn't. i really didn't.

MYRNA: well, you still get a christmas goodie anyway, just because. how's that?

DEREK: i'm too old for christmas.

MYRNA: you will never be too old for christmas.

DEREK: yes, i will. i am already. i have a very bad tattoo, and it's beginning to wrinkle and sag. do you see how it's doing that? o my god, i'm old, i'm like an old man. when did this happen?

MYRNA: just pull yourself together, will you please. *(reaching into her suitcase.)* here, have a sugar cookie. have two.

DEREK: they're the kind with sprinkles.

MYRNA: yes, yes, they are.

DEREK: i love the kind with sprinkles. but wait, don't you see? i have problems. i have deep, unsolvable problems, and i'm basically fucked.

MYRNA: ssh. don't talk, ok? eat, just eat.

(derek eats his sugar cookies. exit myrna. the sound of distant drumming. enter jason holding an axe.)

JASON: hey, derek.

DEREK: hey, jason.

(derek flees. jason follows. the sound of drumming continues. light on wendy. light on joy. each is in her own bubble of light. the bubbles are at separate ends of the known universe. joy is covered head to foot in tattoos. she is a walking tattoo with a face and hair. she still carries her fish. wendy has a plant and is staring at her.)

WENDY: hey, joy.

JOY: hey, wendy.

WENDY: wow. you seem so different.

JOY: i have tattoos over every square inch of my body. i think that's part of it.

WENDY: you know, you seem really faraway right now. you want to maybe come over here?

JOY: you know, i think i'm fine where i am.

WENDY: well, then maybe i should come over there. i'll come over there.

(wendy sidles over to joy. wendy and joy occupy the same bubble of light. it's a small bubble of light. it's a bubble of light made for one.)

WENDY: this is for you.

JOY: thanks.

WENDY: god, look at you. i can't get over it. i never knew you were this wild. were you always this wild?

JOY: you know, i think so. deep down inside, i was very, very wild.

WENDY: i think i love you, joy. i mean, i don't think. i know. i do. i love you. i mean, i love you.

JOY: let's not talk, ok? let's just do other things. can we do that?

WENDY: ok.

(wendy and joy kiss. the sound of drumming continues. the sound of monkeys and birds in the trees. light on a densely foliaged place. the interior of a lush jungle. light on derek and jason. jason swings his axe.)

JASON: derek.

DEREK: jason, please don't kill me.

JASON: derek, man, you never change. you're like exactly the same. such a tense little guy. such a headcase, you're like all in the head. you gotta relax. it's good to see you, man.

DEREK: thanks. what's up with the axe?

JASON: o it's for the tree. i'm looking for a tree, you know, a christmas tree.
every year, it's kinda like my deal. the tree. but this year, man, i don't
know. all the trees are kinda weird. like check these out. these aren't right.
they're all kinda shrubby. and tropical. they've got this whole tropical
thing going on. hey, wait a sec, wait a sec, look at that. see that? now that,
that's a tree. you coming?

DEREK: uh, sure.

(exit jason. derek follows. the sound of drumming continues. enter richard,
disheveled and muddied. he has twigs in his hair. he clutches a komodo dragon.
jed emerges from the underbrush holding a small, flowering plant.)

RICHARD: hi.

JED: hi.

RICHARD: you know, i'm feeling very deja-vuish.

JED: me too.

RICHARD: are the plants very big here or is it just me? maybe it's just me.
maybe i'm just very small. maybe i shrunk. i think i shrunk. i hear you
shrink with age.

JED: i don't think it's you. i think everything here is kinda on the big side. for
example, that lizard, that's a very big lizard.

RICHARD: he's a komodo dragon. from a distance, i thought he was a dog.

JED: do you think he's happy?

RICHARD: you know, as far as i can tell, he eats well. he takes little walks. he
rests in the shade. he's not exactly setting the world on fire, but i think his
life could be a helluva lot worse.

JED: merry christmas.

RICHARD: merry christmas.

JED: i'm going to a christmas party. maybe you want to come with.

RICHARD: o that's so sweet, but you know, i think i'm going to have to pass.
i'm a little pooped. it's been a very long day. i think the lizard and me,
we're going to call it a night.

JED: 'kay.

RICHARD: can i get a raincheck?

JED: 'kay.

RICHARD: i mean it. i'd like that. i'd like that a lot.

JED: 'kay.

(jed exits. richard exits with the komodo dragon. the drumming turns into
christmas music. light on vivian's foliage-filled room. it's christmas. tinsel and

popcorn chains and little colored balls. jed's little fake tree. enter jason with a christmas tree. it's a strange christmas tree. enter vivian bearing a platter. enter jed holding a small, flowering plant. enter lee, sulking.)

VIVIAN: merry christmas. i have eggnog and cookies and ham. i have a ham. look at this beautiful ham your uncle brought. this is a party. we're having a party. i'm very happy. right now, i am very, very happy.

LEE: i smell something burning.

VIVIAN: o my god, i have cookies in the oven. don't go anywhere.

(exit vivian.)

JASON: nice plant.

JED: it's edelweiss. i found it in the jungles of inner borneo. it was a surprise.

LEE: edelweiss grows in the alps. it's like an alpine flower.

JED: as i said, it was a surprise.

LEE: how can an alpine flower turn up in inner borneo? that makes no sense.

JASON: not everything makes sense, dude.

LEE: i would like an explanation.

JED: all right, you want an explanation? fine. this plant was once a little, tiny seed. with me so far? it started one place and wound up somewhere else, carried on the back of a sea turtle, or perhaps on the beak of a bird. these things happen. they happen all the time. mother nature is weird.

JASON: lots of things are weird.

JED: true.

JASON: this tree is kinda weird.

JED: also true.

LEE: why does everything have to be so weird? why can't it just be normal? why can't we just be normal?

JASON: *(to lee.)* just hang some balls, ok?

JED: nice work with the tinsel.

JASON: thanks, dude.

(enter myrna carrying a suitcase and a mummy in a santa hat.)

MYRNA: merry christmas, merry christmas, merry christmas one and all. *(to jed.)* have you been a good boy?

JED: you know, i try.

MYRNA: uh huh, well, that's all we can ask for, isn't it? what about you, kid?

LEE: i've been good.

MYRNA: tell the truth.

LEE: i've been ok.

MYRNA: uh huh. hold that thought. *(to jason.)* and you, what about you?

JASON: i've been pretty good.

MYRNA: good, that's very good. all right, enough chit chat. this is a very busy day for me. spreading good cheer, big kids, little kids. *(to lee.)* hey, don't touch the elf.

LEE: this looks like a mummy. we studied about mummies in school. they shove a straw up their noses, and then they suck out their insides.

MYRNA: she was a mummy in a past life. now she's an elf.

LEE: i shoved a straw up my nose once.

MYRNA: i bet you did. *(to lee.)* now sit down and be quiet. it's time for gifts. everybody sit. *(to jed.)* you, you sit right here, by me. are you excited?

JED: sure.

MYRNA: good, very good. all right, what do we have here? ah, ah. *(removing a letter and giving it to jed.)* i think this is for you.

JED: o my god. it's from demi moore. is this really from demi moore?

MYRNA: well, no, it's actually from her personal assistant, her ex-personal assistant. it's a very nice letter. i read it. i hope you don't mind. he'd like to see you later if you're free. are you free?

JED: yeah.

MYRNA: great.

(exit jed with letter.)

MYRNA: all right, next. *(removing a snowboard and giving it to jason.)* this, i think, is for you.

JASON: o wow, that's just what i wanted. *(to lee.)* snowboard, dude.

LEE: *(to myrna.)* hey. what about me? do i get anything?

MYRNA: a lump of coal. you should be nicer to your mother. myrna knows. myrna hears what's going down. myrna's ears are very big: "you suck. christmas sucks. everything sucks." you should be ashamed of yourself. bad, very bad.

JASON: hey, buddy, don't sweat it. there's always next year. here come on, let's try out the board.

(exit jason and lee. enter vivian with cookies.)

VIVIAN: myrna?

MYRNA: merry christmas. look at you, vivian. time marches on.

VIVIAN: i guess. you know, i'm actually feeling a little left behind.

MYRNA: you're marching, too, vivian. we're all marching along.

VIVIAN: you look great, myrna. i swear to god, you have not aged a day.

MYRNA: you're very kind. what can i say? my work keeps me young. now, vivvie, you didn't ask for anything for christmas, did you?

VIVIAN: no, no, i didn't. i really have everything i need, i really do.

MYRNA: well, be that as it may, everybody gets a christmas goodie. *(taking out a sweater.)* here. it's a sweater.

VIVIAN: gee. thanks.

MYRNA: you don't like it.

VIVIAN: no, no, i do.

MYRNA: sweaters are kinda disappointing, aren't they? who wants a sweater? nobody wants a sweater. what was i thinking? here, i'll take it back.

VIVIAN: no, myrna, no, it's a really nice sweater. it's just i think on some level, i'm just not a big christmas person. i mean, who am i kidding. i burnt the cookies, and so now all i have is this ham, and you know, it's a nice ham, but it's all we have, and i don't think it's enough, you know, a ham, and then there's the tree, look at that tree, i mean, it's a very strange tree, i don't know what my brother was thinking when he got that tree, and also my kid, my kid hates me, and i mean, christmas, you know, it's supposed to be this whole family thing, but i'm not sure i'm a family person. i mean, i think i kinda suck at the whole family thing, i really think i suck.

MYRNA: you don't suck. nobody sucks. well, that's not true. some people suck, but never mind them, just pretend they're not there. o vivvie, honey, you're doing just fine. here, let's put on your sweater.

(myrna helps vivian put on the sweater. it's a very big sweater.)

VIVIAN: it's a little big.

MYRNA: you'll grow into it.

VIVIAN: o myrna i think i stopped growing. i think i stopped growing a long time ago.

MYRNA: phooey. now give me one of these cookies. we're having a party. it's a party. *(eating one of the burnt cookies.)* mm, delicious.

VIVIAN: really?

MYRNA: uh huh. really. all right, myrna must go now, she really must.

VIVIAN: already?

MYRNA: i'll be back. this time, next year. if i get some time off, maybe i'll stop by in the summer, a little alaskan holiday, a little cruise. we'll have to play it by ear. now big kiss. big hug. merry christmas, vivvie.

(exit myrna. enter derek holding a pineapple and a box.)

DEREK: hi.

VIVIAN: hi.

DEREK: hi.

VIVIAN: merry christmas.

DEREK: merry christmas.

VIVIAN: uh, do i know you?

DEREK: i don't think so. i'm a friend of jason's. kind of a friend. not a very good friend. i mean, i want to be a good friend. in the future, i want to be a better friend. is he around?

VIVIAN: you know, no. no, he's not. he just kinda disappeared. everybody just kinda disappeared. this happens to me a lot. i don't know what to tell you. cookie?

DEREK: sure. *(eating cookie.)* good cookie.

VIVIAN: thanks.

DEREK: can i sit down?

VIVIAN: make yourself at home.

DEREK: i like your sweater.

VIVIAN: yeah? thanks. it was a gift. it's kinda crazy. it's kind of a crazy sweater. it's got this whole zig zaggy thing going on, and it's very bright, it's a very bright sweater.

DEREK: it's kinda bright. they'll be able to spot you in a blizzard.

VIVIAN: yes, yes, i guess that's true.

DEREK: this is a pineapple.

VIVIAN: i see.

DEREK: it's from hawaii.

VIVIAN: i figured.

DEREK: i picked it myself.

VIVIAN: just plucked it out of the ground?

DEREK: just right out of the ground. i see you have a ham.

VIVIAN: i do. i have a ham. it's a ham. i think the pineapple, it'll be nice with the ham.

DEREK: that's good, i'm glad. nice plants. nice place. you know, i didn't have anything to do for christmas, and jason, he just, you know, he said, you can come and spend christmas with me and my family in alaska, and i thought, that sounded kinda' nice, christmas, in alaska. i mean, christmas in hawaii, that's ok, too, but christmas in alaska sounded really nice. i hope that's ok that i'm here.

VIVIAN: no, sure, that's, that's fine.

DEREK: good, i'm glad. thank you. thanks. o wait, i, uh, i have this, too. it's just a small thing, it's really, it's nothing. it's just this thing i got in the airport. i was in kind of a hurry, and i just—well, here:

(derek gives vivian the box. she opens it. it's a small glass orb.)

DEREK: it's a snow globe. you shake it. here, see, like this.

(somewhere else, a bubble of light. a parenthesis of foliage. inside the foliage are wendy and joy. two pretty girls. a grass skirt. a tattoo. they are tiny, distant figures. they wave in slow motion. fake snow falls on them. they are happy.)

DEREK: i like how it's snowing, but it's hawaii, i mean, it's supposed to be hawaii, but it's snowing, i like that. and how they're waving, i like how the girls, how they're waving, i like that a lot. it's like they're saying: hello, you know, or good-bye, or help, maybe they're saying, help, "help, help me, i'm trapped, get me out of here." you know, i really, i don't know what they're saying.

VIVIAN: no, now wait, wait a minute, i think i hear little voices. i do, little teeny voices. you don't hear them? you have to listen. you really have to listen. here, listen: "aloha." "aloha."

DEREK: o, ok, yeah. "aloha."

VIVIAN: "aloha."

DEREK: what does it mean?

VIVIAN: i forget.

(darkness. hawaiian music.)

END OF PLAY

Y2K
by Arthur Kopit

BIOGRAPHY

Arthur Kopit is the author of *Oh Dad, Poor Dad, Mamma's Hung You in the Closet and I'm Feelin' So Sad*; *Indians*; *Wings*; *End of the World with Symposium to Follow*; *Road to Nirvana*; and the book for the musicals *Nine*, *Phantom* and *High Society*. Besides *Y2K*, his current projects include: *Discovery of America* (a new play), *Tom Swift and the Secrets of the Universe* (an original musical with score by Maury Yeston); and *Stealing Mother* (an original film).

HUMANA FESTIVAL PRODUCTION

Y2K received its world premiere production at the Humana Festival of New American Plays in February 1999. It was directed by Bob Balaban with the following cast:

Costa Astrakhan (a.k.a. BCuzICan, ISeeU and FlowBare)	Dallas Roberts
Joseph Elliot	Graeme Malcolm
Orin Slake	Fred Major
Dennis McAlvane	Thomas Lyons
Joanne Summerhays Elliot	Lucinda Faraldo

and the following production staff:

Scenic Designer	Paul Owen
Costume Designer	Nanzi J. Adzima
Lighting Designer	Pip Gordon
Sound Designer	Malcolm Nicholls
Properties Designer	Ben Hohman
Stage Manager	Charles M. Turner III
Production Assistant	Amber D. Martin
Dramaturg	Michael Bigelow Dixon
Assistant Dramaturg	Sara Skolnick
Casting	Laura Richin Casting

The New York premiere of *Y2K* was produced by Manhattan Theatre Club in the Fall of 1999.

CHARACTERS

COSTA ASTRAKHAN (a.k.a. BCUZICAN, ISEEU and FLOWBARE) (20)
JOSEPH ELLIOT (early 50s)
ORIN SLAKE (looks to be in his 40s)
DENNIS MCALVANE (a bit younger than Slake)
JOANNE SUMMERHAYS ELLIOT (late 30s)

TIME
Now.

The play is to be performed without an intermission.

"To choose one's victims, to prepare one's plan minutely, to slake an implacable vengeance, and then to go to bed…there is nothing sweeter in the world."
Josef Stalin

Dallas Roberts (above), Graeme Malcolm and Lucinda Faraldo in
Y2K by Arthur Kopit

23rd Annual Humana Festival of New American Plays
Actors Theatre of Louisville, 1999
photo by Richard Trigg

Y2K

A narrow spot of light illumines Costa Astrakhan (a.k.a. ISeeU, BCuzICan and FlowBare), taking us all in through almond-shaped sunglasses.

Astrakhan is nineteen, but one might not guess it, for he looks so wasted and haunted that were we told he was in his middle twenties we wouldn't be surprised.

His hair is neon blue; his shoes, suede and electric green. He wears black leather pants and leather coat, a la Mel Gibson in The Road Warrior. *Under his jacket is a T-shirt that says "Nemesis."*

ASTRAKHAN: Though you think you see me now, I promise you, you do not. It is not possible. In fact, I am everywhere—on the outskirts of your mind, in the ether, in the darkness. And when I'm on the hunt, as relentless as the wrath of God.
(Lights up on: three men standing in a room lit by one bare dangling bulb. Under the bulb is a solitary chair. Across from the chair is a table with two chairs behind it.
Of the three men, one seems confused by where he is. His name is Joseph Elliot, he's in his mid-forties, and wears a casual but elegant tweed jacket and well-pressed jeans.
The two men with him, Orin Slake and Dennis McAlvane, wear the kinds of dark undistinguished suits, white shirts and ties favored by the Secret Service.
Slake, in his forties, has an open friendly face and an easy smile. McAlvane, being younger, and still a trainee, tries to emulate Slake.
Joseph looks around in surprise.)

SLAKE: I imagine, right now, you are wondering why we have brought you here and not to our office. Tell him.

McALVANE: Bringing you to our office would only attract attention.

SLAKE: To *you*. And who wants that?

McALVANE: Rumors, you know. Hard to stop 'em once they start!

SLAKE: I'm sorry: can we get you something?

JOSEPH: Yes. A phone. So I can call my lawyer.

(Slake hands him a cell phone.)

SLAKE: There is really no need, you know. *(Joseph starts to dial.)* We just want to ask you a few questions.

McALVANE: You can leave any time you wish. Really.

JOSEPH: *(Into phone.)* Dotty, hi, it's Joe Elliot, is Larry in by any chance?

SLAKE: We mean that.

JOSEPH: Well when do you expect him?

SLAKE: Any time at all.

JOSEPH: Well when he calls, tell him I've been picked up by two Federal Agents—yes, dear, Federal Agents—who've brought me to a room in a warehouse in Soho George Orwell would feel happy in.

SLAKE: If you prefer, we can do this in a restaurant.

JOSEPH: No, no, this is fun, I'm enjoying this. *(Into phone.)* Yes, that's right, Federal Agents. They showed me a badge. *(To Slake and McAlvane.)* What are your names?

SLAKE: It doesn't matter.

JOSEPH: *(Into phone.)* Did you hear what he just said? *(To Slake and McAlvane.)* Larry will be pleased with that! *(Into the phone.)* Anyhow, tell Larry if I'm never heard from again, this is a clue. *(To Slake, re the cell phone.)* Can Larry call me back on this?

SLAKE: No.

JOSEPH: *(Into the phone.)* From this moment forward, it seems I am in the hands of the gods. *(He clicks off; hands back the phone.)* I'm curious. What would you have done if I'd said no, sorry, fuck off, I am not going anywhere with you. Would you have let me continue on my way?

SLAKE: Of course.

JOSEPH: Really!

SLAKE: As I said, you're just doing us a courtesy.

JOSEPH: Then you should know I have a luncheon in one hour.

SLAKE: Yes, at the Gramercy Tavern, we know. I'm sure we'll be done by then.

(Joseph stares at Slake, startled.)

McALVANE: Would you like to sit?

(McAlvane gestures to the solitary chair under the light; not the sort of place one would choose, given a choice.)

JOSEPH: Could I sit over there instead?

McALVANE: We'd prefer if you sat here.

JOSEPH: Why don't we just all sit together!

SLAKE: Fine. Mac?

MCALVANE: Coming up!

(McAlvane carries the two other chairs toward the one in the middle.)

JOSEPH: So what is it you want to know?

SLAKE: Does the name Feted mean anything to you?

JOSEPH: ...*Name?*

SLAKE: Yes.

JOSEPH: You sure you don't mean "word"?

SLAKE: No.

MCALVANE: Name.

JOSEPH: First or last?

SLAKE: It's an alias.

JOSEPH: "Fetid."

MCALVANE: Yes.

JOSEPH: As in—

MCALVANE: Wined and dined.

JOSEPH: Ah! No. Means nothing.

SLAKE: What about— *(Opens a notepad; reads.)* ShortCurlies, BungHole or ISeeU.

JOSEPH: I'm sorry—but are you aware how odd these questions are?

MCALVANE: Very.

JOSEPH: Well that's encouraging! So. ICU—as in "Intensive Care Unit?" or—

SLAKE: *(Miming it out as he speaks.)* I see you.

JOSEPH: I see. To the best of my knowledge, I have never met or conversed with anyone who refers to himself as I-See-You.

SLAKE: What about corresponded?

JOSEPH: Nor corresponded.

MCALVANE: Are you sure?

JOSEPH: Is that another name?

MCALVANE: No, a question.

SLAKE: Have you ever received anything—

MCALVANE: —by either hand or mail—

SLAKE: —from a man who calls himself ISeeU.

JOSEPH: Not that I recall.

MCALVANE: Which means you may have.

JOSEPH: Only if he called himself something else. I say that with trepidation, knowing it opens the door to almost limitless possibilities. He could for example be one of our authors.

SLAKE: That's what I was going to ask next.

JOSEPH: To my knowledge, not one Random House author, and I am including there both current and backlist, has ever used the name I-See-You.

McALVANE: What about BungHole?

JOSEPH: Now there I'm not so sure. *(They look at him with intensity.)* I'm joking! I mean—All right, the truth: on several occasions I have heard people in my office, generally in the heat of argument, say, "You bunghole!" Were they in fact saying, "You comma Bunghole?"—of that I am not sure.

SLAKE: What about your wife?

JOSEPH: My wife, to my knowledge, has never uttered the word bunghole in her life. But then, I've only known her since she was twenty-eight—no, sorry, twenty-seven. Who can say how her youth was spent?

SLAKE: Exactly. In such matters, who can really say?

McALVANE: Is it possible that *she* is acquainted with ISeeU?

JOSEPH: I wouldn't think so.

SLAKE: How can you be certain?

JOSEPH: I am certain because if she WERE acquainted with someone named I-See-You, I assure you she'd have told me by now.

SLAKE: He knows *her.*

JOSEPH: Well he's LYING!

(They stare at him. Beat. Lights back on Astrakhan.)

ASTRAKHAN: And though you cannot see where I really am, I can see all of you! In fact, can see any part of you I wish—your cunts, your bank accounts, your charge accounts. Is that fair? Not at all. That's just how it is. I'm being honest now. Which is not to say that usually I'm not. Because I am. Usually. I mean honest. Honest as the day is long. So when I tell you that you cannot hide from me so don't even try, you should fucking well take my word for it.

(Lights up on Joseph, dressed as before, staring at his wife, Joanne, late thirties, dressed in a simple, understatedly elegant suit.)

JOSEPH: *(Finally.)* I'm sorry; you don't find this…"odd"? *(She turns and looks at him; no idea what he's talking about.)* What I've been telling you. *(Still a blank.)* …For the past hour. *(That notion startles her.)* …All right, twenty minutes.

JOANNE: Give me a hint.

JOSEPH: Two Federal Agents; a warehouse down in Soho—

JOANNE: You'd think that would be enough.

JOSEPH: Wouldn't you?

JOANNE: I'm sorry, Joseph. This has not been a good day for me. Would you like a drink?

JOSEPH: Sure.

JOANNE: Vodka and tonic?

JOSEPH: Vodka and vodka. *(She exits.)* By the way, did Larry call?

JOANNE: *(Offstage.)* No. Only Emma.

JOSEPH: Emma?

JOANNE: *(Offstage.)* She's in Paris.

JOSEPH: What's she doing there?

JOANNE: *(Offstage.)* Didn't say.

JOSEPH: Well why didn't you ask?

JOANNE: *(Offstage.)* It was on the machine.

JOSEPH: Ah.

JOANNE: *(Offstage.)* Do you want vermouth?

JOSEPH: No. Not even ice. So wha'd she say?

JOANNE: *(Offstage.)* That she received an obscene phone call this morning.

JOSEPH: In Paris?

JOANNE: *(Offstage.)* Obviously! That's where she is.

JOSEPH: And she called from Paris just to say that?

JOANNE: *(Offstage.)* No, she called to say that the man who phoned her… *(Pokes her head back in.)* …sounded exactly like you.

JOSEPH: Jesus.

JOANNE: She thought you'd be interested. Any idea where I might find the corkscrew?

JOSEPH: You don't need the corkscrew for vodka.

JOANNE: I've decided to have wine.

JOSEPH: Ah. No. No idea. *(She disappears again.)* Did she say what hotel she was in?

JOANNE: *(Offstage.)* No. Sorry.

JOSEPH: Right.

JOANNE: *(Offstage.)* She said it was a very disturbing call.

JOSEPH: …Yes…I'm sure…

(He stares out, puzzled. Lights back on Astrakhan. During the following, the lights dim on Joseph, but do not fade completely. He stares out, vaguely troubled.)

ASTRAKHAN: My original mentor was the group known as MoD—that's capital M, small "o," Capital D—and stands for Masters of Downloading, a rowdy bunch, quick with the quip and by and large I would say fearless,

but I quickly moved away from them into a hitherto unknown region of digital hyperspace that was, to be blunt, beyond their imagining. Yet I am a gracious soul, and left them a farewell gift—a password cracker I call Willie Sutton. This little gem, currently available at www.nemesis.com will defeat UNIX, DOS, Windows 95, 98, NT and is compatible with Linux x86/Alpha/SPARC/FreeBSD86 and OpenBSD. Even more astonishing, out of the box, Willie Sutton supports standard and double-length DES-based and OpenBSD's Blowfish-based ciphertext! If you have understood nothing of what I have just said, don't go near this stuff. It could only do you in. A hint: learn it. With what I know, I can go anywhere, and you can too. I have done the math. *Do you have the courage?*
(Lights off on Astrakhan and back up on Joseph as Joanne enters carrying vodka and wine on a tray.)

JOANNE: So, two Federal Agents...

JOSEPH: *(Going for the vodka.)* Interrogated me in a seemingly abandoned warehouse somewhere in Soho for about an hour-and-a-half.

JOANNE: *What?*

JOSEPH: An appropriate reaction!

JOANNE: Joseph...

JOSEPH: But do not fret. As I left, they said they were sure it was probably all a mistake.

JOANNE: *Mistake?*

JOSEPH: I think they meant of identity, but I'm not certain.

JOANNE: Did they say anything about obscene phone calls to Paris?

JOSEPH: This is not funny!

JOANNE: Sorry. *(She sips some wine.)* ...Well you should call Larry!

JOSEPH: I did, but he hasn't called back.

JOANNE: Are you worried?

JOSEPH: No-no, he'll call.

JOANNE: I mean about the Feds.

JOSEPH: Do I *look* worried?

JOANNE: No, but I can't always tell with you.

JOSEPH: Well I am not worried, I am fucking PISSED OFF!

JOANNE: That seems like a very healthy attitude. Cheers!

JOSEPH: It's outrageous!

JOANNE: To a *warehouse?*

JOSEPH: "So as not to attract *attention.*"

JOANNE: You're not serious!

JOSEPH: It's what they said! Place smelled of dead meat. Oh, guess who was in with Perry.

JOANNE: Perry?

JOSEPH: When I got back to the office.

JOANNE: …Give up.

JOSEPH: Tom Clancy.

JOANNE: I thought he was with Putnam.

JOSEPH: He is, but Perry was all smiles, so I think something may be up. Anyway, I gave them a brief account of my morning's adventures, and they both agreed they had never heard of such a thing, but that if I played it right it could lead to all sorts of wonderful dinner invitations. You can even come along!

JOANNE: Are you sure you're not in trouble?

JOSEPH: No, I am not sure, not at all. Anyway, that was my day. How was yours? Terrible, I know. Tell me.

JOANNE: Compared to yours, it was nothing.

JOSEPH: To compare *anyone's* with mine is unfair. This is not a competition. What happened to you?

JOANNE: Francis called.

JOSEPH: Oh God…

JOANNE: I can't stop him from calling me.

JOSEPH: What about a restraining order?

JOANNE: Joseph, be sensible.

JOSEPH: Well certainly you don't have to *take* the call.

JOANNE: Francis is nothing if not persistent.

JOSEPH: That doesn't mean you have to take the call!

JOANNE: If you're going to shout—

JOSEPH: I am not shouting! *(Softer.)* Not shouting.

JOANNE: I took the call because he'd been calling every fifteen minutes for two days straight and Stephanie was getting tired of telling him I wasn't in.

JOSEPH: What about telling him you *are* in but prefer not to take his call, today, tomorrow, and forevermore.

JOANNE: We tried that.

JOSEPH: And?

JOANNE: He started faxing me and it tied up the line. The fax machine is a significant tool at Sotheby's.

JOSEPH: So you spoke to him.

JOANNE: Yes. I spoke to him.

JOSEPH: And I trust told him to fuck off.

JOANNE: That sort of approach only inspires him.

JOSEPH: So what did he want?

JOANNE: I think it may be time to switch to vodka.

JOSEPH: *What did he want, Joanne?*

JOANNE: What do you think?

JOSEPH: It is nice, I must say, to have someone in your life whom you can despise so intensely that you need only conjure up his name when you are bored to get an instant rush of adrenaline. Sometimes I think I could kill him.

JOANNE: No you can't; he's already dead. Read Anne Rice.

JOSEPH: I meant a stake through the heart.

JOANNE: Ah.

JOSEPH: So what did dear Francis say?

JOANNE: The usual.

JOSEPH: Jesus!

JOANNE: Complete with anatomical details. I said, "That's nice, Francis, keep dreaming," and hung up.

JOSEPH: Does he think you get some kind of charge from this?

JOANNE: I'm afraid to say, I've never actually inquired.

JOSEPH: Do you?

JOANNE: Think he gets a charge?

JOSEPH: *Get* one.

JOANNE: Yes, I get all wet. You should see my legs, right now, dripping, just from this.

JOSEPH: Joanne—

JOANNE: No, I do not get a charge.

JOSEPH: Even in a creepy sort of way?

JOANNE: Oh my God—

JOSEPH: What, you don't think it's possible?

JOANNE: Joseph, darling, making lampshades out of human skin is possible. Does it follow therefore that you'd like to see how it's done?

JOSEPH: I might.

JOANNE: You *might?*

JOSEPH: In the abstract.

JOANNE: Doesn't sound very abstract.

JOSEPH: But if it were, if it somehow could be, you know, presented...

JOANNE: *Tastefully.*

JOSEPH: Kind of hard to imagine.

JOANNE: Still!

(She pours herself another drink.)

JOSEPH: Anyway, in this spirit of abstract unfettered inquiry—

JOANNE: You were wondering if I get any sort of rush when Francis calls to ask how my pussy's doing.

JOSEPH: Yes.

JOANNE: The answer's no. I am in fact revolted. Is that clear enough?

JOSEPH: Yes.

JOANNE: Are you disappointed?

JOSEPH: No.

JOANNE: *Pleased?*

JOSEPH: Neither pleased I'd say *nor* disappointed.

JOANNE: What about "surprised"?

JOSEPH: A bit.

JOANNE: Sometimes, I have to tell you, I am really staggered at how little you seem to understand me.

JOSEPH: Actually, I don't think I understand you at all.

JOANNE: Well that's comforting!

JOSEPH: No-no, please, it's exciting.

JOANNE: Part of the adventure!

JOSEPH: Yes.

JOANNE: I can see that, yes, waking up each morning, a blank slate with tits lying next to you in bed…

JOSEPH: Not quite what I had in mind.

JOANNE: Good. I've made an impact then.

JOSEPH: So is that it?

JOANNE: What?

JOSEPH: Francis called you up and that was it?

JOANNE: If that were it, I would not be on my second or is it third glass of vodka now.

JOSEPH: So…?

JOANNE: When I left, he was waiting by the curb.

JOSEPH: For you?

JOANNE: Yes, Joseph, for me, big black umbrella in his fucking hand, limo double-parked, back door open. "Hi, it's raining, thought I'd give you a lift home."

JOSEPH: Tell me you didn't get in.

JOANNE: I did not get in.

JOSEPH: Well thank God for that.

JOANNE: Think I could use another drink.

JOSEPH: Well did you get in his fucking limousine or not?

JOANNE: I got in.

JOSEPH: Well then why did you say you didn't?

JOANNE: Because that is what you asked me to say, and so naturally I assumed it was what you wanted to hear. You've had a rough day, too, and I am trying to be a helpmate.

JOSEPH: So you got in.

JOANNE: It was pouring out.

JOSEPH: Then take a fucking cab!

JOANNE: There weren't any.

JOSEPH: This is really wonderful.

JOANNE: So he drove me home.

JOSEPH: Took the long route, I'm sure.

JOANNE: With all the traffic, going straight was long enough.

JOSEPH: I can't believe you got in his fucking car!

JOANNE: If it makes you feel any better, I can't believe it either.

JOSEPH: What did he do to you?

JOANNE: In the car?

JOSEPH: Yes!

JOANNE: Nothing.

JOSEPH: Well I don't believe it.

JOANNE: All right, fine, he fucked me.

JOSEPH: Jesus!

JOANNE: First on the back seat, then on the floor. He did NOTHING to me, Joseph, not a THING! He was a gentleman.

JOSEPH: *Francis Summerhays?*

JOANNE: Yes, Joseph. When he wants, Francis can be a perfect gentleman.

JOSEPH: "Perfect gentleman!"

JOANNE: Mostly, he asked after you.

JOSEPH: Fuck him!

JOANNE: And I told him not a thing.

JOSEPH: What does *that* mean?

JOANNE: It means I refused to speak about you in any way.

JOSEPH: Why?

JOANNE: Because I didn't want to sully you.

JOSEPH: "Sully?"

JOANNE: Francis has this ability of turning any remark into something untoward. I was not pleased to find myself in his car, and I thought the least I can do is keep you out of it.

JOSEPH: Did he touch you?

JOANNE: On my arm, guiding me in, and that was all.

JOSEPH: Hard to believe.

JOANNE: Believe it.

JOSEPH: So *then* what did you talk about, if all he wanted was to inquire after me?

JOANNE: Nothing.

JOSEPH: Nothing?

JOANNE: Nothing! I was silent the whole way home. And eventually, he shut up too.

JOSEPH: So then what did he do?

JOANNE: What do you mean?

JOSEPH: If he is silent in the back, how was he occupying his time? With what endeavor was he filling his fucking time?

JOANNE: *(Barely audible.)* ...He was watching me.

JOSEPH: *Watching* you.

JOANNE: Yes.

JOSEPH: And what are you doing during this?

JOANNE: Staring out the window.

JOSEPH: So then how did you know?

JOANNE: I could see his reflection.

JOSEPH: *Watching* you.

JOANNE: Yes. And there you are, there you have it. Would you like another drink?

JOSEPH: No.

JOANNE: Look, I'm sorry. I should not have gotten in. And I've no idea why I did, I just did. Next time, I will be prepared.

(She pours herself another drink. Pause.)

JOSEPH: The men who questioned me asked if I knew anyone who uses the name "I-See-You" as an alias. I said I didn't. They said, "Well he knows your wife."

JOANNE: If you're thinking that it might be Francis, I can assure you it is not.

JOSEPH: How can you be certain?

JOANNE: Because Francis does not like playing games. It's not his "style." When Francis wants a thing, he goes straight for it. It's his only honest trait.

JOSEPH: Then why did you marry him?

JOANNE: Joseph…

JOSEPH: *WHY?*

JOANNE: We've been *through* all this! It does no good!

JOSEPH: Are you still in love with him?

JOANNE: Are you serious?

JOSEPH: Yes.

JOANNE: Then lighten up.

JOSEPH: You got into a car with a man you swear you despise!

JOANNE: It was raining out!

JOSEPH: Is *that* all it takes?

JOANNE: Apparently, some days yes! Then again, some days no. With me, it's hard to say in advance.

JOSEPH: I am trying to get a grip on this!

JOANNE: I've been trying that for years. It's slipp'ry stuff!

JOSEPH: Jesus…

JOANNE: One of these days, your blasphemy is going to catch up with you, Joseph. And the earth is going to open. Watch.
(She starts to leave.)

JOSEPH: Joanne!

JOANNE: *(Stops; defiant.)* I married him because I thought I loved him, and believed he would be my rock. On both counts I was wrong. You are my rock, and the only man I've ever truly loved. Why? I've no idea. Life is fun, isn't it?
(She leaves. He stares after her, shaken. She comes right back.)
I'm sorry, I didn't handle that quite right. Let's try that again. Even at moments such as this, Joseph, you are who I love, and the only one I've ever loved. And my rock, my one true rock, to whom I am most profoundly tethered, and in whose lee I am sheltered from all storms. *That felt a little better!*

JOSEPH: *(Genuinely moved.)* Thank you.

JOANNE: Proves it can be done!

JOSEPH: Yes. Proves it can be done.
(She smiles. The light dims. She moves toward him. He takes her in his arms. Lights back on Astrakhan, staring out, blank and pitiless.)

ASTRAKHAN: *(Flat; expressionless.)* Joanne Summerhays, born Joanne Elizabeth Simpson, October fifth 1961 in Ann Arbor, Michigan, where her father taught moral philosophy at the university and her mother taught the flute.

(In the shadows, Joseph slowly begins to remove Joanne's blouse. But Astrakhan continues to stare out.)

In 1983 Joanne graduates from Princeton with a summa in Art History, and the next fall accepts a position at Sotheby's as an administrative assistant specializing in jade and Chinese porcelain.

Two months later, she meets Francis Summerhays, a venture capitalist, at an auction of Asian art at which Summerhays pays three hundred thousand dollars for two matching porcelain tea cups of the Sung dynasty, whose luster, he tells Joanne, pales in comparison to the luster of her skin. Three months later, she marries him.

(Joseph stares at Joanne in awe.)

But the marriage does not go well, and before the year is out she seeks a divorce—this, according to a journal she starts to keep on her lawyer's advice, first in a notebook, then, later, on her computer at Sotheby's believing it's "more secure."

(Joseph kisses Joanne.)

Then, one night, with Francis out of town, Joanne goes to a dinner party where she meets Joseph Elliot, an editor at Random House.

(Joanne and Joseph move to the couch.)

The next morning she calls her host, supposedly to thank her for the lovely evening but in fact to inquire about Joe Elliot, whom Joanne had found, quote: "a delightful dinner partner; most intriguing."

Which is when she learns that Joseph is married—to a fragile beauty named Annabel. When Joanne asks what Annabel does, she is told: Annabel is dying of cancer.

Undeterred, Joanne calls Joseph at his office with an idea for a book about Chinese jade which Joseph finds so fascinating he invites her to lunch, where he offers her a book deal. For the next year, their relationship is business-like.

Then, on August the fourth, with Annabel at New York Hospital recovering from yet another round of chemotherapy, Joseph and Joanne become lovers, the event occurring at approximately 11 P.M. on a couch in Joanne's office.

(Joanne and Joseph decide the bedroom is better for this, and exit.)

Apparently, remorse almost instantly overcomes them both and they decide, while still on the couch, to refrain from any further screwing until Annabel is gone for good—which turns out to take far longer than her doctors had predicted.

But, eventually, it does occur. And three months later, recently widowed Joseph Elliot and recently-divorced Joanne Summerhays marry in a ceremony which Joseph and Annabel's twelve-year-old daughter, named Emma, refuses to attend. Four years after that, I enter the picture. Which is to say, that is when I first see Joanne. Joseph is my way in. No, let's be honest: to me he is far more than that. In fact, always has been. I just hadn't discovered it yet.

(Lights to black on Astrakhan and up on Joseph's office at Random House. It is late afternoon, and Joseph is at his desk, Slake and McAlvane standing just inside the door, staring at him. McAlvane carries a slim leather pouch. During the course of this scene, the afternoon light fades imperceptibly until, near the end, it becomes so dark that Joseph has to turn on a desk-lamp. But the lamp sheds little light. At the start, Joseph, in contrast to the last time these three met, seems at ease. Joseph believes he is in charge.)

JOSEPH: *(Rising from behind the desk.)* Come in, come in! Sorry! Did I keep you waiting?

SLAKE: Not at all.

JOSEPH: Oh good! The other day—well I've just never had an experience like that! Nor, actually, has anyone else I know. So when you called to ask if we could meet again—and this time here!—well I was overjoyed! As was the rest of Random House. *(Sotto voce, gesturing out toward his workers.)* Half of them didn't believe you were real. *(Calling out the door.)* I'm shutting the door now! Sorry! *(Joseph shuts the door.)*

SLAKE: So you've told them.

JOSEPH: Oh yes. Right down to marketing. No secrets here. And the consensus is, play your cards right, you could get a book deal out of this. That's assuming you've done this sort of thing before and are willing to tell all. Perhaps you're not. Anyway, no need for an answer now.

SLAKE: You're not worried?

JOSEPH: About…

SLAKE: Rumors.

McALVANE: You know how they spread.

JOSEPH: Heavens no! We're used to that in publishing. No, I'll tell you what I am. I am outraged and morally appalled by the both of you! How *dare* you do this to me!? *Or to anyone?* Is there some right you have that the rest of us don't know about? Some arcane Inquisitional law? I don't think so. I mean who the fuck do you think you are?

McALVANE: *(With a cold grin.)* Don't you mean "whom"?

JOSEPH: *Whom* the fuck? *(Turns to Slake.)* I had no idea—you employ the handicapped! No, really, that speaks well for you. First thing that does.

McALVANE: Fuck you.

JOSEPH: Temper, temper! *(To Slake, re himself, with a laugh.)* Look who's talking! *(To McAlvane.)* Sorry. Let's forget this part. Can we be friends again?

McALVANE: No.

JOSEPH: No, you're right, of course we can't. None of us will ever be what I'd call "friends," will we? So how long will this take?

SLAKE: Not long.

JOSEPH: Good. Oh by the way, I'm sure by now you've noticed that my lawyer isn't here. Are you surprised?

SLAKE: No.

JOSEPH: Really!

SLAKE: As I said, all we want is some information. I would assume you passed all that on to him, and he concurred.

JOSEPH: "No need for a lawyer!"

SLAKE: So why waste money?

JOSEPH: What *else* do you think he said?

SLAKE: "Call me when they leave?"

JOSEPH: Besides.

SLAKE: I give up.

JOSEPH: He said, "If at any point you feel even remotely uncomfortable—"

SLAKE: "Just say stop."

JOSEPH: His very words!

SLAKE: And we stop.

JOSEPH: Just like that.

SLAKE: Just like that!

McALVANE: Wouldn't have it any other way.

SLAKE: So then… *(Opens a notepad.)* How often would you say you use your computer?

(Joseph stares at Slake, surprised. Slake and McAlvane stare back, expressionless. Lights up on Astrakhan.)

ASTRAKHAN: *HOW IT'S DONE. (Beat.)* Assuming your target's well protected— because where's the challenge if it's not?—what you look for is what we "in the business" refer to, politely, as a back door, and, impolitely, bunghole. It's no accident! The whole thing's highly sexual, it is, I'm erect almost the entire time. Really, breaking into where you're not supposed to go— it's a kickass fucking turn-on. And I do it…*because I can.*

(Lights back on Joseph, et al.)

JOSEPH: My *computer?*

SLAKE: Yes. How often would you estimate that you use it in, oh, say, an average week?

JOSEPH: Just about every day.

McALVANE: But not *every.*

JOSEPH: No. For example, today I probably won't touch it at all.

SLAKE: Then why's it on?

(Joseph turns to look at his computer. Beat. Lights back on Astrakhan.)

ASTRAKHAN: So what you look for are these entranceways. *(Beat.)* And when you finally make it through there is such intense pleasure it's like electronic cum. It's the truth! Really, I keep expecting the screen to get all blotchy! I only tell the truth. That's because lying is obscene. My mom used to lie. Or rather, the woman I *thought* was my mom. Astrakhan, Glenda, 43, dental hygienist and sometime prostitute, stomped to death by her former husband, a tapdancer with Tourets Syndrome. Lucky thing they were not my *real* folks. I'd be all fucked up by now.

(Lights back up on Joseph, et al.)

JOSEPH: The computer's on because of E-mail.

SLAKE: E-Mail!

JOSEPH: Yes. Except for that, I don't use it much at all. And even then...

McALVANE: What?

JOSEPH: Well, most of my business correspondence, I dictate. And if it's personal...

SLAKE: Don't tell me you write longhand!

JOSEPH: Yes! In fact, I prefer it.

McALVANE: *(To Slake.)* He's just an old-fashioned fellow!

JOSEPH: That's why I publish books.

SLAKE: Like that big one over there?

(Joseph looks at a book on a table.)

JOSEPH: You mean the Mapplethorpe?

SLAKE: Yes.

McALVANE: Are you proud of that?

JOSEPH: What?

SLAKE: That book.

McALVANE: Proud that you published it?

SLAKE: I'll bet he is.

McALVANE: Why else would he have it out?

JOSEPH: Would you like a copy of your own?

SLAKE: No. But thank you anyway.

JOSEPH: Why? Have you ever looked at it?

SLAKE: Yes, Mr. Elliot.

McALVANE: We all have.

SLAKE: Had to.

McALVANE: Part of the job.

JOSEPH: So *this* is why you're here!

SLAKE: Not at all. No.

McALVANE: Not even close.

SLAKE: *(To McAlvane: a correction.)* Well…

McALVANE: *(Back to Slake.)* …It's *sort* of close.

> *(They turn to Joseph.)*

SLAKE AND McALVANE: *(Together, to Joseph.)* It's *sort* of close.

> *(Lights back on Astrakhan.)*

ASTRAKHAN: And you find these secret entrances because they were…left there! Yes! Can you believe it? Not for you, oh no, but they might as well have been. No, they've been left by the people who designed the basic system, its security! Because every now and then they like to go back in— *just to see what's doing.* It's like going home again. Really! And you have to understand all that to be any good at this.

> *(Lights back on Joseph, et al.)*

SLAKE: What about the Internet?

JOSEPH: The *Internet?*

SLAKE: Yes.

McALVANE: How often would you say you use the Internet?

JOSEPH: I would say, as little as possible.

SLAKE: Really!

JOSEPH: Yes. I find it mostly a great waster of valuable time. *Like both of you.*

McALVANE: Does that hold for weekends as well?

JOSEPH: *Weekends?*

SLAKE: Yes. How often would you say you use the Internet then?

> *(Joseph stares back, puzzled. Lights back on Astrakhan.)*

ASTRAKHAN: And so you find this back way in because there are certain telltale signs experience has taught you to look out for, the equivalent of footprints, almost ghostly, an extra digit here and there, I mean sometimes that's all it is. And then, once you're in… Well, you're like a mouse in the woodwork, just nestled there, quiet, watching, waiting.

(Lights back on Joseph, et al.)

JOSEPH: On weekends, I would say that if I can help it, I don't use the Internet at all.

SLAKE: And can you?

JOSEPH: What?

McALVANE: Help it.

JOSEPH: The computer is not something I find difficult to resist, especially on weekends, when I use it mostly as a paperweight. Sorry, but I just don't keep records of things like this. I don't "clock in."

SLAKE: But there are records kept.

JOSEPH: Well then check the fucking records!

SLAKE: We have.

JOSEPH: So then you know!

SLAKE: That you in fact use it all the time.

McALVANE: Five, six hours at a stretch.

SLAKE: Sometimes even more!

JOSEPH: I believe you have mistaken me for someone else.

SLAKE: I don't think so.

(Beat. Lights back on Astrakhan.)

ASTRAKHAN: So let's say, now you're "INSIDE THE SYSTEM!" If you choose, you don't have to stay. You can leave a surrogate behind, sometimes called a "sniffer." That's because it—you guessed it!—sniffs. For other telltale signs. Like passwords. Passwords are the key. Because your target has a whole set of 'em, which he uses to go places he'd prefer you didn't know about. And those passwords are what you want.

(Lights back on Joseph, et al.)

SLAKE: *(To McAlvane.)* Mr. Elliot's memory seems to be failing him.

McALVANE: *(Reading from a notepad.)* Three weekends ago, both Saturday and Sunday, you were online almost all day and night. We have your log line, your phone records.

SLAKE: Does *that* ring a bell?

JOSEPH: …Actually, yes, that does.

SLAKE: Why were you online so much?

JOSEPH: I was online because I was trying to get help.

McALVANE: About what?

JOSEPH: My computer. I had somehow screwed it up. I'm sorry: what exactly do you *think* I did?

SLAKE: Show him.

(McAlvane shows Joseph a sheet filled with data. As Joseph starts to examine it, lights come back up on Astrakhan.)

ASTRAKHAN: And this "sniffer" senses when a password's been given, and instantly freezes the screen. "Sorry!" says the message. "Didn't catch that. Could you input your password one more time?" And so your unsuspecting target types in his password one more time. And this time you *capture* it! *(Beat.)* And with that, the system's yours. You are the owner now. Which is when the *real* fun begins.

(Lights back on Joseph, et al.)

JOSEPH: *(Re the list.)* What the hell is this supposed to mean?

SLAKE: The time has come to stop pretending.

JOSEPH: I am not pretending!

McALVANE: *(Sly grin.)* Nor is your wife, it seems.

JOSEPH: My *wife?*

McALVANE: Should I show him those as well?

SLAKE: No, let's just send the whole thing to his lawyer. I'm getting tired of this man.

JOSEPH: What the fuck are you talking about!?

McALVANE: You don't have to go to jail for this, you know.

JOSEPH: I said what the hell are you—

SLAKE: We *heard* what you said!

McALVANE: In fact, neither *one* of you needs to go to jail for this.

JOSEPH: Neither one?

SLAKE: Well, she might.

McALVANE: Yes, sorry. She might.

SLAKE: Still, who knows, maybe not.

McALVANE: Assuming you "cooperate."

(Joseph pushes an intercom button.)

JOSEPH: Could you get me my attorney, please?

(They stare at him. Lights off on Joseph, et al. Lights up on Astrakhan.)

ASTRAKHAN: I did not set out to discover Joseph Elliot's secrets. My sole intention was to take his writing class at the New School, in New York, where I'd just arrived.

Lest you jump to any wrong conclusions, I should point out that my interest in his class had nothing to do with writing. Put simply, there was a girl enrolled in it whom I wanted very much to fuck.

That was before I saw Joseph's wife. *Met* his wife. *Fucked* his wife! Eight times! In three days, ten more in the next two months, once in their very own apartment, which I thought was a little risky, but she said no, let's do it here, on the pool table, and then there was the stain, but she said that doesn't matter, he won't notice it. Joseph doesn't notice things like that. Am I being indiscreet? I'm sorry but there's no avoiding it. Not if honesty is to be our policy. And truth to be told.

In that regard, I must add this: To get into Joseph's class, you had to submit a sample of your work. Unfortunately, I had nothing to submit. I hate writing; always have! So I submitted someone else's—an unpublished piece, relentlessly erotic, written by a demented friend of mine who'd died of an overdose so, I mean, *he* wasn't going to know.

Mind you, I'm not proud of this. I simply tell you this so you may know the truth. It's important to be truthful, and, whenever possible, I am.

Which means I probably should tell you this as well:

Though this particular event occurred almost four years ago, it so reshaped my life, not a day passes that I don't bring it back to mind, with, somehow, each time, some new detail emerging until now it actually seems even clearer than it was back then. Funny, how memory works.

(Lights up on Joseph, big smile.)

JOSEPH: Ah! Right on time! Come in.

ASTRAKHAN: Thank you, thank you.

(Astrakhan enters Joseph's apartment.)

JOSEPH: So nice of you to come.

ASTRAKHAN: No, please, so nice of you to have me—your house, your I mean apartment, this is such a beautiful place!

JOSEPH: Thank you.

ASTRAKHAN: What is this street called again?

JOSEPH: Park Avenue.

ASTRAKHAN: Ah! Yes! Good name. When I publish my first novel, this is where I think I'll live. I don't mean *here* of course! With…

JOSEPH: I understand.

ASTRAKHAN: You and your wife.

JOSEPH: I understand!

ASTRAKHAN: Nice as that might be.

JOSEPH: Right! No, I understand. Not a problem. *(Awkward silence.)* So… would you like a drink?

ASTRAKHAN: Sure.

(Joseph heads for the bar.)

ASTRAKHAN: …Is she here?

JOSEPH: Joanne?

ASTRAKHAN: Is that her name?

JOSEPH: My wife's. Yes. Joanne. No, she'll be here soon. *(Heading back with drinks.)* She works at Sotheby's and an installation's going up that— *(Off Astrakhan's look.)* It's an auction house. *(Again off his look.)* Art.

ASTRAKHAN: Ah.

JOSEPH: You're not from New York.

ASTRAKHAN: No, California. Irvine.

JOSEPH: That's…

ASTRAKHAN: South of Los Angeles. Lot of airport noise. I'm sorry, should I take this off, or…

JOSEPH: Oh! Please! Of course!

ASTRAKHAN: I don't have a regular—you know, *sports* coat, just this which I actually even sleep in, so I didn't know if—

JOSEPH: No, no, you look fine, you're dressed fine. Here, I'll take mine off too. *(They both take their jackets off. Under Astrakhan's is the T-shirt that says "Nemesis." Joseph stares at it.)*

ASTRAKHAN: So you liked my story!

JOSEPH: Liked? No, if I had only liked it, you wouldn't be in the class.

ASTRAKHAN: Guess it's a hard class to get into.

JOSEPH: People have actually tried to bribe me to get in.

ASTRAKHAN: Wow.

JOSEPH: The fact that you are—what?

ASTRAKHAN: A student.

JOSEPH: No. Your age.

ASTRAKHAN: Fifteen.

JOSEPH: *Fifteen!* It's amazing!

ASTRAKHAN: I look older.

JOSEPH: I'd have guessed…

ASTRAKHAN: Eighteen, nineteen…

JOSEPH: Even twenty!

ASTRAKHAN: It's the drugs.

JOSEPH: Ah!

ASTRAKHAN: But I don't do drugs anymore. Not since I began *your class.*

JOSEPH: …Really.

ASTRAKHAN: Absolutely. First day of class, when that old lady read, the one you invited in—

JOSEPH: Grace Paley.

ASTRAKHAN: Her, yeah, I said, hey, your head has to be clear for shit like this, crystal clear—I don't mean crystal, I mean…

JOSEPH: I know.

ASTRAKHAN: No, crystal clear, I was right. My mind has got to be crystal clear. You didn't think there was too much sex?

JOSEPH: Sex?

ASTRAKHAN: In my story.

JOSEPH: Ah! No, well, I mean, there was a lot!

ASTRAKHAN: My English teacher thought there was too much.

JOSEPH: I'm sorry. You wrote this—

ASTRAKHAN: —for sophomore English class.

JOSEPH: Must've caused quite a stir!

ASTRAKHAN: Stir? They kicked me out of the fuckin' school over this. Over THIS! Unbelievable! Especially when you consider that I was merely carrying out a fuckin' assignment!

JOSEPH: *(Incredulous.)* This was an *assignment?*

ASTRAKHAN: "Write about something you consider significant that happened to you during the past summer." Simple.

JOSEPH: Wait.

ASTRAKHAN: What?

JOSEPH: This *happened?*

ASTRAKHAN: What?

JOSEPH: This "story." What you have described in it, the events—

ASTRAKHAN: All true.

JOSEPH: All the fucking.

ASTRAKHAN: All the fucking!

JOSEPH: Let me get this straight.

ASTRAKHAN: I fucked 'em all.

JOSEPH: In what sort of time frame?

ASTRAKHAN: I'd say about a week.

JOSEPH: A *week?*

ASTRAKHAN: Wild fuckin' week. Didn't get much sleep, I'll tell you! But, hey, fuckit, when you're fifteen—

JOSEPH: Why sleep?

ASTRAKHAN: Why sleep? And my teacher—I'm reading this in class—

JOSEPH: *Aloud?*

ASTRAKHAN: That's how we did it.

JOSEPH: To your sophomore class.

ASTRAKHAN: Sophomore English class. I'm reading this aloud. And my teacher turns like purple. "Stop! Stop!" Talk about rude! I wasn't even through the first fuckin' sentence. So I said, shut the fuck up, this is our assignment, cunt!

JOSEPH: You didn't.

ASTRAKHAN: What?

JOSEPH: Say that.

ASTRAKHAN: Of course! I took homework very seriously. Or at least till this. "Stop! Stop!" So finally I stopped, because frankly I just couldn't take it anymore. "What I am reading here is the truth," I said. "Would you prefer it if I lied?" And she said—you won't fuckin' believe this, a certified high school English teacher!—she said, get this: "Yes! You're just are a sophomore. In the sophomore year, you LIE!"

So I said adios, cuntface, and out I went. Fuck school I said! Then I heard about the New School. And came east. I mean this is something else. I'm like in heaven here.

(Joseph stares at him, speechless. Beat. A door opens. Joanne rushes in.)

JOANNE: Sorry, couldn't get a cab, so I ran, I mean it. I'm drenched, through and through. Hi. I'm Joanne. *(To Joseph.)* Is he the one?

JOSEPH: What?

JOANNE: Wrote that story.

JOSEPH: He's the one!

JOANNE: *(Back to Astrakhan.)* That story's positively filthy! And I loved every filthy word of it. *(To Joseph.)* Tell him.

JOSEPH: She's a fan.

JOANNE: Even Xeroxed it so I could show it around the office. My God! Who does your hair?

ASTRAKHAN: I do.

JOANNE: Not bad, not half-bad. Let me see your eyes. *(She lifts his shades.)* Jesus! *(Lowers them instantly.)* How *old* are you?

ASTRAKHAN: *(Hesitates before saying.)* Sixteen.

JOANNE: What the hell have you been doing?

JOSEPH: If you read his story, you know.

JOANNE: It's *true?*

JOSEPH: "Autobiography."

JOANNE: And you're still *standing?* Oh my God! Those shoes! Where'd you get those shoes?

ASTRAKHAN: Stole 'em.

JOANNE: Well steal me a pair!

JOSEPH: Joanne!

JOANNE: He's got style! *(To Joseph.)* How's the dinner?

JOSEPH: Done.

JOANNE: *(To Astrakhan, re Joseph.)* The man's a miracle! Literary taste, and he cooks! Joseph doesn't invite just any old student here for dinner you know. You've been honored! *(To Joseph.)* Start the clock. Five minutes, quick shower, out of these and I'm back. Go! *(As she rushes off, calls.)* Wouldn't mind a martini!

(Exit Joanne.)

ASTRAKHAN: I don't think I've ever met anyone quite like her.

JOSEPH: Few have.

ASTRAKHAN: You're very lucky.

JOSEPH: Yes.

(Joanne returns, blouse almost off.)

JOANNE: Change that to white wine.

JOSEPH: Gotcha.

JOANNE: *(To Astrakhan.)* We must go shopping, someday. Love those shoes!

(Exit Joanne, undressing as she goes. Astrakhan turns out.)

ASTRAKHAN: *(To us.)* I remember him saying something about—I'm not sure, a writer I believe.

JOSEPH: *(Voice barely audible; distant; faint sense of an echo.)* Have you read William Burroughs?

ASTRAKHAN: Burroughs, yes, but don't hold me to it, because at that point all I could think about was her. *(To Joseph.)* I think I'll go freshen up if that's all right. *(To us.)* "Freshen up." I'd heard that in a movie somewhere, and it seemed the right sort of thing to say.

JOSEPH: *(Distant sound, vague sense of an echo.)* Of course. First door on the left.

ASTRAKHAN: *(To Joseph.)* Thank you. I'm so glad you invited me. *(To us.)* And then I walked down the hall, past the first door on the left toward a door at the far end that was slightly open. I could see a light. It was a bedroom. And I walked there. And pushed the door open the rest of the way.

(A door opens revealing Joanne, in an odd light, completely naked, her back to us, drying herself with a towel, but so slowly it feels like a dream.)

(To Joanne.) Oh! I'm sorry.

(She turns slowly, making no effort to cover herself with the towel.)

I have no idea how quickly she turned. I would suppose she turned at a normal rate. But the moment has become so minutely defined that it now seems timeless, and I can replay it at whatever speed I choose, and yet know that it is right. That it is true.

(She stares at him, fully naked, still no attempt to cover up.)

JOANNE: The bathroom's at the other end.

ASTRAKHAN: End?

JOANNE: Of the hall.

ASTRAKHAN: Ah. Sorry. My mistake.

JOANNE: Not a problem. These things happen.

(As if by magic, "the door" shuts on her. And she is gone. Astrakhan turns back out.)

ASTRAKHAN: When she came back out—maybe five minutes later, maybe ten, she was in a light blue dress, loose fitting, delicate, and instantly I knew— or thought I knew, no, felt certain that I knew, that she was wearing nothing under it.

Whether that in fact was true or not, I could see in her eyes that she realized that's what I was thinking. So in a sense it didn't really matter if she was naked underneath. Because she might as well have been, for that's how I saw her now. And she understood that. And that is the truth of this moment, as I remember it.

(Joanne enters in a dress that, when lit a certain way, shows her to be naked underneath. Which is how Astrakhan obviously sees her—though Joseph looks at her as if she were perfectly clothed.)

JOSEPH: Hi.

JOANNE: *(Eyes on Astrakhan.)* Hi.

JOSEPH: Feeling better?

JOANNE: Much.

(She walks up behind Joseph and puts her arms around him, adoringly, and smiles past him—at Astrakhan.)

JOSEPH: Mr. Astrakhan was saying just now that I've changed his life.

JOANNE: How so?

ASTRAKHAN: He's given me a sense of purpose.

JOANNE: In what way?

ASTRAKHAN: Well, for example, the other day in class, he quoted Flaubert.

JOANNE: Flaubert!

ASTRAKHAN: And I had never heard of him.

JOANNE: Well then, you have a great deal of pleasure ahead of you.

JOSEPH: That's what I told him!

ASTRAKHAN: *(Eyes on Joanne.)* I hope you're right.

JOANNE: I'm sure of it.

ASTRAKHAN: Would you like to hear the quote?

JOSEPH: She knows it already.

JOANNE: He tells it to *all* his students. *(With a smile.)* "Everything you invent is true."

(Lights off on everything but Astrakhan.)

ASTRAKHAN: *(To us.)* It was in Chicago, at the Palmer House, that we fucked for the last time. No warning! Nothing! Though I thought she did seem a little distant as we went at it. But then, that could just be me, now, looking back. Can't be sure.

Anyway, when it was done—can't even conjure it, don't want to!—she put on a robe, which was unusual; I mean, for her to cover up—and then, said, straight out:

(Lights up on Joanne, in a robe.)

JOANNE: That's it. No more. It is over.

ASTRAKHAN: *Over?*

JOANNE: Yes, love, over. I mean, what more can we possibly get out of this?

(Lights start to fade on Joanne.)

ASTRAKHAN: *(As the lights fade—an icy calm.)* So then I ripped her robe off. "Stop!" she said. But of course I didn't. Not till I was good and done. *"What more can we get out of this?"* Showed *her* a thing or two. Yes, that scared her, I believe. Scared her quite a lot. And she was right to be. *"NO ONE DOES A THING LIKE THIS TO ME!"*

Then, I just *waited.*

And of course *watched.* I love watching her...

During which time—totally by accident!—I discovered what Joseph's "secret" was.

It's so fucking mysterious, isn't it? I mean the way paths sometimes cross, for no apparent reason, yet, when you look just a bit more closely... Almost makes you believe there's a god.

(A light—in the front hallway of the Elliot's apartment—is switched on by Joanne, who has just returned from work. It is night. The rest of the apartment is dark. From somewhere within, music can be heard, softly: the first movement of Beethoven's Quartet, Op. 131. Astrakhan disappears from view.)

JOANNE: ...Joseph?

JOSEPH: *(Muted, flat.)* In the living room.

(She moves forward, startled that he's sitting in the dark, and peers into the living room, where a dim light from outside now reveals a shadowy unmoving form sitting in a chair.

She switches on a lamp. It's Joseph in the chair, staring out, expressionless, a bottle of vodka and glass on a table next to him. Also nearby: a CD player, the source of the sound.

She turns off the music.)

JOANNE: *Joseph!*

JOSEPH: …Yes, dear. What?

JOANNE: *(Staring at him, startled.)* What is it? What has happened?

JOSEPH: Well, believe it or not, I'm still actually not absolutely sure. But it would seem nothing good. In fact, it may well be catastrophic. Besides that, I'd say everything is fine! This chair is as it was, the floor is at it was, the front key still worked. And how was *your* day?

JOANNE: Why didn't you return any of my calls?

JOSEPH: Well, probably because I was at Larry's. I didn't go back to the office after that, just sort of walked around. Drink?

JOANNE: No.

(He goes to pour himself a drink.)

JOSEPH: *(As he pours.)* Oh, guess what I did at Larry's!

JOANNE: What?

JOSEPH: Threw up. No warning. Projectile vomit, I think they call it! Went halfway across the room! Splat! Right on the Aubusson! Never done a thing like that. Amazing feeling. Womp! Like a cannon. Larry said not to worry. I like that in a lawyer. You sure you don't want a drink? I bet you do. You're just feeling shy. *(Pours her one. Hands it to her.)* Here's looking at you!

(He smiles, clinks her glass, then downs his drink in a gulp. She just stares at him.)

JOANNE: Joseph…

JOSEPH: The funny thing is, it's not just me who doesn't understand how this has happened, Larry doesn't either! In fact, he says he's never come across anything quite like it—as if that would reassure me. Annals of law! I'll tell you what did reassure me. Him saying it's going to be all right. Wait! No. Sorry. That was his secretary. Said it to me on the way out! Guess I looked upset. Or maybe it was the shirt.

(She stares at his shirt, which is spotless.)

Oh, Larry sent out for a new one. That was nice of him, don't you think? Thoughtful! I told him to charge it to me, but he said no, no, it's on him. That gives you some idea of how bad things are.

JOANNE: How bad are they?

JOSEPH: Would you like the short version or the long? Actually, in this case, the long's not much longer than the short. So let's do that. You haven't touched your drink!

(To placate him, she takes a sip.) Little more... *(She drinks down the rest.)* There we go! *(He refills her glass, speaking as he does.)* Well, the nearest I can figure, and Larry, too—assuming now that I'm innocent, which by the way Larry does believe! Or at least he says he does. No, I think he does. Pretty sure he does.

JOANNE: Innocent of what?

JOSEPH: Of the charges. Against you as well!

JOANNE: *Me?*

JOSEPH: Yes, you're in this. It's you an' me, babe. The fat lady's singing for us both! Anyway, nearest we can figure is that I made some sort of terrible blunder inadvertently three weekends ago, when you were up in Boston visiting—can't even remember now!

JOANNE: My mother.

JOSEPH: Oh yes! How is she?

JOANNE: Joseph.

JOSEPH: No, I mean it.

JOANNE: Doing fine.

JOSEPH: Really?

JOANNE: Yes, Joseph, really.

JOSEPH: I like your mother. She's got a lot of guts.

JOANNE: What did you mean by "blunder"?

JOSEPH: Ah! Well now. There it gets a little murky. I *thought* I was doing nothing of any consequence. *(Heads for the bar.)* How about a freshener?

JOANNE: Joseph!

JOSEPH: We have an author who has written a book called "Crisis," filled with endless data on the Year 2000 Problem, and whose central thesis, in a nutshell, says, head for the hills Jack, it's all comin' down. So I thought, if this author's right, there goes his book tour! In fact, everybody's book tour, to say nothing of everybody's salary, yours and mine included. In short, if he's right, we're all fucked! On the other hand, if he's wrong, why are we publishing his book? You see what I mean?

So I said to myself, you'd best look into this! I was curious. Nothing more. You were away. So out I went to the beach house—armed with this weighty tome and my new light-weight state-of-the-art portable computer, which I'd hardly used, but the author mentions all these supporting Web sites so I thought, I'll kill two birds with one stone—I'll read his book, and as I'm doing it, learn how to use my lovely new machine. It seemed an innocuous and foolproof plan.

So there I was, on the back deck, in a deck chair, pitcher of Bloody Marys by my side, mucking about on this new computer, which I was actually rather liking, merrily bopping from one Web site to another, all dedicated to The Year 2000 Problem, and each one by and large backing up our author's dire contention.

And you know what? I was persuaded. I was! Not because of all the data—I get book proposals every day proving that the world is flat, and with data, really, BUT!—because this crisis, even if it never happens, seems so *appropriate*. Really, it's the Parthenon of jokes! Who are those computer assholes who dreamed up that two-digit idea? I am going to sue them. I mean it. For substance abuse.

(She looks at him.)

Yes, dear. For they have abused us of our substance. We are nothing but abstractions now. Strings of digits, signifying anything you want, floating in the ether.

And then I thought of Yeats. That pleased me! Always pleased when I think of him. And I thought, no, he had it wrong. That rough beast slouching toward Bethlehem isn't coming through a desert; it is coming through cyberspace, its body built of naughts and ones.

The ceremony of innocence has been drowned, Joanne—*in naughts and ones.*

(Pause.)

So there I was, musing about the end of things, when all at once this message appears on my computer screen: "Possibly Fatal Error has occurred." And I think, "Surely you exaggerate!"—and give the thing a little shove, whereupon the screen just sort of shrinks, amazing sight! as if Saran Wrap had squeezed everything together. Which lasts only a moment. Bang!— it's back. Only this time it is telling me where I might FIND this "possibly fatal error!" It's trying to help! It's my FRIEND! Which I appreciate so much I believe I actually said thank you to the machine. I think I'm going to need another bottle.

JOANNE: I'll get you one.

JOSEPH: You're an angel.

JOANNE: So what did it say?

JOSEPH: "Possibly Fatal Error in partition 0001-CF-BX forward slash V"—or something like that. Anyway, I think, "Well this at least is helpful!" *(She brings a fresh bottle.)* And this is helpful too! *(He takes the bottle.)*

So I call IBM, because they made this fucking machine, and after about thirty minutes of waiting, a human voice is heard. And the fellow couldn't be nicer! "These things say fatal error all the time; they don't really mean it." "Ah!" So he asks where the error is, in what particular partition, and I read him the information, and he says, "There is no such partition." So I say, "Well, I guess that's the fatal error." And he laughs and says yes, maybe so. I say, "So what do you think caused this?" He ponders for a moment. Then says, "Gremlins prob'ly."

What's really scary is, he's not kidding. I mean he is; of course he is. But the fact is, he doesn't know what's gone wrong any more than I do.

But he does have a suspicion: which is that somehow I've done something wrong. I say, "I hope you don't mean with my *life!*" He says no, laughing, "With the computer. You've probably given it one too many commands. Or have a virus. Did you check for viruses?" "No." "Well, too late now. Do you have *another* computer around?"

"Yes, my wife's." "Well, use that one." And that's his advice. "Nice to speak to you," he says. "Same here," I say. "Have a good day!"

So I hang up. And to my surprise, find I am in a state of seraphic bliss. Because, *because*, Joanne, at long last I know, and with a certainty that comes maybe once in a lifetime, know that I do not ultimately in any way shape or form NEED THIS FUCKING COMPUTER! Fortified with this knowledge, I march inside and bring out *your* computer.

JOANNE: Didn't know I had one.

JOSEPH: Got it for you on your last birthday.

JOANNE: Oh yes…

JOSEPH: Working now swiftly but calmly, I mix up a fresh batch of Bloody Marys, bring out our second phone line, plug it into your "modem port"—

JOANNE: Without asking?

JOSEPH: Without asking. Yes. And *"access your modem."*

JOANNE: *(Shivering with excitement.)* My God!

JOSEPH: Which I found oddly stimulating.

JOANNE: I can imagine!

JOSEPH: Using *your* modem now, I call up our main phone line, to which my inert useless piece of shit is still connected, thinking maybe the gremlins inside will hear that telltale ring-a-ling and wake the fuck up.

JOANNE: Do they?

JOSEPH: Amazingly enough they do. And my machine comes alive!

JOANNE: You should have called Oliver Sacks.

JOSEPH: Good thing I didn't. Bad stuff is about to happen.

JOANNE: Your machine goes back into its coma.

JOSEPH: No, yours does.

JOANNE: My beloved little machine!?

JOSEPH: Your beloved little machine.

JOANNE: Why?

JOSEPH: You are asking *me*? It shut down! "A Fatal Error has just occurred!"

JOANNE: What happened to "potentially?"

JOSEPH: Guess yours just took a more direct route.

JOANNE: Just from dialing *yours?*

JOSEPH: I think there may have been some kind of lethal feedback.

JOANNE: Are things like this supposed to happen?

JOSEPH: One assumes not. But for reasons humankind will never comprehend, in this case it did. Zap. So I disconnected you. And got back to work on mine. Was I right?

JOANNE: To disconnect me?

JOSEPH: Yes. I figured you wouldn't want to just sort of, you know…

JOANNE: *Linger* there.

JOSEPH: Yes.

JOANNE: No, you did right.

JOSEPH: You'd do the same for me I'm sure.

JOANNE: Of course.

JOSEPH: It may come to that sooner than you think.

JOANNE: Joe!

JOSEPH: Somewhere in this next stage of my euphoria is when I suspect it must have happened.

JOANNE: What?

JOSEPH: According to this man in Larry's firm—Thompson, I think, Jim? Yes! Anyway, he's their new computer guru, maven, on this Year 2000 Problem—they've set up a whole division!—anyway, according to this guy, all it takes is one little slip-up and a hacker, if he wants, can get into your machine, your system, and from there, do anything you would do, if not more. Because once he has access to your life, if he wants, he can *revise* it all.

This guy Thompson thinks, can't be sure, but thinks I must have somewhere clicked on something or downloaded something I shouldn't have. Which opened up a sort of door to my system, to my files. And to my life. And with this little door, whoever it was who'd been watching me, and waiting—and he had to be, because clearly a lot of very careful planning went into this—whoever it was—well, it was enough for him.

And in he came.

And now it seems he has revised my life. No, rewritten it. I've got a whole new history, Joanne. And it ain't a good one. *Nor is yours.*

(She stares at him, scared.)

We think we know who it is. He's left a trail. Quite openly. Apparently, he doesn't think he can be caught. He may be right. Thompson says it's almost impossible to know where he actually is, his messages are all time-delayed and routed in a Byzantine way Thompson claims is like a work of art; I mean he's good at this. And now—well, he's just sort of taunting us. Which Thompson says in a way kind of helps, since it makes it so clear that he's invented all of this. Or, anyway…*most* of it.

The problem is: it all looks *real,* you see. Really does! In fact, unless you're me, it's just about impossible to tell what's me and what isn't.

He's made it look as if I'm engaged in child pornography.

JOANNE: Oh my God!

JOSEPH: And not just, you know, collecting it, but selling it. And on a massive scale.

JOANNE: But that's ridiculous!

JOSEPH: Of course, of course, but the evidence—if you want to *see* it as persuasive, is. I mean, there are receipts, Joanne, receipts from hotels I never went to, phone calls I never made, photos of me coming out of buildings I never visited. Sometimes…with children.

JOANNE: Joseph!

JOSEPH: The photos, Thompson says, can be done digitally. And the records—well, you just go back in and revise what was there, or add ones that weren't. He says it's not that hard if you know what you're doing. The FBI creates false identities all the time. And while you're busy proving that it's false—which you may not be able to, not in every instance—it all leaks out. And the damage is done.

You're married to a child molester, dear.

And I'm married to a kind of porno star.

(He picks up the packet McAlvane had been holding, and which had been on the table next to him, takes out a photo, and hands it to her.)

JOANNE: Oh Jesus! Oh my God!

JOSEPH: That's Francis I believe. Standing on the side.

JOANNE: …Yes, but—

JOSEPH: I couldn't recognize the other two men.

(She drops the photo and runs out, holding her mouth. He stares out.
In the distance, we can hear the vague sound of Joanne retching. He stares
down at the picture she has dropped, picks it up and stares at it. Joanne
returns, ashen.)

JOANNE: That never happened, never, never never!

JOSEPH: It's all right.

JOANNE: It is NOT all right! How the hell can you say this is all right?

JOSEPH: Well it does look like you.

JOANNE: Oh my God.

JOSEPH: So I was just saying that if it *were*—

JOANNE: But it's NOT!

JOSEPH: Can you be sure?

JOANNE: Can I be sure? Can I be fucking SURE!?

JOSEPH: Because it really does look exactly like you.

JOANNE: Well it is NOT!

JOSEPH: And I believe you.

JOANNE: Really? Then why did you say just now are you sure? Did I ask you
are you sure you didn't fuck a little kid or two along the way?

JOSEPH: Jesus.

JOANNE: No, I did not. I *trusted* you were telling me the truth! Trusted,
Joseph! TRUSTED!

JOSEPH: *And I trust you.*

JOANNE: Well it didn't sound—Jesus. Oh my God. No… *(She's just looked at*
the photo again.) This *is* me. This is, this is, fuck, oh fuck. And this is
Francis, this is him, it is, and this definitely is me in some I believe hotel,
Monterey maybe, not sure, and I…*sort* of remember him taking photos,
but NO ONE ELSE WAS IN THE GODDAM ROOM! I'd remember
that! *Fuck!* How did they get hold of this?

JOSEPH: I wouldn't know.

JOANNE: Thank you for not saying you tell me.

JOSEPH: Francis could have left it somewhere, sold it, dropped it, made a
duplicate—

JOANNE: NO ONE ELSE WAS IN THE ROOM!

JOSEPH: Look, even if they were—

JOANNE: If they WERE?

JOSEPH: I am only saying—

JOANNE: I don't think I want to hear this.

JOSEPH: I am saying—

JOANNE: Joseph!

JOSEPH: I am SAYING! That even if they were, that is not the issue!

JOANNE: Not the ISSUE?

JOSEPH: *(Holding out another.)* What about this one?

JOANNE: Oh my God!

JOSEPH: *(Weakly.)* I find that one *particularly* disturbing since you have always…
  (He stares at it, too shaken to continue talking.)

JOANNE: Who did this? Who is doing this to us?
  (He sets the picture face down, so he cannot see it, even inadvertently.)

JOSEPH: They believe a former student of mine.

JOANNE: Whom you fucked, I'm sure.

JOSEPH: Oh Jesus.

JOANNE: Probably can't even remember her name.

JOSEPH: *Joanne!*

JOANNE: Sorry, that's right, no, you said this was a man.

JOSEPH: Joanne!

JOANNE: *Sorry!* You were saying?

JOSEPH: …I was saying…

JOANNE: Francis happened *before* you, Joseph! Before, do you understand what that means? BEFORE!

JOSEPH: Of course I understand.

JOANNE: Do you really!

JOSEPH: Yes!

JOANNE: So then why don't I believe you?

JOSEPH: Look—
  (She rips up the two photos he has shown her.)

JOANNE: *(Icily calm.)* So now. You were saying…

JOSEPH: I don't know anymore.

JOANNE: This student's name.

JOSEPH: Oh yes. Astrakhan. Costa Astrakhan.

JOANNE: Never heard of him.

JOSEPH: Four years ago, we had him here for dinner.

JOANNE: By *HIMSELF?*

JOSEPH: No! No-no. With all my other students. My "annual bash."

JOANNE: Ah.

JOSEPH: Neon hair. Neon shoes…

JOANNE: …Wait-a-minute!

JOSEPH: About *sixteen.*

JOANNE: The student you kicked out for plagiarism!

JOSEPH: The very one.

JOANNE: *Neon shoes…*

JOSEPH: He remembers you vividly.

JOANNE: From one crowded party?

JOSEPH: According to him, that's where it all began.

JOANNE: What?

JOSEPH: The affair.

JOANNE: The *affair?*

JOSEPH: Which he refers to as "a fuckfest."

JOANNE: Joseph, this is *Alice in Wonderland!*

JOSEPH: So did you fuck him or not?

JOANNE: I'm going to assume that is a joke.

JOSEPH: He lists all the dates.

JOANNE: He came for dinner once, Joseph! ONCE! The place was crammed with students. I do not remember what he looked like, and except for maybe a "good-night, nice of you to come!" doubt that I even spoke to him.

JOSEPH: Do you remember taking a shower that night?

JOANNE: Why, does he remember me *smelling?*

JOSEPH: No.

JOANNE: I take a shower before *every* party, Joseph. It's a long-standing habit.

JOSEPH: I mean *during* the party.

JOANNE: I would not think so.

JOSEPH: He says he saw you nude.

JOANNE: In the *shower?*

JOSEPH: No, toweling off afterwards.

JOANNE: No, no, that's the sort of thing I'm sure I would remember.
    (Pause.)

JOSEPH: He also believes… *(Hardly able to say it.)* …that I am his long-lost father.

JOANNE: *What!*

JOSEPH: Whom it seems he'd not actually *realized* he had lost till he met me.

JOANNE: Joseph, darling, you have lost your mind.

JOSEPH: But you'll be pleased to hear, you are not his mother.

JOANNE: Well I can't tell you how relieved I am! I mean here we were fucking our brains out—

JOSEPH: He thinks Annabel was his mother.

JOANNE: Oh Joseph, Joseph—

JOSEPH: And he has documents that seem to back it up.

JOANNE: He's insane! How can there be documents?

JOSEPH: Somehow he got hold of some old medical records…
    (He stares off, shaken.)
JOANNE: I don't understand.
JOSEPH: *(With difficulty.)* In 1977, Annabel and I were in Paris when the first signs of the cancer came on. She was in her seventh month. And we decided to abort, because the chemotherapy…
JOANNE: *(Goes to him, moved.)* Joseph, Joseph…
JOSEPH: What's so astonishing is that he somehow got into the files at the American Hospital in Paris, where the abortion was done, and *altered* them…so that it now seems Annabel in fact delivered a healthy little boy on that day. Whom we decided to put up for adoption. *My terrible dark secret!* So we could focus all our energy on Annabel's chemotherapy. *(Beat.)* At that point, my real history and the false link up.
JOANNE: And he is that boy.
JOSEPH: But of course.
JOANNE: He is bloody fucking insane!
JOSEPH: I don't think anyone is disputing that.
JOANNE: Then where is the problem?
JOSEPH: Where?
JOANNE: Yes, Joseph. If he is so obviously insane—
JOSEPH: Joanne, there are post office boxes scattered like signposts around this country in my name to which more child porno has been sent than anyone in the government has apparently ever seen.
JOANNE: And obviously he set it up.
JOSEPH: But that I cannot prove.
JOANNE: Of course you can! Just sue the little fucker!
JOSEPH: How? Where is he?
JOANNE: I don't know. Hire a detective! Hire ten!
JOSEPH: With what?
JOANNE: With *what?*
JOSEPH: We have no money left.
JOANNE: Joseph, wake up. Wake up!
JOSEPH: It's evaporated!
JOANNE: Money does not evaporate. Stocks and bonds do not evaporate.
JOSEPH: That's true only if they are made of paper. Something you can hold.
JOANNE: We have back accounts, Joseph!
JOSEPH: No more.
JOANNE: I have records, we have records!
JOSEPH: They've been closed.

JOANNE: *Closed?*

JOSEPH: Electronically. And our money transferred halfway to the fucking moon and left there to drift, in the ether, in the gloaming. I mean it's somewhere! No one's eaten it. It's just unobtainable, digitally speaking.

JOANNE: Did you call the bank?

JOSEPH: Of course I called the bank, our brokers, everyone! Larry had three lawyers on the phone all day. They're all baffled. It's just gone. Puff the magic dragon. Ah, but not to worry. He says he'll take care of us.

JOANNE: Who?

JOSEPH: Astrakhan. "My son." It's really rather nice of him! After all these years, you'd think he'd be bitter.

JOANNE: It's…

JOSEPH: Yes, sort of unexpected.

Larry thinks he must have had it all in place, the altered records, photos, everything, just waiting to move in, like Hitler's Panza Division. One night is all it took. For the *anschluss.* And by next morning…

Well, we had been *annexed.*

If I could just step back, I would admire it. Because what he's done of course is written a kind of novel. Only not in the old-fashioned linear one-sentence-follows-the-other sort of way, but, somehow, simultaneous.

A novel made of naughts and ones.

And we are its characters.

(She stares at him.)

JOANNE: *(Finally.)* …Can't Larry—

JOSEPH: What? Can't Larry what? What would you have him do?

JOANNE: Well,…explain this to those two Federal Agents.

JOSEPH: Explain what?

JOANNE: That all of this is fake.

JOSEPH: But all of it is *not* fake. *(Staring at her; coldly.)* …Is it?

(She stares back. Pause.)

Speaking for myself, there are things he has found—about me—and which he's tucked in with all the really dreadful "invented" stuff—which is going to come out, and which you will see and will not I think be especially pleased to see—nothing really vile, nothing criminal, but then again…nothing anyone would be proud of.

And for all of that I am very deeply sorry.

And though I can't be sure, I would suspect a similar situation may hold for you.

(Pause.)

At Larry's suggestion, I have resigned from Random House, effective immediately.

JOANNE: Oh my God…

JOSEPH: Larry also thinks you will have to resign from Sotheby's. It's all going to come out, you see; once again, overnight—the credit card records, the phone records, all showing "where I've been." And then the photos. Of me fucking all the kids. Proving it. And then of course there's you.

I'm afraid there are more photos. Many more. Even some video tapes.

JOANNE: *(Barely audible.)* Have you seen them?

JOSEPH: *(Barely audible.)* Yes.

JOANNE: Well I can tell you right now—

JOSEPH: *(Just words—numb.)* I'm sure it's not you.

JOANNE: Oh Jesus.

JOSEPH: Well what do you *want* me to say?

JOANNE: "I *know* it's not you!"

JOSEPH: I know it's not you.

JOANNE: Could you try that again?

JOSEPH: Joanne…

JOANNE: Please? One more time?

JOSEPH: *(Still nowhere close to convincing.)* Of *course* I know it's not you!

JOANNE: Good.

JOSEPH: Joanne—

JOANNE: I said good. Good, Joseph! I'm glad you don't believe it's me. Can't tell you how much it means.

(She stares at him. He stares back. She turns and stares out. The lights change. Astrakhan enters the room. But they don't notice him.)

ASTRAKHAN: Like any homecoming, it will be difficult at first. For all of us. So much to get used to! But we will.

In time.

And then…

Yes…

It will all be, once again, as I remember it.

(He reaches out and, with one arm around each, draws them towards him, gently, lovingly.)

And I will take care of them, forever and ever.

(Lights fade.)

END OF PLAY

The Cockfighter
by Frank Manley
Adapted by Vincent Murphy

115

BIOGRAPHIES

Frank Manley was raised in Atlanta and educated at the Marist School, Emory University and Johns Hopkins University. He taught at Yale University before returning to teach at Emory University, where he is now the Charles Howard Candler Professor of Renaissance Literature. He has published a number of books in his field, most notably on John Donne and St. Thomas More. His other works include *Within the Ribbons: 9 Stories*; *Among Prisoners: Tales from the American Outback* (Fall 1999); *Resultances*, winner of the Devins Award for poetry; *Two Masters*, which was produced at the 9th Annual Humana Festival; and a novel, *The Cockfighter*. His other plays include *The Evidence*, *The Trap*, *Married Life* and *Learning to Dance*.

Vincent Murphy's credits include directing his own literary adaptations of works by John Barth, Wole Soyinka, Samuel Beckett, Michael Ondaatje, James Baldwin, Athol Fugard and William Blake. Other regional directing credits: The Alliance Theatre, Sundance, Alabama Shakespeare Festival, American Repertory Theatre, TheaterWorks, the 1994 Humana Festival and a decade of work at Theater Emory at Emory University in Atlanta, GA, where he is the Artistic Producing Director and developed *The Cockfighter* in the Brave New Work Series.

HUMANA FESTIVAL PRODUCTION

The Cockfighter premiered at the Humana Festival of New American Plays in March 1999. It was directed by Vincent Murphy with the following cast:

Father	Phillip Clark
Mother/Uncle	Ellen McQueen
The Boy	Danny Seckel

and the following production staff:

Scenic Designer	Paul Owen
Costume Designer	Nanzi J. Adzima
Lighting Designer	Pip Gordon
Sound Designer	Malcolm Nicholls
Properties Designer	Ben Hohman
Stage Manager	Paul Mills Holmes
Assistant Stage Manager	Jennifer Wills
Dramaturgs	Michael Bigelow Dixon & Kae Koger
Assistant Dramaturg	Sara Skolnick
Casting	Laura Richin Casting

CHARACTERS

FATHER

MOTHER/UNCLE

THE BOY

TIME & PLACE

The present. Rural America.

Phillip Clark, Danny Seckel and Ellen McQueen
in *The Cockfighter*

23rd Annual Humana Festival of New American Plays
Actors Theatre of Louisville, 1999
photo by Richard Trigg

The Cockfighter

PART I

MOTHER AND FATHER: "The Spirit of Man is descended not only from the Stars and the Elements, but there is hid therein—"

BOY: "—a Spark of the Light and Power of God."

(Shift.)

FATHER: The boy waited until the moon rose and the aluminum frame of the window beside him was full of cold light. He watched as it crept up on the bed, and when it finally got to the slash of electrified red that ran up the middle of the quilt his mother made, defining him, he got up and crept down the hall. The linoleum was cold and slick. It felt like the hard skin on his heels. He went to the door and eased it open inch by inch, as he had been doing every night for the last couple of weeks. When he was certain no one had heard, he went out on the concrete steps.

BOY: The cold hit like a hammer.

FATHER: He went down the steps across the gravel to the gash the bulldozer cut when we leveled off the side of the hill to move in the trailer.

BOY: It was ten or fifteen feet high. Pure red clay. Nothing would grow on it, so Daddy put the cages there. They fit it so perfect.

MOTHER: There were twenty cages in all, set up on legs so foxes and rats and dogs couldn't get them. Underneath the cages the ground was white with their droppings. It looked like it might have been limed, it was so bright.

BOY: I used to think the earth opened up, and the light inside was leaking out.

MOTHER: Each cage had a couple of milk jugs wired to the side. One was for water, one was for feed. They looked like a shed full of skulls in a movie.

FATHER: The Gray was in the first cage he came to. The others were Clarets and Arkansas Travelers and Butchers and mixtures of all three or more, bred for speed and guts and endurance, not for the purity of their bloodlines. There are no thoroughbreds among cocks.

BOY: The Gray was the only Gray we had. When Daddy gave it to me two weeks ago and told me to put it on the keep and get it ready for the next derby, I couldn't believe it. It was my first cock, the best one my daddy had—a real champion, the only one that ever won three derbies. It was known for miles around as the toughest, meanest son of a bitch of a chicken there was.

MOTHER: The Gray was sitting on its perch sleeping, its head buried under its wing. The feathers looked like scales of metal shining in the light. They came down in layers from his ruff, where they were darker, more mysterious looking.

BOY: I loved the ruff best of all. It made him look just like a lion, so that's what I called him: Lion. I didn't tell my daddy about it because he never gave a name to a chicken in his entire life.

(Shift.)

FATHER: They're not pets. You want pets, get your momma to buy one at Easter and raise it by hand. These are wild animals. What you call a deer, you see it running in the woods, lifting its scut?

MOTHER: Tell him deer.

BOY: Deer.

FATHER: The little shit. Listen to that little son of a bitch, Lily. Say deer, you little shit.

BOY: Deer.

FATHER: Damn right! And these are cocks. Remember that. Deers and bears don't have names, and these don't either, except what God gave them, and that's enough. You call them cocks.

BOY: Yes, sir.

MOTHER: God didn't name them. Adam did. *(Reciting.)* And out of the ground the Lord God formed every beast of the field, and every fowl of the air; and brought them unto Adam to see what he could call them. And Adam gave names to all cattle, and to every fowl of the air, and to every beast of the field.

FATHER: That don't include chickens. Chickens don't fly.

BOY: Momma was right, like it says in the Bible. But I didn't care. Lion was mine, and I could call him whatever I wanted.

MOTHER: He was still enough of a child himself not even to be able to think of it without giving it a name. It would be like having a child of his own and not ever naming it, just calling it child.

(Shift.)

BOY: Lion.

MOTHER: It was a secret. He felt the cage tremble when Lion shifted. The head rotated, and its ancient eye looked out. The eye was so dark there was no light reflected in it. It looked like a hole or vacancy.

FATHER: Then it blinked. The wrinkled eyelid shut and opened, then shut again. The bird slept, and the boy stayed there with it until he felt something drain away from him. All the warmth he brought out of the house with him was slowly leaving his body while something else was flowing into him, spinning off the white sheen of the feathers and the cold, translucent light of the moon and entering him, slowly filling him up.

BOY: I knelt there in front of the cage, holding the wire with both hands. It was almost like praying.

MOTHER: Then he got up and ran as fast as he could back to the house. Soon it would be dawn, and the seed of light the boy believed the cock had in it would flare in the sun, and it would start crowing.

FATHER: Later the boy would take the same seed and set it on fire in the pit.

(Shift.)

MOTHER: I didn't know you gave it to him.

(No response.)

MOTHER: What you do that for?

FATHER: Because it's time.

MOTHER: Time for what?

FATHER: Time for you to let go of him, that's what.

MOTHER: I'm not holding on to him.

FATHER: He won't get hurt.

MOTHER: How do you know?

(No response.)

Leave him be.

(No response.)

You hear what I said?

FATHER: I heard what you said.

(The boy wakes, listening.)

MOTHER: It's too rough. Men and women like that.

FATHER: Like what?

MOTHER: Drinking and whoring and fighting and gambling. I don't want my child there.

FATHER: He ain't a child. You seen his pecker?

MOTHER: Don't talk like that! Don't ever dare talk to me like that!

FATHER: How come? I thought you might be interested in that.

(No response.)

FATHER: I thought you might be interested in the fact that boy got a pecker almost as big as mine is now. But you ain't interested in that, are you, Lily? Peckers never been high on your agenda.

MOTHER: Not my son's.

FATHER: Husband's either. You ain't much on peckers, Lily. Never have been. That's the main complaint I got about you.

MOTHER: You don't have anything to complain about me. I've been a good wife to you, Jake. You get what you want to.

FATHER: What about you? That's what I mean. You ever get what you want, Lily?

MOTHER: We aren't talking about me. We're talking about Sonny.

FATHER: Don't call him Sonny. He don't like you to call him Sonny.

MOTHER: You teach him that?

FATHER: What? Hell no! I don't have to teach him a thing. He's thirteen goddamn years old.

MOTHER: Twelve and a half.

FATHER: Who gives a shit! You know what I mean. It's happening, Lily. I don't have to do a thing. I just tell him where to point it, see he don't go off half-cocked.

MOTHER: Don't talk like that!

(Shift.)

(Father laughs. Boy joins in, trying to suppress it.)

FATHER: When you were little, I had to leave you home with your momma. That's the woman's part. Take care of babies. But now you're grown up and getting balls on you, we're going to be buddies.

BOY: That's all I wanted. There wasn't anything else in the world I wanted more than that. He was just waiting for me to grow up.

MOTHER: I don't want him to turn out like you.

FATHER: Like what? You mean disgusting?

MOTHER: I'm sorry. I'm just upset.

FATHER: Like what?

(No response.)

(Shift.)

FATHER: Answer me, Lily. Talking about peckers, fucking, or what? Fucking upset you?

MOTHER: I didn't mean that. You know what I mean. He's just a child. That's what I've been trying to tell you. He's just a baby. You're rushing him too much. You're too rough.

FATHER: What you mean rough?

MOTHER: You know what I mean.

FATHER: You still going on about that? I told you about that. I'd been drinking.

MOTHER: I didn't mean that. I meant all the rest of it.

FATHER: The rest of what?

MOTHER: The whole thing. The way you do. You're one kind of person, and I love you for it. I wouldn't want you to be any different. You believe that, don't you, Jake? You do what you do because that's what you are. I knew that when I married you. But he isn't like that. He's different from you. He's more like me. I'm the one raised him.

FATHER: I raised him too.

MOTHER: You know what I mean. You were off carrying on. That's what I mean. You live rough, and it shows, Jake. Anybody looking at you knows that. Look how you look.

FATHER: What do you mean?

MOTHER: Look what you got on.

FATHER: What's the matter with it?

MOTHER: It's just rough, that's all. Nothing the matter with it. It's just rough.

FATHER: It ain't dress-up. That's what you mean. I ain't dressed up to go to a party.

MOTHER: You aren't dressed up at all. You're dressed to go fighting.

FATHER: Damn right. You don't get dressed up to go to a cockfight unless you're Benny Easley, maybe.

(Shift.)

BOY: Benny Easley's the county commissioner and the only man ever known to go to a cockfight dressed up in a suit and tie. He always said he had an appointment later on.

FATHER: An appointment with an undertaker, they said. Haw! Haw!

(Shift.)

MOTHER: You know what you look like, Jake?

FATHER: Yeah. I know what I look like.

MOTHER: You look like you're going hunting, that's what. You look like a soldier. What you trying to hide from, Jake?

FATHER: Hide? That ain't hiding. That's camouflage, that's all. You know why I got these coveralls on?

(No response.)

FATHER: It's cold at a cockfight, that's why. These're insulated. These are insulated hunting clothes. That's how come I got them on.

MOTHER: You give him a gun?

FATHER: What?

MOTHER: I said, are you going to give him a gun?

FATHER: If he asks me, I will. I won't buy it for him. I'll make him earn it, but I'll go with him and pick it out. Then I'll show him how to shoot it. You know I will.

MOTHER: I know you will.

FATHER: Damn right, I will. When the time comes, I will.

(Shift.)

BOY: I couldn't believe it. I never even thought about wanting a gun, but now that my daddy mentioned it and my momma didn't seem to mind, that's all I wanted. I already had me a cock. All I needed now was a gun. Growing up is the most exciting thing that ever happened to me. Every day it's something new. Today me and Lion. Next week a gun—

FATHER: If she had her way, you'd be a girl. She always wanted one, you know.

BOY: How come?

FATHER: Damn if I know. She don't like men—that's one thing. Except me. She likes me all right. That's how come she married me. But she doesn't like the general run of them. They're too rough.

BOY: What about me?

FATHER: You aren't a man. I'm talking about men. I'm not talking about little children. They're all pretty much the same when they're little, girls and boys both, till they grow up. Then they get different. I don't mean between the legs. I mean up here— *(Tapping his head.)* Their thinking's all screwed up. You're going to have to wait a while. You're still something in between. She might like you all right till you change. Then you're going to start having some problems. Women ain't men, and they don't much like them. They love them all right. That's how come they marry them. But they don't much like them.

(Shift.)

(Brief pause.)

FATHER: You know what's the matter with you, Lily? You worry too much, that's what. If you didn't worry, you'd be all right.

MOTHER: If I didn't worry, I wouldn't be nothing.

FATHER: What the hell's that supposed to mean?

MOTHER: I don't know.

FATHER: I know you don't. Half the stuff you say, you don't. That's another thing about you, Lily—you talk too much. I'm going to go get him.

MOTHER: Let him sleep. Go get Homer.

FATHER: He's going to meet us. You know what Homer is?

MOTHER: I know it.

FATHER: A son of a bitch, that's what. A no-good, goddamn son of a bitch, that's what.

MOTHER: I know it.

FATHER: If he wasn't your brother— *(Breaking off.) (To the boy.)* Get up, you little fucker. It's time to get up and go get them cocks. *(Giving him a knuckle rub. The boy rolls over and pretends to wake up, flinging him off.)*

BOY: What time is it?

FATHER: Time to get up. You want some breakfast, you better get going.

MOTHER: Take your time.

FATHER: Time hell, we got to get going.

MOTHER: The boy's got to eat his breakfast.

FATHER: He should have thought about that before. *(To the boy.)* Come on out when you finish eating. I'll be getting them in the truck.

BOY: They haven't even waked up yet.

FATHER: How the hell you know that? That boy's a fucker, ain't he, Lily?

MOTHER: Don't talk like that.

BOY: Because they aren't crowing yet.

FATHER: They will be. By the time you get finished—hell, I'll be gone— *(Cramming a large orange insulated hunting cap on his head and exiting.)*

MOTHER: Sit down. I'll fix you some eggs.

BOY: I don't have time for eggs. Where's my hat?

MOTHER: That big old Orange Crush like your daddy's? I'm working on it.

BOY: Doing what?

MOTHER: Altering it.

BOY: I don't want it altered. What you mean, altering?

MOTHER: Making it little.

BOY: I don't want it little. I want it big. I already stuffed newspapers in it.

MOTHER: Sit down and eat.

BOY: I can't. You heard him.

MOTHER: He'll wait a while.

BOY: No, he won't.

MOTHER: He ate his breakfast.

BOY: Why didn't you wake me?

MOTHER: I wanted to let you sleep. Let me get you something to take.

BOY: She looked around like she was scared. There was nothing there but a dirty plate with streaks of yellow egg yolk on it and a couple of crusts of toast.

MOTHER: That's the only neat thing about him—the way he eats toast.

FATHER: Neat? You want to see neat? *(Unzipping his trousers and laughing.)*

BOY: *(Laughing with him.)* That's how he is—always joking and carrying on. Momma says he's full of high spirits. That's how come I like to be with him.

FATHER: It ain't all chores. That's the main difference between a man and a woman. Women worry, and men have fun.

MOTHER: What about a choke sandwich? *(Laughing.)*

BOY: I don't have time.

MOTHER: You don't have time for a choke sandwich?

FATHER: One time he was eating too fast. He was always eating too fast, according to her, only this time it was a peanut butter and jelly sandwich, and he couldn't seem to get it down. I said, Do like a dog. Do like this— *(Thrusting his neck out two or three times, pretending to swallow it whole.)*

BOY: It was like chewing a mouth full of tar. That's how come he called it a choke sandwich. It was daddy's idea about what to call it, but I did the choking. *(Shift.)*

MOTHER: Lion was busy grooming himself, smoothing his feathers and picking mites. The boy dragged his finger across the wire, and the cock looked up. Then he reared back and started crowing. The ruff on his neck stood out like it did when he was fighting, and his head was thrown back furiously, and the cry that was coming out of his throat was different sounding than the others—shriller and crazier sounding, full of rage and fury and all sorts of things he couldn't identify yet.

BOY: Daddy loved the equipment and trappings and all the business of getting ready just about as much as he loved the birds. Maybe more.

FATHER: Trappings are what makes it special. If it was up to the cocks, they'd fight anywhere, in a pit or a dunghill. It doesn't make any difference to them. They do it by instinct. It's men that put the art in it. That's the only thing that makes it worthwhile. If it was just chickens killing each other, it wouldn't be worth a goddamn shit, but knowing the rules and working the chickens, knowing the art, bringing something out in them they didn't even know was there—that's what makes it interesting.

BOY: What about the cocks? They're interesting.

FATHER: Of course they are. You use the cocks. They got all that bravery and steadfastness in them, and that's what you use.

BOY: Use for what?

(Pause.)

FATHER: She keep you for breakfast?

BOY: No, sir.

FATHER: What the hell you eating, then?

BOY: A piece of bread.

FATHER: That's all?

BOY: Yes, sir.

FATHER: You hungry?

BOY: No, sir.

FATHER: About to shit in your pants, ain't you?

(No response.)

FATHER: Polish these gaffs. I'll get the rest of it.

BOY: They already looked polished to me, but I opened the box and took out the gaffs and rubbed them with Brasso. Then I polished them with a clean rag and put them back in the box and snapped the lid. It had his name on the top near the handle stamped in gold: SNAKE NATION COCK FARM. JAKE CANTRELL, PROPRIETOR. Snake Nation was the name of the mountain that rose up behind the cages.

FATHER: These are boxes full of pills and ointments and medications and waxed string to tie on the gaffs and spur saws and scissors of all sorts of different sizes for all sorts of different things. Each one is special.

BOY: That the first thing I learned. You don't cut the spurs with the hackle scissors. You want to trim the comb a little, dub him out, you use the dubbing scissors set aside in a special place just for that purpose.

MOTHER: I wish you were as neat about your person as you are about those cocks.

FATHER: If I had a reason to do it, I might. Cocks, I got a good reason for it. There's a whole lot more to it than just giving them feed.

BOY: Yes, sir.

FATHER: You finish them gaffs?

BOY: Yes, sir.

FATHER: Then get the boxes and start loading up.

BOY: I reached in with one hand and slipped it under Lion's belly, and took him out and held him in my arms a minute the way you would a cat or a puppy. *(He glances over to check on his father, then bends over and burrows his face inside the cock's feathers.)*

FATHER: Get away from that cock, goddamn it! You don't want to get them used to you. Standing there with your thumb up your ass looking at them like it was a girl showing her tits, they turn into chickens. You want to turn him into a chicken?

BOY: No, sir.

FATHER: Then get away from him, like I said. Leave him alone.

(No response.)

FATHER: You hear me?

BOY: Yes, sir.

FATHER: It takes the edge off. That's what I'm saying. The less they see of human beings, the wilder they are, and the wilder they are, the better they fight. What the hell you think we breed them for?

(No response.)

FATHER: Well, what are you standing there for? Load them up.

BOY: Yes, sir.

FATHER: Goddamn it! Don't run with those chickens. You'll shake them up, I told you about that. Don't ever run with a cock, you hear?

MOTHER: He put the traveling boxes in the bed of the truck behind the cab, out of the wind. Then he got a rope and tied them down so they wouldn't go sliding around. Then he picked up Lion and went to the passenger's side and got in.

FATHER: What the hell is that? What the hell you doing with that cock in here?

(Mother tries to open the door of the truck.)

FATHER: What the hell you doing, Lily?

MOTHER: He hasn't had his breakfast yet. He can't go without breakfast. I made him some.

FATHER: What is it?

MOTHER: Peanut butter and jelly sandwich.

(Father laughs.)

BOY: I told her I didn't want any.

FATHER: It wouldn't matter to her if you did. She gets something like that in her head, you can talk till you're blue in the face, she wouldn't listen. She ain't got good sense sometimes. Stand back, Lily. We're late already. *(To the boy.)* Goddamn it, I told you to get that chicken out of here.

MOTHER: Let him alone. Don't be so hard. Why you want to be so hard like that?

FATHER: Keep out of this, Lily.

MOTHER: Let him alone. *(To the boy.)* Here, eat this sandwich.

FATHER: Listen, Lily, we're going to be late. Leave him alone.

MOTHER: When are you coming back?

FATHER: When it's over.

MOTHER: What time is that?

(No response.)

BOY: Daddy put the truck in gear, and I tried to close the door. Momma wouldn't let me at first.

MOTHER: You all be careful, you hear?

BOY: She was still running along beside the truck, trying to keep up. All I had to do was turn my head, and there she was. I hated to see her. She was too crazy looking. We picked up speed, and then she was gone. I didn't even turn around to see where she was for fear I'd turn into a pillar of salt like it says in the Bible. I kept my eyes straight ahead—it wasn't just a whole new day. It was a whole new life. There was no telling where we were going or what we were going to do when we got there.

FATHER: I told you about that chicken.

BOY: He'll get cold out there.

FATHER: Damn right. That's why he got feathers.

BOY: He's a champion bird. It won't do to let him get cold.

FATHER: You little shit, that's good. Keep him warm—that's good. You're thinking like a cock now, boy.

BOY: It won't do to treat a champion bird like the others.

FATHER: Damn right. That bird's worth a lot of money. The other ones are mostly all chickens. That one's a real son of a bitch.

(The boy leans over and puts his eye to one of the airholes in the traveling box, trying to look in.)

FATHER: *(Shouting.)* Don't do that! I've seen them peck an eye out like that. Think it's a button or piece of glass—some shiny shit like that—and peck at it. Son of a bitch ain't got no sense.

BOY: I didn't know who he was talking about, me or the cock.

(He suddenly rolls down the windows and throws out the peanut butter and jelly sandwich.)

FATHER: What you do that for?

BOY: I'm going to get me a bar-b-que sandwich.

FATHER: A bar-b-que sandwich. Where you going to get a bar-b-que sandwich?

BOY: When we get there.

FATHER: When you start eating bar-b-que sandwiches for breakfast?

BOY: When I started handling cocks.

FATHER: You ain't started handling them yet.

BOY: I ain't got a bar-b-que sandwich for breakfast yet either.

FATHER: You little shit. You handle that cock, I'm going to buy you a bar-b-que sandwich. I'm going to get you one for breakfast every goddamn day you want it, and that's a promise.

BOY: I don't want it every day. I just want it this one time.

PART II

MOTHER: I didn't know that when I had a boy, I'd have to lose him. A daughter would be mine for the rest of my life, but if I had a boy, and I really loved him, I'd have to let him go. And not just now. I was going to have to do it over and over the rest of my life. *(Pause.)* One time at church the preacher said a woman had twins, and one of them died, but nobody knew it. The woman didn't even know it was twins. One was born, but the one that died stayed up in her and never came out. The preacher said it turned into stone. Every little cell it had in its body turned into stone like a worm in the ocean that died a million years ago and fell to the bottom, and little by little it turned into stone. Later on, the woman got pregnant and had another baby, and that's how they found out. She passed it along with the other. It looked just like a regular baby. The preacher said it had little ears and little hands and little fingers and toenails and a little bow on top of its lip. Everything was sharp and crisp. There wasn't a dull edge anywhere on it. It was just perfect. *(Brief pause.)* It was just like meeting a total stranger and hearing him tell your whole life story up to and including the future. Pretty soon it would be as though they had walled me up inside. The whole thing will turn into stone. Not just the little baby inside me, like my own dearest twin, but my heart and my soul and my tender affections. Pretty soon there won't be anything left except me, and inside me, if you broke me open, a perfect little petrified baby—like a jewel. And it will be everything I ever wanted. It will be the perfect child I always dreamed of when I was a girl. It will look just like Jake when he was a boy, not like he is now, when the drinking and running around tore him down, but like he was in the tenth grade, when we first met. And it will be mine. He won't be able to lay a hand on it. He won't even know it's there because he won't be able to see it. It will be mine, and it will always be with me—flesh of my flesh, bone of my bone. The great, sheltering wings of my pelvis will close in around it like valves of stone, protecting it from all harm until we become one thing: one man and one woman, one husband and one wife, one mother and one child.

PART III

HOMER: Where's your daddy?

BOY: Signing in. You been drinking, Homer?

HOMER: Of course not, you little shit. Who told you to say that?

BOY: Nobody. I said it myself.

HOMER: You little shit, I told him I wouldn't. He said to come help him cover the bets. I told him I would. I don't give a shit for cocks. I'll have mine for Sunday dinner. The only way I like chicken, I told him, is cut it in pieces and fry it for dinner. But I don't mind money. I don't mind making money. You got a proposition about money, that's serious business. I don't drink when it's serious business.

BOY: I thought you quit drinking.

HOMER: I did. Ever since I got out of Detox. He knows that. Your momma knows that. I told him I quit.

BOY: That's good. *(Brief pause.)* How long ago you get out of Detox?

HOMER: Two weeks. A little over. When's he coming?

BOY: When he gets through.

HOMER: I want to get started.

BOY: Doing what?

HOMER: Whatever he says to.

BOY: You can't get started till they get started.

HOMER: I can get started setting it up. I just need the money.

BOY: He'll be along.

HOMER: I hear you're going to handle one of them.

BOY: Yes, sir.

HOMER: Your daddy says that'll set it up. A twelve-year-old boy handling a champion.

BOY: Thirteen.

HOMER: You thirteen?

BOY: Just about.

HOMER: Just about's not it. I'm going to say twelve. That sounds better. That's going to attract a lot of attention. Folks going to want to bet on that.

BOY: How come?

HOMER: How come? It's unusual—that's how come. Folks going to want to bet on the unusualness of it.

BOY: I wouldn't do it if my daddy didn't say I could. I wouldn't want to. He said I was ready.

HOMER: Of course you are. That's what fools them. That and the fact it's a champion cock. Your daddy said your momma could handle that one and win. It ain't the handler, it's the cock.

BOY: They say it's the handler. They say a good cock's no good without a good handler.

HOMER: That right? Well, I don't know a damn thing about it. I know how to bet. That's all I know. I know how to take folks' money and give them change. Except in this case there ain't going to be any change. Your daddy says it's a sure thing.

BOY: That's right.

HOMER: You're damn right, that's right.

(Shift.)

MOTHER: Homer was the black sheep in the family. Every family has a black sheep, and Homer's the one in mine. He was my pet before he got drinking, and even now I can't help but love him.

FATHER: I can. I don't like the son of a bitch.

MOTHER: He isn't your brother, that's why. If he was your brother, you'd love him too.

FATHER: I doubt it. It takes a man with an awful strong stomach to put up with Homer, let alone love him.

MOTHER: I'm not talking about a man. I'm talking about a woman. If you were a woman, you'd love him like I do even if you felt sorry for him.

FATHER: Shit.

(Shift.)

BOY: Daddy says it's an art.

HOMER: *(Acting like somebody put him in neutral.)* I reckon it is.

BOY: I put him on the keep.

HOMER: That right?

BOY: You know what it is?

HOMER: What?

BOY: I said, I put him on the keep. You know what that is?

HOMER: Not exactly. When's he coming? I got something I got to do.

BOY: Pretty soon. I exercised him. That's one thing. Hold him up and make him fly. Strengthen his wings. That makes him strong. That and strychnine.

HOMER: *(Pulling out of it.)* What?

BOY: Strychnine.

HOMER: What strychnine?

BOY: I fed it to him.

HOMER: Bullshit! Strychnine's poison. That'd kill him.

FATHER: *(Coming up.)* It's poison for people, but not for cocks. You know what's poison for cocks? Sweet milk. That'll kill a cock every time.

HOMER: Bullshit!

FATHER: No sir. That's the truth. Sweet milk'll kill them, but strychnine sets them up. It's the opposite from the way it is with people. Amphetamines. You ever take amphetamines?

HOMER: *(Evasively.)* I might have.

FATHER: Same thing. That's how strychnine does to a chicken.

BOY: And vitamin B-12.

FATHER: That's right. And Jake's Special Conditioner. You know what that is?

BOY: It grows balls on them! *(Laughing.)*

FATHER: That's right. That's how I got a four-thousand-dollar bird sitting right there in that cage waiting to go out and make me more money. I got a Special Conditioner. My own secret formula.

BOY: He taught it to me.

HOMER: When are we going?

FATHER: As soon as it starts. Now listen, goddamn it. This is important. Here's the plan. I handle the first three cocks.

HOMER: How many you got?

FATHER: Look there. How many cages you see?

HOMER: Four.

FATHER: That's right. That's what I got. I put up a hundred dollars to enter. Winner takes all. There're sixteen handlers in the derby. That's sixteen hundred dollars right there, besides what else we take in on bets.

HOMER: What you got to do to win it?

FATHER: Shit, you don't know as much as that boy.

HOMER: I didn't say I do. I just asked a question. I don't give a shit about cocks. I don't like the fuckers. I'd just as soon fight a snake as a cock.

BOY: You can't fight snakes. They won't fight.

HOMER: Who gives a shit? That's my point. You're missing the point.

FATHER: The one that wins the most matches wins.

HOMER: All right. We bet on them all?

FATHER: Just the ones I tell you to. Now listen. *(To the boy.)* That Gray's a shake. I talked to the judges, and they agreed to run them last.

HOMER: What's a shake?

FATHER: More than six pounds. All the others fight by weight within two ounces. Shakes, though—it doesn't matter. They put them together. It doesn't matter what they weigh.

HOMER: Heavyweights. *(Laughing.)* Heavyweight chickens.

FATHER: *(To the boy.)* Listen. You help me out.

BOY: Yes, sir.

FATHER: I want you to get them ready for me. If they get in the drags, you take over.

HOMER: What's drags?

FATHER: *(Ignoring him.)* Homer and I'll work the crowds, and when it gets to that big Gray, you take over and handle him. We'll do the betting, and you win that fucker, and we'll clean them out.

HOMER: What about the other ones?

FATHER: The other what?

HOMER: The other chickens. We bet on them?

FATHER: I'll tell you what to bet. A man who doesn't even know what a drag is doesn't have any business betting—ain't that right, boy?

BOY: Yes, sir.

FATHER: Betting's a serious business, Homer. You don't just do it.

HOMER: I know that.

FATHER: Then act like you do. You going to be betting my money, you better listen and do like I tell you.

HOMER: What about the money?

FATHER: What money?

HOMER: The money to bet with.

(Father hands him the money and a pencil and paper.)

HOMER: What's that?

FATHER: An IOU. Sign it.

HOMER: What for?

FATHER: So I get my money back, that's what. That paper says I get back whatever I give you plus whatever you make on the bets.

HOMER: You don't need that. You got my word on it. Besides that, we're family, Jake. That just ain't friendly making me sign something like that.

FATHER: Go ahead.

HOMER: What do I get? Put that on it.

FATHER: Ten percent.

HOMER: Plus expenses.

FATHER: What expenses?

HOMER: Getting over here and eating.

FATHER: *(To the boy.)* That's right, you haven't eaten. Homer, you shit-ass, sign the paper, and I'll give you your fucking expenses. *(To the boy.)* Come on.

HOMER: Where are you going?

FATHER: Get this boy a bar-b-que sandwich.

HOMER: I might have me one too. *(Following them out.)*

PART IV

BOY: We checked the pits. There were three of them, a main pit and two drag pits. The main pit was in the middle, and it was about twice as big as the others. They all had dirt floors and were fenced in with hogwire three or four feet high. At one end of the main pit was a gate and a chair for the scorekeeper. It looked like a lifeguard's chair at the beach.

HOMER: The bleachers were already filling up. The men had on jeans and field jackets and camouflage hunting clothes. They looked like a unit in a rebel army somewhere in Central America. The women were mostly wrapped up in quilts—Bridal Wreaths, Dutch Girls, Baskets of Flowers, Log Cabins. They had them pulled up over their heads like Indian blankets or tucked in around their legs. They looked gaudy as flowers.

FATHER: Looks good.

BOY: Yes, sir. Looks real good.

HOMER: What's the lines for?

FATHER: *(To the boy.)* Tell him what the lines are for.

BOY: That's where you pit them.

FATHER: That's where all the action is. You keep your eye on that, you hear? Come on, they're starting.

HOMER: A fat man climbed up in the scorekeeper's chair and called out, "Numbers two and eight, weigh in."

FATHER: Come on. That's us.

HOMER: I'll wait here.

FATHER: Not with all that money you won't. I want you with me—me or the boy, either one. I don't want you going off by yourself.

HOMER: I'm not going off.

FATHER: I know you're not. Not as long as you're with me, you're not. Come on.

HOMER: We went back to the cockhouse, and Jake got out the Arkansas Traveler.

BOY: Daddy trimmed the tail a couple of inches, shortened the wing primaries, cut a little off the saddle in back.

FATHER: All right. Let's go. Homer, you bet on this one, you hear? Go up to seven or eight. No odds. Even bet.

HOMER: *(Working the crowd.)* Goddamn son of a bitch! Look at that one! I just got to bet on that one. I don't care if I lose or not. Who's going to take it?

FATHER: An old man in a Bush Hog cap and no teeth but a real sharp nose nodded his head. He looked like a chicken pecking at something.

HOMER: You're on. Who's another? You're on. Who's another? All right! You're on. Who's another?

FATHER: Go up there and tell him to shut up. Tell him I said it ain't a show. He's making a damn fool out of himself, carrying on like that. Tell him I said to wait till later, after we got it built up a little. He's liable to spend himself too soon and get them suspicious. Looks like he's selling peanuts, don't he? What the hell's the matter with him?

BOY: He doesn't know what he's doing, I reckon.

FATHER: Damn right. Son of a bitch takes after your momma. That whole damn family's born with something wrong with them, boy. I don't know what the hell it is. Something's missing. They ain't got a lick of sense.
(Shift.)

MOTHER: That had him worried. I was his momma. He could have inherited it from me the same way you inherit noses or mouths. He didn't want to look like me. He wanted to look like his daddy and act like him too, not like me and Homer, going through life with something missing and never even knowing what it was. He imagined it as a body part—a hand or a foot—except it was inside where no one could see it. Something was missing, something he should have been born with left out.
(Shift.)

FATHER: The first fight was a clean kill. I set my cock loose, and it hit the other one and bounced off the hog wire, and by the time it came down the other cock was already uncoupled. Its spinal column was cut in two, and it couldn't even use its legs to stand up or crawl. It tried to steady itself with its wings, but my cock was all over it, jumping up on it and gaffing it till it couldn't move. Then it got hung up, and neither one of them could move. They laid there on top of each other. "Handle!" We pulled them apart, and that was it. The other cock was already dead.

FATHER: Keep on like that, I'm going to have me another champion here.

HOMER: Looks like luck to me.

FATHER: Shit. There's no luck to it, except what you make yourself, Homer. The reason that damn cock's so good is I knew how to breed him. I knew how to put him on the keep.

HOMER: That your secret?

FATHER: That's one of them.

HOMER: Secret feed?

FATHER: It might be.

HOMER: You could sell that for a lot of money, a secret formula like that.

FATHER: If I was fool enough, I might. But that's not all. It's the handle.

HOMER: What handle? *(To the boy.)* What handle's that?

(No response.)

HOMER: The handle on a shovel maybe, shoveling bullshit. There's no handle. Not in that. Not in what I saw. You turned him loose. You call that a handle?

FATHER: Look at my shoes.

HOMER: What about them?

FATHER: What color are they?

HOMER: White.

FATHER: Damn right. White shoes. I bought them special. What color the other handler have on?

HOMER: I can't remember.

FATHER: That's right. *(To the boy.)* You remember?

BOY: No, sir.

FATHER: That's right. You don't remember because they were just shoes, that's all. They blended in. That's what I mean.

HOMER: What's shoes got to do with it?

FATHER: Everything. That's the handle.

HOMER: What handle?

FATHER: I flashed my shoes at him. He turned that bird loose, and I shuffled my feet like this. *(He makes a slight movement. His shoes flash in the light.)* My cock couldn't see it. Because why?

HOMER: Because why?

BOY: He had his back turned! *(Laughing.)*

FATHER: That's right. And that other bird didn't know what it was. He thought it was two or three of them coming—one cock and two shoes. That threw him off just for a second, enough to get a gaff in him.

HOMER: That fair?

FATHER: Fair? Shit. He won, didn't he?

HOMER: What about rules?

FATHER: They didn't see me. They got rules about handkerchiefs and clucking and blowing and waving your hands, but they ain't got around to shoes. They ain't even thought of them yet. That's what I mean. You don't just turn them loose, see what happens. There's an art to it. *(To the boy.)* That right?

BOY: Yes, sir.

HOMER: *(Amazed.)* That's all right. I didn't even see what you did.

FATHER: Hell, no. You weren't supposed to. If you could see it, I wouldn't have done it.

(Shift.)

BOY: The second match was just like the first. It was over in less than three minutes.

HOMER: What happened? *(Coming up from betting.)*

FATHER: Son of a bitch cut and run. Didn't you see it?

HOMER: I mean, did he kill him? Is he dead?

FATHER: Who gives a shit? Goddamn dunghill son of a bitch! I don't think my cock killed him, but the one that owns him probably will.

HOMER: How come?

FATHER: Homer, I can't believe it. You're a dumb son of a bitch. You can't keep a cock like that. What the hell's the matter with you?

(No response.)

FATHER: How much money you make on the bets?

HOMER: Three hundred and eighty-two dollars.

(Shift.)

FATHER: Not counting what he knocked down for himself. By the third match the tension was building. There were four winners left in the derby. The field was narrowing. The next round it would narrow even more.

BOY: Daddy was fighting a Red this time. It had a lot of Claret in it and a lot of something else.

FATHER: That's another secret. The secret of breeding and knowing when to let good enough alone and when to go forward.

BOY: The Red was a big bird, almost a shake. Daddy had a lot of trimming to do and feeding him on vitamins to get his weight down. It hadn't eaten in a couple of days. We gave him some water, and he pecked at it, looking for food.

FATHER: That's one thing I hate about chickens. They're all heart if you breed them right, but they ain't got a lick of sense.

HOMER: I saw one they taught how to dance. The Southeastern World Fair. They had a chicken in a box. You put in a dime like a pinball machine. The music came on, and the chicken started dancing.

FATHER: I saw that. They had it wired.

HOMER: What you mean wired?

FATHER: The floor of the box. They had it wired. You put in the dime, it turned on a heater, the floor got hot, and the chicken started lifting its feet to keep them from burning—and they called it dancing.

HOMER: Well, I'll be damned.

FATHER: You're getting a real education.

HOMER: Seems like it. Ever since I got out of Detox, things have been happening.

FATHER: They happened before. You just didn't notice.

HOMER: I noticed. They just didn't happen. Not like they've been happening lately.

FATHER: Well, I'm not going to argue about it. I got this here cock to fight.

(Shift.)

MOTHER: The match lasted three or four minutes. The referee was just about to move it out to one of the drag pits when the other cock started running. It hit the fence and tried to climb up it. His daddy's cock was on it as soon as it hit the wire and got its gaffs in, and they hung up.

MOTHER AND BOY: Handle!

BOY: The other handler picked up his cock and said, He's rattled.

HOMER: Listen to that. *(Listening to the bird.)* He's rattled.

FATHER: Goddamn right. He ought to be.

HOMER: He took a lot of steel.

FATHER: That don't matter. He cut and run. *(Exits.)*

HOMER: What's rattled?

BOY: The way he sounds.

HOMER: I don't hear him.

BOY: You're too far away. Daddy says when they get rattled, it sounds like a coffee pot perking inside.

HOMER: Is that right? Wonder what does it.

BOY: Blood in the lungs.

HOMER: Goddamn!

BOY: Daddy says they get a hole in it like a balloon, and the air lets out, and it fills up with blood, and that's what you hear rattling in there. You hear them breathing.

HOMER: You ever hear it?

BOY: Not yet. I might if they get over here with it.

HOMER: Why don't they just suck it out?

BOY: What?

HOMER: The blood.

BOY: The lung'd collapse.

HOMER: Oh shit! I don't mind betting on them, but I don't want to know what they're doing.

BOY: Not me. I want to know all about it.

HOMER: That's because you're going to be a cocker. You got to know. You don't have any choice in the matter.

(Shift.)

BOY: By that time there were just two of us left—Daddy and a man from Ocoee, Tennessee. The man at the mike announced the last and final round. He told about Daddy and the name of his cock farm and the name of the man from Tennessee and his cock farm and how the next round was shakes and that was going to determine the derby.

FATHER: *(Shouting.)* Tell them about my boy. *(To the boy.)* Listen to this.

MOTHER: That's right. The handler for Snake Nation Farm in this round is the owner's son. He ain't but twelve years old, and this is the first cock he ever handled. Go get yourself a little refreshment or let out some of what you took in already. The big show's about to commence. You all get your money ready. This is the main event of the day.

(Brief pause.)

MOTHER: The boy's heart swelled with pride. The cock was like the root of his root, the knot in the ropes that tied him together. Seeing him fight was like seeing his own soul go forth from his body.

FATHER: *(To the boy.)* You fight him right, there's no way that son of a bitch can lose.

BOY: Maybe you better handle it.

FATHER: No way. I told you, he's yours. Young son of a bitch like you—you'll steal their hearts. They'll look at you and think of themselves when they were your age and bet their hearts out. Besides, this bird's a three-time champion. Your momma could handle him and win. You ready?

BOY: Yes, sir!

MOTHER: His heart rose up and almost choked him, he was so happy. His daddy believed in him, and he wasn't ever wrong about that. Not about him, not about cocks, not about nothing.

FATHER: All right, then! Let's go!

(Shift.)

MOTHER: The handler from Tennessee was about fifty-five years old. He had on a pair of cowboy boots with high heels and pointy toes and a straw hat, despite the cold, with cock feathers stuck in it all around the brim. He had on a black nylon jacket. It was unzipped, and his belly stuck out like a rock he was carrying—hard and round and gray from his tee shirt. He had a cock slung under his arm like a melon.

BOY: I went into the pit. The referee came over and took Lion and started to weigh him, but the Tennessee man said:

FATHER: It don't matter. Let's get to fighting. It don't matter what it weighs. We already agreed to that.

MOTHER AND FATHER: OK, you ready? *(Brief pause.)* OK, bill them up. *(Brief pause.)* Pit them! The cocks flew at one another like they were fired out of a barrel. They hit and went rolling over and over on top of each other. It was hard to tell where one left off and the other one started. They looked like some kind of ball of fire or wheel of feathers, kicking up dust. Then they hit the wire, and it knocked them apart, and they ran at one another again and got hung up with the gaffs in each other so deep they couldn't move. They just lay there on top of each other kicking their feet as though they were wired, trying to get up.

MOTHER: Handle!

BOY: Lion was on bottom. I slipped my hands under him when all of a sudden the Tennessee man came up and ripped his bird off. Both its gaffs were driven in Lion, one in the head, the other through the neck at the shoulder. He wrenched the gaffs out, twisting them, making the wounds much worse than they were. *(Shouting.)* Hey! Don't do that!

FATHER: *(Innocently.)* Do what?

BOY: Tearing him up like that.

MOTHER: We don't allow no rough handling.

FATHER: I know you don't. Tell him about it. I don't like messing with boys. I'd just soon a woman handle that cock as a boy like that. I've been fighting cocks all my life.

MOTHER: I know you have. You ready to pit them?

BOY: We pitted them again, and again they hung up, and again the man from Tennessee ripped the gaffs out, twisting them, enlarging the wounds. I didn't know what to do. I figured if it got bad enough, the referee would do something about it. That's how come he was there.

HOMER: *(Shouting.)* Tear him up! Your daddy's got a lot of money on this, and I got a little. Don't let me lose it. I need all I can get and then some.

BOY: Go get Daddy!

FATHER *(Coming up.)* What's the matter?

BOY: Something's wrong. It can't move.

FATHER: It's in shock, that's all. Blow on his back. Not like that. Put your face in it. Give him some heat.

HOMER: *(Coming up.)* What happened?

FATHER: Goddamn cock. Wore himself out killing that fucker.

HOMER: Look at the other one. It doesn't look wore out to me. Look at it walking around like that, pecking that shit. You sure it's all right? I got a lot of money out on this.

FATHER: You got a lot of money out? Whose money you think it is?

HOMER: Your money. I'm just taking an interest, that's all.

FATHER: Like shit. *(To the boy.)* Put his head in your mouth and blow.

BOY: I could taste the blood.

HOMER: Goddamn! Looks like he's eating it.

FATHER: Not like that. You act like a woman. Let me do it. *(Taking the cock's head in his mouth.)* There. That ought to do it. *(Wiping his mouth with the back of his hand.)* Look at that son of a bitch. Look how he's looking.

HOMER: It was like it had come back from the dead. Even the blood on its bill had stopped running, and the other wounds were so deep the bleeding was mostly all inside. It took a lot of searching around even to find where it had been gaffed.

FATHER: *(Inspecting the cock.)* It took a lot of steel, all right. I count ten, but it's OK. It hasn't hit anything vital yet.

HOMER: Hell, yeah. It ain't even bleeding, and that stopped.

FATHER: Oh, shit.

BOY: What is it?

HOMER: *(Crowding in.)* Nothing there. I don't see a goddamn thing.

FATHER: White head. This chicken's goddamn head is white.

HOMER: What do you mean white?

FATHER: The skin on its head. Look there. *(Ruffling the feathers.)* White-headed chicken's no goddamn good.

HOMER: How come?

FATHER: Don't ask me. I'm no doctor. Something's wrong with them makes them like that. They can't fight. They ain't got any lead in their pencils, that's what's the matter. *(To the boy.)* How long's it been like that?

BOY: I don't know. Just now, I reckon.

FATHER: Just now, hell. He's been that way. It don't just come on all of a sudden. It takes a while. What the hell I got you for? Go on and fight it.

BOY: What's going to happen?

FATHER: He's going to lose. He got the white head. I never heard of one like that winning.

BOY: What do I do?

FATHER: The best you can. That's all you can do.

BOY: They going to kill him?

FATHER: Damn right they're going to kill him. That goddamn fucking champion bird. Well, that's it. *(Turning to leave.)* There's no help for it. People and cocks are a lot alike in a lot of different ways and dying's one of them. I don't care how game they are, it's going to happen sooner or later, and the best thing to do is go off and leave them and get on with the rest of your life.

BOY: *(Calling after him.)* I'll fight him for you!

HOMER: You want me to help?

BOY: What can you do?

HOMER: I don't know. I thought you might tell me.

BOY: There's nothing to do. You heard what he said.

HOMER: You never can tell. Looks like you all fixed him up, blowing on him.

BOY: They ain't got a lick of sense.

HOMER: I know that. I never could tell what you all were carrying on about, anyway. Chickens are chickens, no matter if you bet on them or not. Betting doesn't change a thing.

BOY: They ain't chickens. These got heart. These are game. These are what you call game fowl. A cock's the only animal God ever made that's courageous and steadfast. That and a lion.

HOMER: So is a man. What about a man?

BOY: *(Piously.)* A man's not an animal. God just made two animals like that. The cock and the lion. The Bible says that.

HOMER: I don't doubt it. The Bible says lots of shit like that. But I ain't going to argue the point.

BOY: It might not lose.

HOMER: Damn right! *(With an air of false bravado.)* Your daddy's been known to be wrong before. Shit fire! He's been known to be wrong about me! How are we going to fight this cock?

FATHER: Pit them!

HOMER: I'll be right over here. Just call if you need me.

(Shift.)

BOY: The fight lasted two or three minutes, and it was just like before. The cocks kept getting hung up, and the man from Tennessee would twist the gaffs out, hurting Lion each time he did it.

FATHER AND BOY: Handle!

HOMER: You want to concede?

BOY: What's that mean?

HOMER: You want to give up?

BOY: Go get my daddy!

HOMER: What for?

BOY: Tell him I need him!

HOMER: That bird's wore out.

BOY: Wait for my daddy.

FATHER: *(Coming up.)* What's going on here? What? Hell, no! Fight it out. I don't give up.

HOMER: That's you. That ain't that chicken. Why not let the boy have it?

FATHER: Hell, no! White-headed son of a bitch. Get on with it.

HOMER: *(To the boy.)* That's what you want to do?

FATHER: What the hell you asking him for? I'm the owner. I already told you. *(Starts the count.)* One, two…

HOMER: He's the handler of record.

FATHER: *(To the boy.)* Three, four…

HOMER: How about it?

FATHER: Five, six…

HOMER: Keep it. Don't let them kill him.

FATHER: Seven, eight.…

HOMER: You got a dog?

(Boy shakes his head no.)

HOMER: Go on and keep it, then. Chickens make good pets. Follow you around wherever you go, if you let them.

FATHER: Nine, ten.

BOY: Fight it out!

FATHER: PIT THEM!

BOY: I did what my daddy showed me to do. *(Cupping the bird in his hands, ministering to it.)* But he was exhausted. His eyes were glazed and not able to focus. They kept drooping shut.

FATHER: PIT THEM!

BOY: I turned him loose, and Lion just stood there. The other bird leaped up and gaffed him. Lion went down, and the other cock kept leaping up on him, gaffing him and pecking his head till the blood ran out of his eyes and Lion was dead.

FATHER: The other cock was still gaffing him. The boy started to pull them apart. Let him alone. Let him enjoy himself a little. He got to come down. It's part of his nature.

HOMER: The bird was already dead, but the other cock kept gaffing him till the boy finally went over and picked his cock up by the legs and carried him out upside down so he wouldn't get the blood on his trousers.

BOY: Daddy?

FATHER: What the hell you got there?

BOY: What you do with it?

FATHER: Throw it over there till they finish. They'll get it later. Unless you want it. *(Turning to a woman beside him.)* You want you some cock?

MOTHER: Not no dead cock. I had enough of that to last me a lifetime already. *(Laughing.)*

FATHER: We'll have to get you a live one, then.

MOTHER: You might have to. It's been a long time if you do. *(Cutting her eyes at him.)*

BOY: I tasted something in my mouth that wasn't my own spit and wasn't the taste of chicken blood either. It tasted like dirt when I had to eat it one time at school when another boy beat up on me. It was gritty and dead like dirt. It was filling me up from inside like dirt somebody poured in a bottle. When it got filled up, I'd be dead. It was the start of something that would go on for the rest of my life—like Homer. I never knew that before. Nothing happened like it was supposed to.

HOMER: Can't win them all. Look at me.

BOY: I'm going to go sit with my daddy.

HOMER: Good idea.

BOY: Daddy must have known something I didn't. Some kind of secret. That's how come he didn't care. He knew how to handle it. I just started handling things, and if I was going to learn how to be a good handler, I was going to have to stick with my daddy. Homer didn't know shit.

FATHER: Come on, let's go. I'm getting sick of this place, ain't you?

(Homer starts to get up with them.)

FATHER: Not you.

HOMER: I thought you might drop me off.

FATHER: How'd you get out here?

HOMER: Somebody took me.

FATHER: Then somebody might want to take you back.

HOMER: They're already gone.

FATHER: OK. You ride in back with the chickens, you hear? Those that are left. *(Pointedly.)* Those that aren't dead already.

BOY: He can ride in front with us. There's room.

FATHER: Not for me. I don't want him crowding in. Unless you want to sit back there.

BOY: I don't mind.

FATHER: All right. Let's go!

BOY: And that's when I saw him. It was as though he had risen from the dead and was coming out from under the bleachers, stopping every now and then to peck at a feather or piece of paper or scrap of food just like he would in a barnyard.

(The boy runs over and scoops up the cock and cradles him in his arms like a puppy. Then he stands up and offers him to his father.)

FATHER: What the hell is that? That's that goddamn chicken that's dead.

HOMER: What chicken? *(Crowding in.)*

FATHER: *(To the boy.)* What the hell you giving me that for?

BOY: *(Confused.)* He ain't dead.

FATHER: The hell he ain't.

HOMER: Don't look dead to me.

FATHER: That's you. Just because he's walking around don't mean he ain't dead.

BOY: You could fix him.

FATHER: What the hell I want to do that for? That cock's no good. Wring his neck, and let's get going. A cock takes a beating like that, it might live a day or two, but it's bound to die sooner or later. There're some things you just can't fix. That's the first rule about cockfighting. It's a sport, and the first rule of sport is be a good loser. Besides, even if it did get better, it had all the spunk knocked out of it. A chicken takes a beating like that, it isn't ever the same again. They're like Homer, then—ain't that right, Homer? They know what can happen to them. They lost their cherry, and they aren't ever going to do that again. *(Changing tone.)* I don't raise dunghills. I'd just as soon kill them all if they turned into chickens. A boy of mine don't need a pet. He's too old for pets. I'm training him to be like me. *(To the boy.)* Wring his neck.

BOY: What?

FATHER: Wring his neck. Take him back there and wring his neck.

HOMER: Goddamn, Jake! Back off a little. Let the boy keep it. What the hell's it matter to you? I'll pay you ten dollars. Here, take twenty. *(Thrusting the money at him.) (To the boy.)* Go on and keep him.

FATHER: I told you about that.

HOMER: *(Backing off.)* I don't mean to mess with your business. You know that, Jake. I was just talking. Seemed to me it wouldn't hurt.

FATHER: That's you. I just don't need you butting in, that's all. I get enough of that from Lily.

HOMER: I know you do.

FATHER: He's my boy.

HOMER: I know that, Jake.

FATHER: I'm going to raise him like I want.

HOMER: I know that. Lily already told me about that.

FATHER: I got a responsibility to him.

HOMER: I know that. You're right about that. There're different ways of seeing it, that's all.

FATHER: My way and yours.

HOMER: I don't mean that.

FATHER: I do. *(To the boy.)* Do like I said. I'm going to be right here watching you.

HOMER: Let me do it. There's no sense making him do it.

FATHER: It's his bird.

HOMER: All the more reason. He doesn't want to kill his own bird.

FATHER: Goddamn, Homer! He's got a responsibility to it. Just like a dog. Say you hit a dog with your truck. I figure it's your duty to kill it. You don't just go off and leave it there. You already bought it—that's what I figure. You hit it, you bought it. That makes it yours. *(To the boy.)* You fought that cock, and now it's dead, and you got to kill it. Go on, do like I said.

MOTHER: He put his hand on Lion's neck and slung him around in a circle— once—twice—then threw him underhand into the corner. The bird kept on going, leaping and flailing and ramming itself into the corner. Then it turned and came hopping and rolling all over itself, coming right at him. He was surprised by how much life the bird had in it, coming out in hysterical, frenzied rushes and jerks, this way, then that, trying to get through the wall. It climbed up the wall boards a little way and then fell back and lay there twitching. Sonny watched while the life drained out.

FATHER: Leave it alone. They'll come and get it.

BOY: I reached out and touched him, and something went out of me when I did it. Everything my momma taught me about the Bible and everything else drained out of me, slow at first, then faster and faster. It was like believing in God and going out one morning and finding him dead, you already killed him, and he wasn't ever coming back, no matter what it said in the Bible.

FATHER: All right. That's enough of this shit. Let's get going. You're acting like a baby about it.

HOMER: Let him alone. The boy's grieving.

FATHER: I don't see what the hell for. It's my cock. I'm the one lost all the money.

BOY: *(Surprised.)* I thought it was mine.

FATHER: It was in a way— *(Glancing at Homer, looking for help.)* I gave it to you, but it was mine, else I couldn't have given it to you. That stands to reason.

BOY: I thought it was mine.

FATHER: Of course it was yours— *(Fishtailing.)* You fought it, you killed it, that makes it yours. I'd say he earned it—don't you, Homer? I might have given it to him at first, but I'd say he earned it now, don't you?

HOMER: That's right. You did enough damage for one day.

BOY: I did what I had to. It was my bird.

FATHER: *(To Homer.)* He's learning. He's going to be all right in a while.

HOMER: *(Smiling at the boy.)* He already is.

FATHER: Not yet. But I'm working on it. He's going to get better. *(Laughing.)* Hell, the son of a bitch is bound to. He can't get much worse.

PART V

HOMER: I said, you married? She said, Yeah, I used to be. That's how come I'm sitting here drinking. I got a bunch of marital troubles. I didn't give a shit about that, so I said, Let me tell you something. What you think about a boy lost his cock? You got any opinions on that? She said, Yeah. Lots of them. I said, Like what? Give me one of them. She said, Tough shit. I said, All right. Give me another. She said, Who gives a shit? I said, He does. If you had a cock, you'd know what I mean. She said, Well, it seems like I don't, in which case, I don't give a shit. My former husband had a cock, and I know for a fact he'd have been a whole lot better off if he didn't. I said, What if I told you it was a chicken? She said, What? I said, His cock. She said, I've known some I wished they were. I said, I mean it. It made him real sad. It was a chicken, and it got killed, and he felt real sad about it. She said, Well, shit! Get him another. As soon as she said it, I knew what to do. I said, All right! Where do I get one? One of them told me, and I said to the woman, You want to help? She said, Do what? I said, Get me a cock. She said, You already got one. I said, Damn right! How about you and me joining forces? She said, Doing what? I said, Looking for cock. She said, That's what I'm doing! I let out a whoop and said, You want another drink or what? Don't mind if I do, the woman said. We kept on drinking, and after a while, I felt like crowing, I was so happy. Whatever the boy lost in that cock fight, and whatever I lost whenever I lost it, so long ago I can't even remember, the whiskey gave it back for a while, and it felt so good, I kept on drinking till I was too drunk to move. I woke up the next morning and saw the blank wash of light at the window and wondered how a man could lose so much, over and over and over again, and still have more to lose even after he lost it all.

PART VI

FATHER: As soon as we cleared the woods and pulled up in front of the house, Lily came rushing out like she was attached to the truck with a spring.

BOY: We hadn't even quit rolling good when she was already running along beside the truck, trying to open the door and climb in or pull me out, one.

MOTHER: You all right? You do all right? He do all right, Jake? How'd he do?

FATHER: He did all right.

BOY: *(Trying to push past her.)* Let me out.

MOTHER: Tell me about it.

FATHER: Leave him alone. He lost his cock.

MOTHER: *(Confused.)* Lost it?

FATHER: It was killed. Leave him alone now, and go get us some supper. We're mighty hungry. *(To the boy.)* Ain't that right?

BOY: Yes, sir.

FATHER: Fighting like that makes a man hungry. Come on, Lily. Leave him alone. Let him unpack and do the chores. He got all those chickens to tend to, and I got a few beers waiting, I reckon.

MOTHER: I'll help him a minute.

FATHER: He don't need it. He knows what to do. Come on in the house.

(*Shift.*)

MOTHER: Tell me about it.

FATHER: Nothing to tell.

MOTHER: What happened then?

FATHER: Little shit blew it.

MOTHER: It wasn't his fault.

FATHER: The hell it wasn't. Whose fault was it?

MOTHER: He was too young.

FATHER: You mean it's my fault.

MOTHER: I didn't say that. I'm not talking about fault.

FATHER: I am.

MOTHER: I told you. He's just a boy. You shouldn't have trusted him.

FATHER: I didn't trust him. I didn't trust him any more than I trusted that brother of yours.

MOTHER: He had a hard time.

FATHER: Don't give me that, Lily. I had a hard time. You had a hard time. We all had a hard time. That's how it is. As long as you're alive, you're going to have a hard time. The only time you're not is when you're dead, and he's working on that. He's working on that every chance he got. *(Brief pause.)* Neither one of them got any sense. I got to do all their thinking for them, and that wears me out. I get tired sometimes.

MOTHER: I know you do.

FATHER: I get tired, Lily. It wears me out, and I get discouraged. I'm discouraged right now.

MOTHER: I know you are. We're all discouraged. Who wouldn't be, considering what happened.

FATHER: All that money.

MOTHER: That isn't important.

FATHER: It isn't to you. It is to me.

MOTHER: I'm thinking about Sonny.

FATHER: He's all right. He's just a boy.

MOTHER: That's what I mean.

FATHER: That's right. I thought it was time to start him on cocks, but I was wrong. He's too young for it.

MOTHER: You put too big a burden on him. He wasn't ready.

FATHER: Damn right he wasn't ready. He didn't do shit.

MOTHER: You got to train him.

FATHER: That's what I'm doing.

MOTHER: And not get discouraged. Getting discouraged isn't going to help.

FATHER: Neither is losing that cock. That was the best cock I ever saw. I don't mean the best one I raised. I mean the best one I ever saw. If they had a hall of fame for cocks, that'd be the first one they'd want to let in it.

MOTHER: You said it wasn't Sonny's fault.

FATHER: It was, and it wasn't. I thought he couldn't lose with that cock, and he did.

MOTHER: You said it had some kind of disease.

FATHER: It did, but he should have told me about it.

MOTHER: He didn't know.

FATHER: I know he didn't.

MOTHER: He's just a boy. Let him stay here with me next time.

FATHER: Damn right. I wouldn't take him.

MOTHER: Let him feed the birds and clean out their cages. That way he won't have to know about it, you not taking him next time.

FATHER: One thing I hate is that he didn't tell me. He just threw that cock away.

MOTHER: I don't see how he could have known.

FATHER: I'd have known. If it was me, I would have told.

MOTHER: That's silly, Jake. You don't know what you'd do if you were him.

FATHER: I'd have taken an interest in it. You know me. I'd do it like I do right now. I always have, and I always will.

MOTHER: I know that, Jake.

FATHER: I'm not like him. Never have been and never will be.

(Shift.)

BOY: As soon as he said that, I knew what it was. The last piece snapped into place. I wasn't him and never would be, and not only that, I never would want to. Each one was different. That was the puzzle.

FATHER: Just because you went out the first time and lost doesn't mean you're going to do it next time. You were too young, that's all. We'll just wait a year or two, and then you'll be ready. You get knocked down or fall off something, you don't just lay there. You get up and try again and keep on trying till sooner or later you beat the son of a bitch. That's how you do.

MOTHER: But it wasn't that. It wasn't the white head or the man from Tennessee cheating on him. It wasn't even Lion's dying. It was having to kill him himself. And not only that, being willing to do it.

BOY: If that's what it's like to be like my daddy, I wouldn't want it. I 'd just as soon be like Homer. But I wasn't him, either.

MOTHER: Killing that cock was like killing himself and what was left over after he did it was what he was now. There wasn't nothing left but himself.

(Shift.)

(A cock crows. Then another. Then all of them together.)

FATHER: He tiptoed to the door and turned the knob so it wouldn't rattle, then eased on down the hall and opened the front door. The cold took his breath away, it was so sharp. Then he got ahold of it.

BOY: I closed the door till I heard it click. The moon was fading, but the sun still hadn't come up yet, and it was like the air was lit. That or the gravel.

MOTHER: Each thing held its own light in it. That's how he could see what it was.

BOY: It was like first thing in the morning after it snows. There were no colors. Black was white, and white was black. To get it straight, you had to turn the whole thing around backwards.

MOTHER: He went straight to the line of cages. The first one he came to was empty. He went on past it and came to the second and looked in and saw the beady eye looking at him.

BOY: It was like a seed of light. That's what makes them crow in the morning. They got that seed of light in them, and it flares in the sun, and they start crowing. God made them like that the same way he made them courageous and steadfast.

FATHER: The cock rubbed its beak on the side of the perch. It was a Claret. The ruff was bright red in the light. He opened the cage, and the cock tried to back off. He got his hand under it and felt the stiff grain of the feathers and lifted him out. The cock tried to pull away, but he clapped his other hand on its wings—

MOTHER: —and pulled it against his chest and held it there for a minute the same way he used to hold Lion.

BOY: Then I put my hand on its neck and jerked it around one quick turn— then another—and let go. The bird went spinning in the dust and dirt of the yard, bouncing off the legs of the cages and running around, over and over on top of itself.

MOTHER: Then it was quiet. The dust settled down, and he went to the next cage and took out a Butcher and killed it the same way. Then he went faster. He could hear them flapping behind him, but he didn't turn around to look. He just kept on going.

BOY: Then I was through. I could hear a couple of them still going on like dogs that were poisoned. Then it was quiet, and I saw the sunlight and knew it was morning. The dust they raised drifted on past me, and I couldn't tell the grains of light drifting down from the top of the pines from the grains of dust that were falling through it. Everything was just like it used to be. It was just like a regular, ordinary day. Except it wasn't. It was all brand new.

(*Shift.*)

MOTHER: I was in the kitchen, fussing around with some plants in the window. They were mostly all cactus. Some bloomed in the spring and some in the winter, around Christmas.

BOY: She always said they were just like her. They got by on nothing. That's why she loved them.

MOTHER: Where you been?

BOY: Out.

MOTHER: Doing what?

BOY: Messing around.

MOTHER: Messing around with those chickens.

(*No response. He starts to get a glass of milk.*)

MOTHER: Leave some of that milk for your daddy.

BOY: There's some.

MOTHER: You hear what I said?

(*Father enters carrying his shoes and socks in his hand.*)

FATHER: Hear what? (*Sitting down, putting on a pair of socks. One of them has a hole in the toe. He pulls it off and puts it on the other foot.*)

MOTHER: Cut your toenails, you wouldn't have a hole in your sock.

FATHER: Keep up with the mending, I wouldn't either. (*Grunting as he bends over to tie his shoes.*)

(*The boy grunts back. It sounds like a pig.*)

FATHER: What?

(*The boy grunts again.*)

What's that? (*Standing up.*) What the hell you think you're doing? You making fun of me, or what? What the hell's he doing, Lily?

MOTHER: (*Looking alarmed.*) I don't know.

FATHER: (*To the boy.*) You do the birds?

(*The boy nods his head yes.*)

Talk to me, you little shit. You water them?

(*The boy shakes his head no.*)

You feed them?

(*The boy shakes his head no.*)

You clean the cages?

(*The boy shakes his head no.*)

You didn't feed them, you didn't water them, how the hell you do them, then?

MOTHER: He opened his mouth, but it wasn't a mouth. It was too hard for a mouth. It was more like a beak. And it wasn't words. It was a roar like the roar of a lion.

BOY: I remembered what Homer said.

FATHER: The cock and the lion are the only animals God ever made that are courageous and steadfast.

BOY: Except for a man, Homer said. Except for a man.

(The boy silently roars. His mother and father join in for real. It goes on for a moment, then almost immediately turns into a general chorus of crowing that sounds like a Jubilee. Blackout.)

END OF PLAY

God's Man in Texas
by David Rambo

for Ted Heyck, a remarkable Texan

155

BIOGRAPHY

David Rambo is making his ATL debut. Mr. Rambo's *Speaky-Spikey-Spokey* was named one of the "Ten Best" by the 1998 Bay Area Playwrights Festival and was presented at the Ashland New Plays Festival, where he was 1998 Host Playwright. His farce, *There's No Place Like House*, was a recent Los Angeles hit. These plays and *God's Man in Texas* have been developed by A.S.K. Theater Projects.

HUMANA FESTIVAL PRODUCTION

God's Man in Texas premiered at the Humana Festival of New American Plays in March 1999. It was directed by John Dillon with the following cast:

Dr. Jeremiah "Jerry" Mears . . . . V Craig Heidenreich
Dr. Philip Gottschall . . . . William McNulty
Hugo Taney. . . . . Bob Burrus

and the following production staff:

Scenic Designer . . . . Paul Owen
Costume Designer . . . . Michael Oberle
Lighting Designer. . . . . Mimi Jordan Sherin
Sound Designer . . . . Jeremy Lee
Properties Designer . . . . Mark Walston
Stage Manager. . . . . Juliet Penna
Assistant Stage Manager . . . . Dyanne M. McNamara
Dramaturg. . . . . Amy Wegener
Assistant Dramaturg. Ilana M. Brownstein
Casting . . . . Laura Richin Casting

CHARACTERS

DR. JEREMIAH "JERRY" MEARS: Baptist preacher, scholar, and teacher in his early 40s. A seemingly conservative, ordinary man, he gains stature when preaching; his voice is startlingly rich and movingly expressive.

DR. PHILIP GOTTSCHALL: Legendary figure in the Baptist pulpit, 81 years old, vibrant, passionate, stentorian, leonine, proud.

HUGO TANEY: Could be 35, could be 55, or anywhere in between. No one, including Hugo, really knows for sure. Reformed wreckage of a life full of drugs, alcohol and faithlessness.

These men are Texans.

TIME & PLACE

The present. The pulpit, Ministers' Room, and various other locations on the campus of the enormous and exciting Rock Baptist Church, Houston.

AUTHOR'S NOTE

Some Bible quotes in *God's Man in Texas* are taken from the *Holy Bible, New International Version* (see below) in accordance with the published permission guidelines. Other Bible quotes are taken from the Cambridge University Press edition of the King James Version of The Bible.

Scripture taken from the *Holy Bible, New International Version*®. Copyright 1973, 1978, 1984 by International Bible Society. Used by permission of Zondervan Publishing House. All rights reserved.

The "NIV" and "New International Version" trademarks are registered in the United States Patent and Trademark Office by International Bible Society. Use of either trademark requires the permission of International Bible Society.

William McNulty, V Craig Heidenreich and Bob Burrus in
God's Man in Texas by David Rambo

23rd Annual Humana Festival of New American Plays
Actors Theatre of Louisville, 1999
photo by Richard Trigg

God's Man in Texas

ACT ONE
SCENE ONE

The pulpit of the Rock Baptist Church in Houston, Texas. The pulpit is dark and deeply carved, over a century old. Dr. Jerry Mears, in his early forties, admires the pulpit respectfully. He carries himself with a slouch and a squint that, when he is preaching, slowly evaporate. But this is not his church, not his pulpit. The ordinariness of his appearance is so great that when he speaks the potency and richness of his voice are shocking. Hugo Taney, a reformed wreck of a man wearing a suit, tie, and wireless walkie-talkie headset appears behind Jerry. He could be 35 or 55, nobody, including Hugo, really knows. Such is what a near-lifetime of drink, drugs and faithlessness can do to a soul.

HUGO: Dr. Mears, they're about to open the doors to the congregation.

JERRY: Moody preached at this pulpit.

HUGO: Yes sir, I have heard that.

JERRY: And Truett. The first time I was here, my father brought me to hear Billy Graham. He was on a sales trip to Houston.

HUGO: *(Laughs.)* Billy Graham wouldn't appreciate his Crusade being called a sales trip.

JERRY: My father's trip.

HUGO: Oh! Oh, of course! Sorry. Before I turned my life over to Christ, I did so much drugs and alcohol. Left me with only a little over half a working brain. Sorry.

JERRY: It's always so exciting to be here. I grew up listening to Dr. Gottschall on the radio, watched his first broadcast on TV. When I was an undergrad at Baylor, some of my classmates and I drove all night long many a time to be here Sunday morning and hear Dr. Gottschall preach. The campus outside looks very different now than it did back then, the way it's expanded. But here, inside…this pulpit, this sanctuary, this will never change.

HUGO: *(Listens, then speaks into his headset.)* Copy that. Out. *(To Jerry.)* Dr. Mears, I'll take you downstairs now.

JERRY: Moody, Truett, Graham, Gottschall…

HUGO: I don't want you thinking I'm completely stupid. I know Billy Graham wasn't a salesman.

JERRY: Actually, he was. He was a Fuller Brush Man.

HUGO: Billy Graham?

JERRY: At one time, yes.

HUGO: Well, if he'd stuck with it, I bet he'd have been their top guy.

SCENE TWO

The Rock Baptist Church Ministers' Room. The room pulses with power: English polished mahogany antique furniture, rich fabrics. A royal chamber, if you will. Hugo leads Jerry in.

HUGO: This is the Ministers' Room. Dr. Gottschall and you wait here until the stage manager gives me the word. Then I bring you both out to the church floor and you make your entrance. *(Jerry catches Hugo staring at him.)* Excuse my staring at you, but you look a lot taller on TV.

JERRY: Taller?

HUGO: On your TV shows, do you use a lower-than-average pulpit?

JERRY: No.

HUGO: Oh, man, there I go again, making dumb comments.

JERRY: That's all right.

HUGO: I wasn't all that smart before I started doing drugs and what-have-you.

JERRY: It's okay.

HUGO: The one part of my brain that's just fine, is the part where I have my technical knowledge. My background's video production. I started here at Rock in TVBO.

JERRY: TVBO?

HUGO: TV Broadcast Ops. Operations.

(Hugo takes a wireless microphone and transmitter pack from his pocket.) I need to do your audio. *(Jerry allows Hugo to wire him.)* Yeah, whenever Rock was broadcasting one of your shows from your church in Dallas—

JERRY: San Antonio.

HUGO: Oh, that's right, San Antonio. Well, whenever you came up on a monitor, all the guys in TVBO would stop what they was doing and watch.

JERRY: Oh?

HUGO: That voice. Even non-believers—some of what we had to hire back then was non-believers, this was before Gottschall College had a media production major—even nonbelievers in the studio would stop and listen to your voice. Praise God, what a gift.

JERRY: Thank you.

HUGO: Think of all the Fuller brushes you could have sold with that voice.

JERRY: My father was in sales. A sales trainer, actually.

HUGO: Did he have a good voice, too?

JERRY: He had...he had a remarkable ability to enthuse people. He gave training seminars all over the country for Vite-America.

HUGO: Vitamins, and diet drinks, and what-have-you.

JERRY: Yes. When Dad spoke to a group of prospects, the excitement—it had weight, and energy, and motion. It was like...like aftershave: cool and fluid, running over your palms, you catch it, you get some friction with it, slap it on, let it sting! That's excitement! It wakes you up and says, "Go out and do something important today!"

HUGO: You are good. You are real good.

(Beat.)

JERRY: I suppose Dr. Gottschall watches most of the tapes from other churches on the network?

HUGO: You mean does he watch your tapes?

JERRY: Mine, and anyone else's.

HUGO: Pastor doesn't watch TV at all; not his own network, or even his own shows.

JERRY: Oh.

HUGO: No time for TV. He's got the church here, three services every Sunday: the eight-thirty, then the ten o'clock—that's the one we tape to play on TV—then the eleven-thirty, which is mainly for retakes, but we get a good crowd anyway.

JERRY: Quite a schedule.

HUGO: And he runs the college, and the Christian School, and all the programs. Meetings, meetings, meetings. Eighty-one years old! And he still studies in private four hours every morning in his pajamas, locked up alone in his library at home over on Overbrook. You been there?

JERRY: Oh, yes.

HUGO: He can read the Bible in Greek, did you know that? Greek!

(Jerry starts to respond, but Hugo indicates he's listening on his headset. Then, to Jerry.)

Audio needs you to say something, to get a level.

JERRY: *"HO EXSON OTA AKOUNEON AKOUNETO."*

HUGO: Say, what?

JERRY: "He that hath ears to hear, let him hear." Luke, chapter eight. The original Greek.

HUGO: Oh. *(On headset.)* Ten-four, Audio. Out. *(To Jerry.)* Mrs. G.'s the TV-watcher. Ross Perot gave her a big old satellite dish for the house. She channel-surfs the Christian networks all day long.

JERRY: I see.

HUGO: And *Wheel of Fortune.* She loves word games. Scrabble? If you ever get invited to Overbrook for a Scrabble game, run and hide. Run and hide! Mrs. G. plays to win.

JERRY: I know she's seen some of my broadcasts.

HUGO: It was her idea you come be Sunday night guest preacher this month.

JERRY: Oh?

HUGO: We all do love Mrs. G. around here.

JERRY: Are you a member of her Sunday School class?

HUGO: Me? Lord, no! That class is the Who's-Who of Houston. Of the whole country! She's got every oil company president in there, most of their vice presidents. Half of the top dogs at NASA. She's even got a converted Sakowitz coming now, praise God. You were talking about your daddy, why, she's got Bucky Buckholz, the most famous motivational speaker in the world in that class.

JERRY: I know Bucky. He was a friend of my father.

HUGO: See? That's the Lord at work, bringing you and Bucky together again tonight.

JERRY: He's here?

HUGO: He's on the committee—the pastoral search committee. They're all here tonight.

JERRY: Well…Bucky's a good man.

HUGO: He's got two hundred in his "Fellowship of Success" lunch group on campus. Captains of Industry, up-and-comers, all of them.

JERRY: Quite a group.

HUGO: That's Rock Baptist Houston.

JERRY: The membership at my church in San Antonio doubled since RBC started broadcasting our services.

HUGO: So, what's your membership now?

JERRY: Just over six thousand.

HUGO: Here at Rock, we got more than that in our singles ministry alone. Not to make this a pissing contest.

JERRY: Well…then, let's not make this a contest.

HUGO: I just get so nervous around famous people like you, and say the stupidest—

JERRY: *(Overlapping.)* I'm not famous, so don't be—

HUGO: *(Overlapping.)* Meeting people you'd only ever seen on TV—you must be used to it. I sure as heck am not.

JERRY: I'll admit, I was quite nervous myself recently, meeting President and Mrs. Clinton when they came to worship with us in San Antonio. *(A chill enters the room.)* Does President Clinton worship here when he's in Houston?

HUGO: He wouldn't be well-received if he did. Dr. Mears, Rock Baptist Church *is* Houston. And Houston does not care much for Bill and Hillary Clinton. George Bush on the other hand…

JERRY: Well-received.

HUGO: Hero's welcome every time he walks in the door.

JERRY: He's here often?

HUGO: Sure, him and Pastor are close personal friends.

JERRY: George Bush—the father?

HUGO: Well, of course! Junior's good, but'll never be half the leader his daddy was. We believe when the real history gets told, not the liberal-biased media version, George Bush will go down as one of the greatest presidents ever.

JERRY: He's not Baptist.

HUGO: He's a believer. And a patriot. I'm ex-Army myself. *(Jerry is fidgeting.)* You know, you got plenty of time before the service.

JERRY: I was hoping Dr. Gottschall would be here by now.

HUGO: Don't be nervous. Sometimes he runs in right at the last minute.

JERRY: *(Overlapping.)* I'm not nervous.

HUGO: You're jumpy as a baby Chihuahua. You really want this job, don't you? *(The chill settles in.)*

JERRY: I'm sorry. I forgot your name already.

HUGO: Hugo. Hugo Taney.

JERRY: *(A polite dismissal.)* Thank you, Hugo, for your help tonight.

HUGO: You're welcome. *(Jerry is lost in private thoughts.)* Oh, man, I am such a goof! Of course! You're concentrating on your message, and here I am, jabbering away. I am sorry. Would you like me to fix you some tea?

JERRY: No. Thank you.

HUGO: Pastor always wants a fresh pot of tea handy. Mrs. G. makes sure we got a stock of Earl Grey, chamomile, some herbal ones and what-have-you. They're imported from England.

JERRY: No tea. Thanks.

HUGO: Pastor's very well-known in England. He preaches in London, and in one of their college towns, they named it the same as one of our southern cities…

JERRY: Oxford.

HUGO: That's it. *(Pauses, listens, and speaks into his headset.)* Yeah, Dave?… Copy that. We're waiting on Pastor in the Ministers' Room… Will do. Out. *(To Jerry, as he prepares a pot of tea.)* Big-time show business. You sure you don't want tea? Part of my job.

JERRY: *(Checks his watch.)* I think I'll get some air, collect my thoughts.

HUGO: Did you have to audition to get hired at your church in San Antonio?

JERRY: Beg pardon?

HUGO: Well, these Sunday night services—it's sort of your audition, isn't it?

JERRY: Audition for what?

HUGO: To take over for Pastor. Reverend Bissonette did real good last month. Real folksy, everybody liked him, especially the pastoral search committee. Tough act to follow.

JERRY: Chuck Bissonette was my roommate at Baylor.

HUGO: He's got a big church in Florida now.

JERRY: Yes.

HUGO: He's real tan.

JERRY: Yes.

HUGO: Looks good on TV.

JERRY: Yes.

HUGO: He said you couldn't play ping-pong worth a darn at Baylor.

JERRY: Oh? My name came up?

HUGO: They say Baptist is the first religion at Baylor, and ping-pong's the second.

JERRY: Chuck was the better ping-pong player, and I was—

HUGO: The better Baptist?

JERRY: Our dorm room was full of his ping-pong trophies, little gold plastic men on top, holding a ping-pong paddle in mid-swat. I committed the unpardonable sin of asking Chuck to move some of the trophies off the bookcase to make room for a few books. As he stormed out of the room, he said, "Jerry, winners win, and losers lose."

HUGO: "Winners win, and losers lose." Can't argue that.

JERRY: So, how did my name come up in your conversation?

HUGO: His sources told him the committee was interested in getting a look at you, too.

JERRY: The only reason I'm here Sunday nights this month is Dr. Gottschall invited me to share the word of God in fellowship with Christ and the congregation of this church.

HUGO: This is the biggest, best-known and most closely-watched Baptist church ever. We only had three pastors in 110 years. Pastor's eighty-one years old. Now, it don't take more than half a brain, which is about all I got, to figure out that when you step up to that pulpit tonight in front of twelve hundred people...

JERRY: Twelve hundred?

HUGO: *(Not stopping.)* ...you're auditioning for the top job in the Baptist universe. I'd be nervous, too.

JERRY: Please stop presuming I'm nervous.

HUGO: Rock Baptist Church Houston is the Baptist Super Bowl, Dr. Mears. And you're standing in God's locker room.

JERRY: Hugo, may I please have a few moments alone? *(Beat.)* Are you not allowed to leave me by myself, is that it?

HUGO: The rest room's in there. That's real marble, one of the Texaco heiresses donated it.

JERRY: I'm accustomed to having some time before preaching to myself, for prayer, for concentration.

HUGO: The sink and the toilet, they were gifts from Governor Connally and his wife.

JERRY: Hugo, I'm preaching without notes tonight, and I—

HUGO: Pastor never uses notes, either.

JERRY: I need a moment of quiet.

HUGO: Oh, well, I'll stop talking, if that's what you want.

JERRY: Thank you.

(Jerry tries to concentrate. Hugo clatters a teacup.)

HUGO: Sorry. I can't leave, or Pastor's tea won't be ready when he—

JERRY: Fine, just...

HUGO: Do it real quiet?

JERRY: Thank you.

(Once again, Jerry concentrates. Hugo prepares a tray for the tea, absolutely quietly. He can be nearly invisible when he wants to be. Moments pass, and Jerry forgets he is not alone as he runs his message fast-forward silently to himself. Hugo, reading a tea box label, nonchalantly breaks the silence.)

HUGO: This dang tea's a laxative. *(Before Jerry can respond, Hugo motions that he's listening on his headset.)* Yeah, Dave?…I copy. Standing by. *(To Jerry.)* Pastor's just pulling in on Fannin Street.

SCENE THREE

The pulpit. The choir, congregation, organ and church orchestra conclude a rousing hymn as Dr. Philip Gottschall (81)—vigorous, leonine, magnetic— kneels beside the pulpit, praying silently, bathed in a shaft of heavenly light from the TV-broadcast-strength spotlights above. Jerry is seated just behind him, waiting his turn to preach. Gottschall rises and speaks Heavenward, his voice vibrating thrillingly with richness and drama.

GOTTSCHALL: "The unfolding of your word gives light." Psalm 119, that beautiful, beautiful hymn of praise to God's word. Tonight, we continue in our study series, "Exodus: United in Faith, A Nation Prevails." We are blessed and privileged to have God's revealed word illuminated tonight by one of his most erudite and devoted servants, a fundamentalist—a true fundamentalist—Dr. Jeremiah Mears. I've had my eye on this young man since he was a puppy-faced preacher-boy at Baylor. Couldn't play ping-pong at all, but, oh, the Lord blessed this lad with an unshakable faith that recalls the most compelling preachers of our great Southern Baptist heritage. Now, over the last six months, we've welcomed a number of guest pastors from all over the country to our Sunday evening services. "Pastors on Parade," as our music director put it. *(He pauses, knowing the congregation will laugh at this.)* Consensus, with which I am proud to concur, has been that the most impressive of these visiting pastors have been those from churches situated right here in Texas. I know of none more impressive than my young colleague, from Crockett Avenue Baptist San Antonio, pastor, professor, and former president of the Southern Baptist Leadership Forum, Dr. Mears.
(Gottschall sits, and Jerry takes the pulpit. For a moment, it seems that he can't quite find his voice; he squints and slouches. Then, he begins. As his resonant, liquid voice pours forth, he gains stature and a searing focus into the congregation.)
JERRY: The power of our Father's voice… On one of those real-life mystery programs on TV recently, there was a young woman who had been given up for adoption at birth, and now was attempting to locate her real parents.

When she was reunited with her mother, she learned her father had long since died. The young woman's tears poured forth like a desert creek following a spring storm. She said she was crying because she would never get to hear her father's voice. The power of a father's voice; so terrifying when it thunders, and so reassuring when it's a whisper… I thought how healing it would be for that emotionally devastated young woman to be able to hear the voice of her Heavenly Father. A whisper. A gentle whisper. *(Beat.)* Who among us, though, has heard—actually heard—the voice of God? What does God's voice sound like? I asked my mother that question, and she replied, "Well, I imagine like Walter Cronkite." I challenged her on that, "Not Orson Welles? Charlton Heston?" She gave it a good deal of thought, and loyally decided to stick with Walter Cronkite. God speaks to man a great deal throughout the Old Testament; there is a wonderful description in the 29th Psalm: "The voice of the LORD is powerful; the voice of the LORD is majestic. The voice of the LORD breaks the cedars of Lebanon." Power! Majesty! *(Beat.)* Has God ever whispered to man? The Bible mentions one specific occasion, yes: First Kings, chapter 19. The prophet Elijah is alone, in a cave, when God speaks to him to "stand on the mountain in the presence of the LORD, for the LORD is about to pass by." Powerful, cataclysmic noises surround Elijah: wind, then earthquake, then fire. This was not God speaking, and Elijah knew it. When God chose to speak, to call his servant back to his service, it was in a whisper. "*Kol D'mamah Dakah*," the Hebrew for an almost imperceptible murmur, a quiet voice. A whisper. God's whisper. *(Beat.)* We think of God's voice as a huge voice, a rich voice. Walter Cronkite. But let's look at this beautiful passage in Exodus 33, beginning with verse 7 where Moses describes "the tent of meeting" in their camp. This "tent of meeting," by the way, is not the Tent of Meeting that was the tabernacle, but another structure, on the camp's outskirts: "*Michutz L'Machaneh Harchak*" in the Hebrew, indicating very far away from camp. "*Machaneh;*" far away from all the cries and shouts, and clanging, and laughter, and animals. This "tent of meeting" where God spoke to Moses, verse 11: "Face to face, as a man speaks with his friend." Imagine! Hearing the voice of God "as a man speaks with his friend." A low voice? An intimate voice? A whisper? *(Beat.)* John, writing in his gospel, quotes Jesus, "He who belongs to God hears what God says." Perhaps through the Holy Spirit, God's voice is your voice. And my voice. For we are all God's creation, "in his image." God must be speaking to us every day. He must! "He who belongs to God hears what God says." *(Beat.)* I believe some of you tonight may be hearing God's voice deep within you, calling you; calling you to come home, to make things right in your heart and with God. Come. Come forward now. As God is speaking to you right now, Jesus is listening. Come. This is the moment. All your days on earth have been building up to this moment, right now, when you come forth and let Jesus be your savior. He died for you. His Father is calling you. Hear his whisper. Come. Come.

SCENE FOUR

The Ministers' Room. The service ended, Gottschall and Jerry enter. Gottschall stretches his arms outward, crucifixion-like so that Hugo can remove his microphone.

GOTTSCHALL: Eloquent preaching, lad.

HUGO: That was real fine preaching, Dr. M. Real fine.

JERRY: Thank you.

HUGO: I liked your take on that bit, talking with God like a friend, a lot better than what Reverend Bissonette did with it.

JERRY: Chuck Bissonette used Exodus 33?

GOTTSCHALL: Only a passing reference.

HUGO: I bet the committee liked what you said better.

(Beat.)

GOTTSCHALL: Tired?

JERRY: Long day. But a good day.

HUGO: Driving all the way back to San Antonio…

GOTTSCHALL: You look more worn out than an undertaker's smile.

JERRY: For some reason, my message…every now and then there's one that just drains everything out of you. You know…

GOTTSCHALL: Sure, sure! And you got 'em!

HUGO: They were with you, Dr. M.

JERRY: It's been a while since I spent any time with Exodus.

GOTTSCHALL: I didn't think that was one of your "sugar sticks."

JERRY: No, indeed. I've been working on it all week.

HUGO: You got 'em with it.

GOTTSCHALL: Yes, eventually. I was bit concerned at the start—

JERRY: *(Overlapping.)* Concerned?

GOTTSCHALL: This isn't a criticism, it's an observation.

JERRY: Yes?

HUGO: They like preaching that starts out folksy.

GOTTSCHALL: Dr. Mears is an accomplished academician, Hugo. A scholar. His insight into scripture is extraordinary, and brilliantly informed.

HUGO: What if he starts out with a cute story, something one of his kids said that was real cute? Not so dark, like all that about the adopted woman crying her eyes out.

GOTTSCHALL: Hugo, where are the numbers?

HUGO: Not in yet.

GOTTSCHALL: Well, what is the delay? Get those numbers! *(Hugo exits quickly.)* Should have had the numbers five minutes ago.

JERRY: You said you were concerned at the start of my message…

GOTTSCHALL: I like preaching that starts off with a bang. Something that grabs 'em right off. *(He grabs Jerry at the chest in a sudden, powerful gesture.)* And holds 'em. *(He releases Jerry.)* But there are other ways to get a crowd's attention. You take milk in your tea?

JERRY: No, thank you.

GOTTSCHALL: No milk.

JERRY: No tea, thank you.

GOTTSCHALL: Oh. You don't care for tea?

JERRY: No.

GOTTSCHALL: You've been up to my private office before, haven't you?

JERRY: I've been to two of them, I think. One at Gottschall College, and one across the courtyard here.

GOTTSCHALL: I got a private office in the Gottschall Building—my real office—where I've had tea with every sitting president since Eisenhower.

JERRY: Clinton?

GOTTSCHALL: Except Clinton. I'd like to think whomever God brings to Rock Baptist when my time here is ended will be a pastor a president will want to join for a cup of tea. There are traditions. Don't read into anything here, I'm still healthy and sharp as a young wildcat.

JERRY: Praise God.

GOTTSCHALL: You had 'em, though. Out of all these "Pastors on Parade" through here, you're the one they really listened to. I'd give you a fidget factor of about two-point-five.

JERRY: How's that?

GOTTSCHALL: Fidget factor. Squirming, candy wrappers, yawning, scratching, what-have-you. Parkhurst, down from Dallas, he got a nine-point-nine. They weren't fidgeting, they were having spasmodic fits.

JERRY: Bissonette holds a crowd.

GOTTSCHALL: Not like you, lad. Not like you. The deacons like him, though. The committee likes him. He looks good on TV.

JERRY: Yes.

GOTTSCHALL: Fine preacher. The committee, the deacons…I make up my own mind, and that's just that. So, how do you think you did tonight?

JERRY: Well, I… I… If, as my father always said, the bottom line is the numbers…I was gratified to see so many walk the aisle when I made the call.

GOTTSCHALL: It's all in the numbers.

JERRY: Bucky Buckholz knew my father, Marshall Montgomery Mears. He was a regional sales manager, a motivational speaker.

GOTTSCHALL: Learned at your daddy's knee, did you?

JERRY: He taught me to read from the Bible before I was two.

GOTTSCHALL: Good man.

JERRY: Dad worked for Vite-America—

GOTTSCHALL: Vitamins.

JERRY: Yes. And sometimes, when Dad was holding a recruiting seminar in our living room, I'd sit there with my Bible and read scripture along with him. He used scripture in his talks to—well, to close his prospects.

GOTTSCHALL: Do they sell bee pollen? Ronald Reagan got me hooked on that.

JERRY: Whenever Dad was on a sales trip somewhere, some city, he'd go out on the street and share the gospel with total strangers. He was amazing, people stopped and listened, really listened to him. He called himself "Christ's rabid dog."

GOTTSCHALL: Christ's rabid dog? Meaning exactly what?

JERRY: Well, he'd sort of bite people with the gospel, so to speak. And then they became, well, carriers, so to speak, of, of…

GOTTSCHALL: Rabies?

JERRY: No, I'm not putting this very well…I guess I'm tired. But what I mean to say is that my fundamentalism, well, it's just always been a part of me.

GOTTSCHALL: Praise God.

(Jerry realizes Gottschall is sizing him up. He speaks to break the tension.)

JERRY: Dad said Jesus was the greatest closer, ever.

GOTTSCHALL: I don't follow you.

JERRY: I'm pretty sure Dad got this from Bucky Buckholz, using the gospel as a model for sales technique. See, it all has to do with establishing credibility before closing the prospect. For instance, most of the people Jesus met, and spoke to, were total strangers. His ideas were going to sound terribly radical to them, so he had to establish credibility first, much in the way the car salesman needs you to trust him before he tells you that top-of-the-line sedan you admire has a $50,000 price tag.

GOTTSCHALL: The Son of God was no car salesman.

JERRY: Of course. But to gain credibility, he did something dramatic right off: a miracle, a healing, Lazarus, what-have-you. We can't do that. But Jesus also did something we can do. When he spoke to downtrodden, powerless people and told them, "Blessed are the meek, blessed are the poor in spirit," he was—

GOTTSCHALL: Being folksy?

JERRY: He was saying, "I know how you feel." Any good salesman since then, when the prospect is showing resistance, establishes credibility by saying, "I know how you feel" to that prospect. They sympathize, they bond. Then they close them.

GOTTSCHALL: That's either pure hogwash or outright blasphemy. God did not speak to man through Jesus to teach him how to sell expensive cars.

JERRY: Dad was trying to say that God's word has meaning—understandable, practical meaning—to every aspect and activity of our daily lives, whether we sell cars, preach, pitch vitamins.

GOTTSCHALL: Your daddy passed away, didn't he? No, it was something else…

JERRY: Dad disappeared— *(Beat.)* Sales trip. I was almost sixteen. Dad got a big promotion, moved us to Dallas. The New Orleans police called one morning and said Dad was missing.

GOTTSCHALL: Killed?

JERRY: Just "missing." That's what they said. Last seen preaching on Canal Street for a full day and a half without stopping.

GOTTSCHALL: Never turned up? *(Jerry shakes his head, "No.")* What do you think happened?

JERRY: I think he was called. And he answered the call.

(Beat.)

GOTTSCHALL: Your first church was just outside of Tyler, is that right?

JERRY: Tiny little country church. Fifty members when I got there.

GOTTSCHALL: Fifty. When I was growing up in Clarksville, fifty was a huge church. Huge! We worshipped with six other families in a little white church built on a stone foundation hand-cut by my daddy. I preached my first sermon in that pulpit. I was five years old!

JERRY: Your life has been an amazing journey.

GOTTSCHALL: So they say. I don't dwell on it. Now, tell me, what did you get that first congregation of yours up to by the time you left?

JERRY: Oh, over two hundred.

GOTTSCHALL: How'd you do it?

JERRY: Well, all the usual procedures: stair-stepping, housecalls, young people's programs.

GOTTSCHALL: You did your own housecalling, did you?

JERRY: Like a rabid dog.

GOTTSCHALL: And tonight, at the largest Baptist church in the world, you preached to likely more than six times the number you left back in Tyler.

JERRY: Dr. Gottschall, I'm inordinately grateful for the opportunity to preach here at Rock this month. That pulpit, all its history, it has so much meaning to me.

GOTTSCHALL: I wouldn't give a cracker for a preacher who hasn't dreamed about preaching here. Lad, how about you and I have a word before you drive off on I-10 West; "face to face, as a man speaks with his friend?"

JERRY: Face to face… Isn't the Hebrew for that phrase wonderful: "*panim el-panim?*"

GOTTSCHALL: Yes.

JERRY: It conveys an intimacy and intensity that just doesn't translate in the English.

GOTTSCHALL: How big a church you got in San Antonio?

JERRY: Just over six thousand.

GOTTSCHALL: Six thousand?

JERRY: It's hard to get an exact number, but that's—

GOTTSCHALL: *(Charging on.)* They give you a house?

JERRY: There's a mortgage on it.

GOTTSCHALL: Is the deed in your name, or the church?

JERRY: Uh, mine. My name, and my wife's.

GOTTSCHALL: She didn't come with you tonight, did she?

JERRY: No, Melody's at home, with our boys.

GOTTSCHALL: Two boys, is that right?

JERRY: Yes.

GOTTSCHALL: How would you rate your marriage?

JERRY: Beg pardon?

GOTTSCHALL: You two happy? Don't fight over money?

JERRY: No.

GOTTSCHALL: "Wives, be in subjection to your own husbands."

JERRY: Yes, First Peter.

GOTTSCHALL: Melody have any problem with that?

JERRY: No, none. We're a fairly traditional Christian family.

GOTTSCHALL: Fairly?

JERRY: Quite so. Quite traditional.

GOTTSCHALL: College sweethearts, weren't you?

JERRY: We met my junior year at Baylor.

GOTTSCHALL: Did Melody take a degree?

JERRY: Yes, library science.

GOTTSCHALL: But she doesn't work outside the home.

JERRY: No. Never did.

GOTTSCHALL: That all right with you?

JERRY: Honestly, I wouldn't mind if she did, depending on the job. But she's never asked.

GOTTSCHALL: Family first.

JERRY: Always. Dr. Gottschall, my boys and my wife are more important to me than…than anything.

GOTTSCHALL: You make sure you bring them along from now on. Sit them right up front.

JERRY: They'd like that.

GOTTSCHALL: Let the people get to know you.

JERRY: I will.

GOTTSCHALL: Lad, you're a superstar in some circles.

JERRY: Well, I've been around a long time.

GOTTSCHALL: We've fought some battles together, haven't we?

JERRY: Always on the same side.

GOTTSCHALL: On God's side. Defending his word.

JERRY: Yes.

GOTTSCHALL: I do admire your fundamentalism. The church needs it. This church needs it.

JERRY: It's all there in the word. I just believe in the word with all my heart.

GOTTSCHALL: The word cannot be chopped up, molded, subverted to suit what passes for popular morality these days.

JERRY: No.

GOTTSCHALL: The word is not some roadside fruit stand; pick what looks pretty and tastes sweet, and ignore the rest.

JERRY: No.

GOTTSCHALL: Gotta take the sweet with the sour. You eat dried pitted prunes?

JERRY: Uh…no. No.

GOTTSCHALL: Well, you should. Put some color in that pale face of yours. Folks like a pastor with good color. Keep the stuff of life moving through you, keep it moving. I'm eighty-one years old.

JERRY: Yes, sir.

GOTTSCHALL: Make a fist. Go ahead, make a fist. Now, sock me. *(Points to his stomach.)* Right here.

JERRY: No, I—

GOTTSCHALL: Punch me!

JERRY: Dr. Gottschall—No!

GOTTSCHALL: Think you'll hurt the old man? Think he's soft?

JERRY: No—

GOTTSCHALL: Hit me!

JERRY: I can't!

GOTTSCHALL: Do it!

JERRY: Pastor…

(Jerry suddenly socks Gottschall in the gut. The older man barely feels it, and laughs.)

GOTTSCHALL: Like steel! That's from two hundred sit-ups and a bag of dried pitted prunes every morning.

JERRY: You're a very healthy man.

GOTTSCHALL: And I'm going to live a long time. *(Beat.)* Did you know this pastoral search committee was convened without anybody in this church consulting me? Not one soul thought enough of the sitting pastor to let him know what was going on.

JERRY: Dr. Gottschall, there isn't a pastor more beloved by his congregation anywhere—

GOTTSCHALL: When God gave me this church, with all its history, and all its rich and powerful people, he also gave me a vision: to make Rock Baptist the center of your life from the day you're born to the day you die. See, a baby's born, I dedicate that little baby to Christ. He's cared for in our Little Lambs Day Care, then our nursery school, and our Blessed Flock Sunday School. The very day they took the Lord's Prayer out of the public schools, I went out and raised the money to build Rock School for that little baby's elementary schooling, then Rock High School, and Gottschall College.

JERRY: I was in the crowd the day you broke ground for the college.

GOTTSCHALL: Now thousands of young people come through here, learning the word of God, *living* the word of God, then going out into the world and changing lives through the word of God.

JERRY: It's one of the most inspiring—

GOTTSCHALL: *(Charging on.)* Young people spend their summers at our Camp Galilee, keep their bodies clean and fit for God's work right here in our Family Life Center gymnasium. I built that gymnasium, two swimming pools. Oh, I fought battles to build it. I had to get hold of the movers and shakers and shake the loose change out of their pockets to build it. But I built it, all of it, because I knew more and more young people and families would come if I did. Get 'em in the pool on Saturday, they'll be in a pew on Sunday.

JERRY: And they've kept on coming.

GOTTSCHALL: And coming, and coming. God gave me the vision! You see? Every week, we tape our ten o'clock for TV and radio so that more, and more, and more can see and hear—proof persuasive as the blood-stained hands and feet of the resurrected Jesus—that this is the place to come to rejoice and be in his presence, *right here!*

JERRY: You've made this the place.

GOTTSCHALL: And when that young man, raised in Christ is ready, he joins our singles ministry and meets a pretty Christ-centered girl, they go on dates right here on campus at our dinner theater or our bowling alley. They get married, have children, and with those little babies the process begins all over again. Continuity. *(Beat.)* Continuity is very important to me.

JERRY: Yes.

GOTTSCHALL: My beloved Julia and I were not blessed with a son. We prayed on it, and prayed on it, but the Lord…Julia is so wise about these things. When the Lord gave us our sweet Pauline, Julia said it was because the Lord knew we had the capacity to love her…

JERRY: Mrs. Gottschall's devotion to your daughter is inspiring to so many other parents of…um, *impaired* children.
(Beat.)

GOTTSCHALL: I got ears all over campus, all over Houston… "The old man's mind wanders…memory's going…gets tired…Alzheimer's… Parkinson's…" These committee boys in their fancy suits and shiny shoes got me diagnosed, dead and buried. I've never had so much as a head cold. I've got the prostate of a man half your age! *(Beat.)* But the Lord has his timetable for all of us. I have to think about a successor.

JERRY: And the search committee's been looking for over a year now?

GOTTSCHALL: The seventh trumpet of the Lord will sound before that group of glad-handers agrees on anybody.

JERRY: Still, they'll have to eventually. Our doctrine doesn't allow a departing pastor to appoint a successor.

GOTTSCHALL: No… That's not my intention, lad. Not my intention at all.

JERRY: Sir, am I under consideration? *(Gottschall doesn't answer.)* One doesn't like to pay attention to rumors, yet one can't help speculating. *(Beat.)* The speculation has already reached my congregation.

GOTTSCHALL: Lad, I have nothing to do with this. It's in God's hands. We'll have to wait.

(Jerry takes a moment to carefully phrase his response. As he is about to speak, Hugo knocks and enters with a printout.)

HUGO: I got the numbers, Dr. G. Attendance: twelve hundred and thirty-one in attendance, sixty walked the aisle. *(This pleases Jerry.)* Income: nine thousand one hundred and eighty-four dollars—that's low.

GOTTSCHALL: Leave it.

HUGO: I need to get Dr. Mears' audio.

JERRY: I put it over there.

HUGO: Pastor, removing the audio is part of my job.

GOTTSCHALL: Hugo, Dr. Mears doesn't want your job. Not your job.

HUGO: Dr. Mears, next Sunday evening I'd appreciate you letting me handle your audio.

JERRY: Yes. Thank you, Hugo.

HUGO: Don't forget: folksy. Some of the committee were having punch and cookies just now, and I happened to overhear… *(Gottschall and Jerry pay strict attention.)* They like you. But—God's truth—I actually heard Bucky Buckholz say ordinary folks liked your daddy so much, 'cause when he talked, it was like he was just one of them.

JERRY: Folksy.

GOTTSCHALL: No matter what happens, you do realize that just by bringing you here tonight, God could be working to change your life beyond your wildest dreams, don't you?

JERRY: Um…yes. And thank you. Thank you again.

GOTTSCHALL: Not at all, lad. Not at all. 'Til next Sunday night.

(Jerry exits.)

SCENE FIVE

The pulpit. One week later. Gottschall sits behind Jerry, who begins his message with more than his customary unease.

JERRY: It's a pleasure to be here for a second time this month with all of you, um, nice...*folks*. Continuing with our study series on Exodus... Perhaps it is because I'm a parent—Melody and I have two boys, my "little men," sitting right up here in the front row. Perhaps it is because I'm a parent that in studying Exodus, I see again and again that Moses, who grew up without having a father there he could speak with, records his dialogue with God as a series of a father's commands and a son's attempts to please him by fulfilling them. Indeed, Moses himself says in Deuteronomy, chapter 8 "as a man disciplines his son, so the LORD your God disciplines you." The lesson of Exodus is that only through complete and total faith in God can we obey him completely. Wouldn't our children do what we ask, without questioning, if they honestly believed everything we tell them? For years, John, our younger boy, would not, under any circumstances whatsoever, eat broccoli. We begged, pleaded, threatened, he would not do it. We commanded. He would not obey. He may have heard about the great uproar that occurred when President Bush refused to have broccoli served in the White House. I don't know. He did, however, love cooked spinach, wanted spinach with every meal. But one night, Melody decided to try serving broccoli again. As expected, John refused to eat it, and there were tears, and all kinds of dramatics. Over a vegetable! Well, I'd about had enough. I told John it wasn't broccoli, it was spinach trees. I showed him the little "spinach" buds in each floret, and explained the stalk was the tree trunk—and John's been eating broccoli ever since. Isn't that right, Son? *(Beat.)* So... Enough about my family.

SCENE SIX

The Ministers' Room, later that evening. Hugo is on the phone, reading from a computer printout.

HUGO: Numbers are real good tonight. Income over eleven thousand—that's good for a Sunday night... Yes, Ma'am... Yes, Ma'am, sixty-six walked the aisle. I think they really like him, Mrs. G. And didn't he do just like you told me to tell him? Real folksy. All that about his little boy, they liked that… Well sure, everybody hates broccoli… Okay, hang on a minute, I'll see what's keeping Dr. G….

(Before Hugo can put the phone down, Gottschall strides into the room, followed by Jerry.)

GOTTSCHALL: Broccoli? What in creation prompted you to preach on broccoli?

JERRY: A parable from personal experience on obedience…

HUGO: *(On phone.)* Here he is. *(Hands the phone to Gottschall.)* Mrs. G. From the car.

GOTTSCHALL: *(Snatching the phone.)* It was a story about how you tricked your boy into eating broccoli.

JERRY: Not "tricked"…

HUGO: Mrs. G. thought the broccoli part was real good.

GOTTSCHALL: *(On phone.)* Hello, Beloved. I thought you were staying to join us…

(Hugo hands him the printout and begins removing his audio.)

HUGO: Numbers are up. They like you, Dr. M. Word got out.

GOTTSCHALL: Numbers are always up when President Bush is here.

JERRY: President Bush was here tonight?

GOTTSCHALL: *(To Jerry.)* Upon my invitation. To hear the brilliant young preacher we brought in from San Antonio. *(On phone.)* Well, then send the car back to my office. I'll be home in an hour. Goodnight, Beloved.

(Hugo hangs up the phone for him.)

JERRY: President Bush—I had no idea.

HUGO: He's waiting in your office. I fixed a pot of Darjeeling for you and Tetley for the President.

GOTTSCHALL: Broccoli is not served anywhere on campus, did you know that?

JERRY: No.

GOTTSCHALL: We got a restaurant, a coffee shop, three snack bars, four cafeterias and a dinner theater, all serving complete, delicious meals without one stalk of broccoli. By my order!

JERRY: My message wasn't really about broccoli.

GOTTSCHALL: *(Studying the printout, to Jerry.)* Lord help 'em, they love you.

(Gottschall exits quickly.)

HUGO: I think it was real brave of you to go for "folksy." *(Jerry allows Hugo to remove his audio.)* You're the lead candidate. Everybody's talking about it.

JERRY: That's very flattering.

HUGO: You gonna take the job?

JERRY: First of all, there is no job. Dr. Gottschall is pastor of this church and he has not announced his retirement.

HUGO: The committee—

JERRY: The committee hasn't said a word to me. And there's no sign that Dr. Gottschall's unable to lead the church. So…

HUGO: Okay, okay. I get it. We'll be all polite and "we're not really talking about it" and what-have-you. Let's just say Dr. G. *was* stepping down, wouldn't you take the job?

JERRY: I have a large church—large by most standards—which is the central force, if not the salvation, of the lives of thousands of people. Good, wonderful people. They've trusted me with expansion plans, fundraising, media, a multi-million dollar budget.

HUGO: Here you could get all that plus a dinner theater, bowling alley, 8-screen cineplex for family movies, Christian satellite network—

JERRY: Yes, yes—

HUGO: Restaurants, coffee shops, snack bars—

JERRY: I know!

HUGO: Full-equipped gymnasium, two swimming pools, baby care, day care, counseling center, kindergarten, grade school, middle school, high school, Gottschall College—

JERRY: Yes!

HUGO: Gift shop, book store, music store. *(Beat.)* Ballpark, football stadium, summer camp, singles ministry, full orchestra, three hundred in the choir, two marching bands, the world's biggest Christmas electric light parade they hired show people from Las Vegas to design the floats for, parking for ten thousand cars—

JERRY: You don't have to—

HUGO: And my personal favorite thing on the whole dang campus: that big bowl of peppermints at the reception desk, and they're free, take all you want. *(Beat.)* Yeah, it's tempting. I know you want it. And I can help you get it.

JERRY: Oh?

HUGO: I'll do for you what I did for Reverend Bissonette and all the rest of these pastors coming through here: tell you what I hear, and what people like and don't like about you. All I want is for whoever gets the job to remember who helped them get it, and keep me on here. Because, if I'm out there, I'm dead.

JERRY: Dead?

HUGO: It's no big secret I was once a bit what you might call "wild." Wild! Saturday nights, drinking, all kinds of drugs, sex I don't half-remember with anything on two legs. And I do mean *anything*. Pretty ugly picture, but I was too drugged-up to see it that way. Sunday mornings, my poor momma would drag me out of bed and stick me in the one jacket my daddy left behind when he run off with the divorcee in the next trailer who had three breasts. I'm not making that up, she did; the extra one was halfway between her right breast and her armpit. We all seen it. Well, I'd sit there on them painful wooden benches in church, still half-stoned or hungover, Momma clutching me so I wouldn't run and hide. Surrounded by every ripe young Baptist female in town. Preacher hollerin' in the pulpit. Sweat pouring down my backbone. Head pounding. Room spinning—I up and vomited right there. The first time, the preacher and everybody yelled, "Praise God! Jesus expelled Satan from deep within this sinner's body right out on to the carpet." But after it happened a couple more times, they kicked me out. *(Beat.)* I joined the Army, turned total alcoholic, and one night in Honolulu paid fifty bucks to have "Jesus Wept" tattooed on the right side of my behind.

JERRY: Somehow you got saved and came here.

HUGO: I got a dishonorable discharge out of the Army, and I just drifted, doing motorcycle repairs, odd jobs, video production, burglary, selling drugs and what-have-you. Over the years, I made my way back to Texas. And one night, sitting at a bar in El Paso, I heard a voice. It sounded like...like what I remembered my daddy's voice being like. I hadn't given him a passing thought in twenty years; for all I knew he was long dead. This voice, right in this ear, so close it tickled a bit, said, "How long are you going to keep trying to kill yourself?" And I spun around like that to see who was talking—but the only people in that bar was me, and way down at the other end, the bartender, and a yellow-haired transvestite, and a crippled man trying to get free drinks by doing tricks with hard-boiled eggs and a spoon. I got sick to my stomach and shot right out the door. And right there, under a streetlight, there was a nice sort of middle-aged man, wearing a tie and a real nice jacket, preaching to a crowd. Was he excited about Christ! Man! *(Beat.)* He looked right at me, right in the eye. And he said, "God loves you. He sent his son to die for you. He won't give up on you. You have been running from Christ all your life. But you're not running any more, because I got you. And I'm Christ's rabid dog."

JERRY: Christ's…

HUGO: Rabid dog. And he was. He would not let me go. I was so scared. Terrified. But he stayed there, praying with me, letting me cry right on him and mess up his nice jacket. We talked all night, and he found out I could do video production, and he told me RBC was just getting the network up and running. He said pray, and God would provide me with a job.

JERRY: Here, where Dr. Gottschall—

HUGO: Where my first day in the studio Dr. G. said, "Son, I can tell just by looking at you that you have been the worst kind of sinner—" and of course, I had been, so he had my attention right there. He said, "Stay by my side, and God won't let you slip and fall away from the rock of your salvation." How he spotted me, why he spoke to me out of everybody in that studio that day… *(He looks Heavenward, then gestures around the room.)* This… This is what keeps my grip on that rock.

JERRY: I see.

HUGO: See, the Devil's right down there in ice-cold, black water, swimming there in all that evil from my wild past. There's a part of me that *wants* to jump in, just for a quick dip. But I know if I do, I'll never find my way back. *(Beat.)* And what do you see when you look down from your rock? A pitiful talent for ping-pong and a kid that won't eat broccoli.

JERRY: My story's more interesting than that.

HUGO: Well, Preacher, what you got to do, if you want the job, is you better tell 'em your story. And it better be a real grabber.

JERRY: Hugo, is there any coffee back there? I need to tell you about my father.

SCENE SEVEN

The pulpit the following Sunday evening. Jerry preaches as Gottschall, seated, watches.

JERRY: Not every man who is called to preach actually hears God's voice calling to him in the manner that, say, God called to Moses over the hissing and the crackling of that burning bush. But I believe God did call me. I believe I heard his voice. *(Beat.)* From my mother I developed a love of books, and from my father I inherited a love—a passion—for the Bible. The summer I was ten years old I made my mother drive me every week to wherever the Youth Crusade For Christ set up its tent so I could hear the preaching and compete in Bible drill. It's hot in North Texas in the summer, especially inside a canvas tent full of children. The Crusade evangelists were kind enough to offer a snow cone on the spot to any child that accepted Christ right then and there as their personal savior. I got saved just about every week. The old "right now close": get saved "right now" and get your ice-cold snow cone in any one of five delicious flavors! Dad thought I should have more significant spiritual guidance, so he sent me to Colt Bible Camp, outside Lubbock, founded by the Colt family that made guns. The camp's motto was "Fellowship and Firearms." I got poison ivy the first day and spent two weeks in the infirmary memorizing Matthew's Gospel and learning how to clean, oil and reassemble a .22-caliber rifle.

(Gottschall squirms.)

Shortly after I'd turned fifteen, my parents and I were sitting, one Sunday, in a blue vinyl booth at the International House of Pancakes in Fort Worth. All through church, the McAllister's girl had been smiling at me from the choir, and now, here she was again, doing the same thing to me from the next booth. I recall it was very, very hot in there, and I was perspiring so much my mother thought I was ill. *(Beat.)* The next thing I knew, there was a roaring sound, the blood was rushing through the veins in my ears so fast it sounded like rapids, thundering whitewater rapids. *(Jerry steps forward, isolated in a wash of bright light as lights go out on everything else.)* I felt the whole restaurant vibrating, and then it was like the building blew away, and I was in a bright, blinding desert. I felt the hand of God come down at me, enter my chest and grab my heart, massaging it. My blood flowed through my veins not by my heart's own beating, but by the rhythmic pumping motions of the hand of God. He pulled, jerking me up on my feet. And I heard his voice: "You are mine!" *(Beat.)* And just like that it was over. I had been called.

SCENE EIGHT

The pulpit, the morning service one week later. Gottschall preaches alone, a simmering volcano, clutching his Bible.

GOTTSCHALL: "When?" I hate somebody asking me when something's supposed to happen. "When?" What an utterly useless question. I do not like, I cannot abide, I will not tolerate useless questions. *(Beat.)* When somebody asks, "What time is supper? When is the next bus supposed to leave? What time does *Wheel of Fortune* come on?" you can tell when all that's going to happen because these are *unimportant* things. If you know when something is going to happen, it is an *unimportant* thing. *(Beat.)* When Jesus was resurrected, and showed himself again to the apostles, they said, "Lord, are you at this *time* going to restore the kingdom to Israel?" Would anybody here not agree that restoring the kingdom to Israel is an *important* thing? Of course it is! And that's why Jesus told the apostles, "It is not for you to know the *times* or *dates* the Father has set by his own authority." *Important* things. In God's time. *(Beat.)* Throughout John's gospel—you sit down and study on this when you get home, you'll see what I mean—Jesus says, over and over again, "My time has not yet come." My time. My time… Everybody, even his mother, keeps asking Jesus, "Why can't you do this? Why hasn't this thing happened," or, "When will such-and-such occur?" Over and over, Jesus says, "It's not time." Not time. *(Beat.)* Ecclesiastes, chapter 3: "There is a time for everything." What time would that be? God's time. Read verse 17 with me: "God will bring to judgment both the righteous and the wicked." When will that happen? Well, read on: "For there will be a *time* for every activity, a *time* for every deed." That time is God's time. *(Beat.)* Do you know what day, exactly when, the Lord will take you from this life? Do you know? Can you tell by looking at your Timex watch? Of course not. That happens in God's time. Because it is an *important* thing. *(Beat.)* Jesus speaks in Revelation, "I am coming soon." When is that? When is *soon*? What year will that be? What day? What hour and minute? In God's time. *(Heavenward.)* Lord, I am ready for your coming, I'm good and ready, but when is it going to happen? You commanded us to endure patiently, and we're trying, oh, Lord, we are trying to be patient, but we've been waiting for two thousand years! When, Lord Jesus, when will judgment day come, and the glorious rapture, when the righteous are lifted up to greet you and dwell with you in the New Jerusalem for ever and ever—when? *When?* *(To the congregation.)* In God's time. Because these are the *most* important things. *(He digs in at the pulpit.)* I'm not going anywhere until God says, "It's time."

The Ministers' Room. Hugo wires Jerry's audio.

HUGO: Two hundred forty thousand the first year, raises and bonuses to follow, a Cadillac car, any house in town—so long as it don't cost more than five hundred thousand—two secretaries, personal customized corner office on the top floor of the Gottschall Building—

JERRY: Chuck Bissonette...

HUGO: It's just a feeler offer, nothing official.

JERRY: Winners win, and losers lose.

(Hugo indicates he's listening on his headset.)

HUGO: I copy...yes...uh-huh... Without even stopping for supper?... Keep me posted... Will do. Out. *(To Jerry.)* Mrs. G.'s fit to be tied. She's at Overbrook calling every newspaper and Christian broadcaster in Texas to tell them Pastor has no plans of retiring whatsoever.

JERRY: Who tells you these things?

HUGO: There are no secrets at Rock Baptist Houston. The half of the committee that made the call just did that on their own, without telling the rest of the guys—or Dr. G.

JERRY: Half of the committee?

HUGO: They was split, half for you and half for Reverend B. It's civil war.

JERRY: Well, at least I had half of them.

HUGO: You'd have had all of 'em if—Well, I hate to say it, but you're Dr. G.'s man and that's what's working against you. Some of them don't think that's right.

(Gottschall, ashen, enters the room so silently that Hugo and Jerry don't hear him.)

JERRY: And they're right. No pastor should be able to appoint his successor. It's not Baptist tradition, not our doctrine.

GOTTSCHALL: Our doctrine wouldn't have allowed Moses to appoint Joshua as his successor...

JERRY: Good evening.

(As Gottschall orates, Hugo serves his tea, which is ignored.)

GOTTSCHALL: ...or Peter to hand the early church over to John Mark, for that matter. First, the committee's scared, thinking I'm about to appoint you.

JERRY: I'm flattered that you—

GOTTSCHALL: Don't be. I never said who I wanted. Never said I wanted anybody! Then, I scared them worse this morning. God's time… Oh, I scared them good, so good they ran for the nearest telephone. This is a multi-million dollar operation here. Can't trust a doddering old man to keep it going, keep folks from staying in the suburbs Sunday morning. Get the man with tan and the Pepsodent smile in here, he'll keep 'em coming! *(Beat.)* Insubordination! No one ever asked me what I want. I built this church! Sure as the blood from my daddy's swollen, dusty, cut-up fingers is on every piece of foundation stonework laid in Clarksville for twenty years, the foundation of this church, this multi-million dollar operation, has got my blood on it. And I will not—will not!—leave it in the manicured hands of any smiling, suntanned ping-pong player! I wanted to bring somebody in as co-pastor first, work with me for a brief period, an orderly transition.

(This is news to Jerry.)

JERRY: Oh, of course. I think that's a wise approach.

GOTTSCHALL: *(Charging on.)* I will not have it done any other way. Will not! I got Bucky Buckholz coming up to Overbrook later to strategize. We'll just see who's running things around here. Hugo!

HUGO: Yes, sir, Dr. G.

GOTTSCHALL: Wire me up! We got preaching to do.

(Gottschall strides out of the room. Hugo runs after him with his audio pack. Jerry stays behind, welling with despair. He prays.)

JERRY: Lord, I am so confused at this moment. Why did you lead me here? Was it to test me, test my ambition? My humility? I do confess to you, I wanted this to be mine. I felt—I feel—that here I can serve you, I can spread the gospel and bring souls unto you in a way that is not possible anywhere else on earth. Why won't you let me do this? Am I not up to the job? Lord, tell me your plan for me. Tell me. I'll follow again if you call. Lord? I'm listening…

(Jerry truly is listening. He strains to hear. Nothing. Hugo appears at the door.)

HUGO: Dr. M., we need you to start the service now.

JERRY: Hugo, would you get word to Mr. Buckholz that I'd like to speak with him before he goes up to Overbrook tonight?

SCENE TEN

The pulpit. Jerry preaches. Gottschall is seated behind him, lost in his own thoughts.

JERRY: Exodus: the Latin word for "departure." Before I depart from you tonight, I'd like to share with you something rather personal, and I hope this doesn't embarrass my two "little men" up here. In raising James and John, Melody and I have always felt that discipline begins with praise. It is as important to say, "Good job, Son, you've made me proud of you!" when indeed, one of our boys does well, as it is to reprimand when the situation calls for it. For a son to know he's made his father proud, well, that's everything to that boy… *(Beat.)* Reading Exodus, this book, this dialogue with God that Moses recounts so powerfully, there is one passage that never fails to bring tears to my eyes. It's here, chapter 33, where, after all the drama of slavery, plagues, crossing the desert, receiving the Commandments, all of this, Moses asks God a favor: he asks God to make his presence known to his people; not a small favor to ask. And in response, God agrees to do it because, he says to Moses, "I am pleased with you." *(Beat.) I am pleased with you! (Jerry composes himself before continuing.)* For all the speaking God does to man in the Bible, precious little of it is spent on praise. We praise God, gladly, lovingly, gratefully. But for God to praise man… "I am pleased with you." The moment defies description.

(Hugo appears behind Gottschall, whispering something in his ear. Gottschall smiles in response and Hugo exits. Jerry sees none of this.)

I hope you have been pleased with me these last four weeks. And I pray God brings us all together again very soon.

END OF ACT ONE

ACT TWO
SCENE ONE

The Ministers' Room, Sunday morning, three months later. Gottschall and Jerry enter in high spirits just after the conclusion of the 8:30 AM service.

GOTTSCHALL: There's *excitement* here today!

JERRY: Yes. It went well.

GOTTSCHALL: We got a few minutes to put our feet up before the ten o'clock. *(Hugo enters, carrying a large gift-wrapped box.)*

HUGO: What a crowd! Parking lot looks like a beehive, full of Christians with them fish things stuck on their rear bumpers, mowing each other down to get parking spots. *(To Jerry.)* This was just delivered for you. *(Jerry, puzzled, takes the package. Hugo serves Gottschall's tea.)*

GOTTSCHALL: Jerry? Tea? No, that's right, you don't—

JERRY: No, thank you.

HUGO: There must have been over forty-four hundred in there. And that's just the eight-thirty. You ought to see how super-dressed-up the ten o'clock crowd looks, like they know this is going to be the most-watched broadcast ever.

GOTTSCHALL: You want the girl to come and give your face a litle color?

JERRY: No.

GOTTSCHALL: Just for TV.

JERRY: No, thanks.

GOTTSCHALL: You need a little color. Half of Texas, half the *country* tunes in for the ten o'clock. What is that?

JERRY: It's from Chuck Bissonette.

HUGO: You got time to open that before the ten o'clock.

GOTTSCHALL: Hugo, get the girl on in here.

HUGO: Will do, Pastor. *(To Jerry.)* Pastor. *(Gottschall is not used to anyone else being called "Pastor" in his church. Hugo exits. Jerry opens the box and smiles, pulling out a ping-pong trophy.)*

GOTTSCHALL: What in creation…?

JERRY: *(Reading the card.)* It's Philippians 3:14: "'Forgetting what is behind and straining toward what is ahead, I press on toward the goal to win the prize for which God has called me heavenward in Christ Jesus.' Wishing you congratulations and God's blessing, Chuck."

GOTTSCHALL: Meaning…?

JERRY: Winners win, and losers lose. His benediction.

GOTTSCHALL: If Bissonette hadn't been so arrogant, so greedy, so hog-like about wanting the whole thing for himself, he could have been here right now getting ready to preach in front of what is certain to be record numbers of people watching TV. Forget the *Texas Baptist Standard*, forget the Texas papers, period. Your picture was in *Time* magazine!

JERRY: My name is news only because of your importance in the history of this remarkable church, this country, even. Jerry Mears' new job is not news. The selection of Dr. Philip Gottschall's co-pastor is news.

GOTTSCHALL: *(Still getting accustomed to the term.)* "Co-pastor..." Well, it's always a thrill the first time your picture's in *Time* magazine. *(Beat.)* You getting any exercise?

JERRY: I keep myself pretty fit.

GOTTSCHALL: Get your heart pumping, circulation going. Color in your cheeks!

JERRY: Believe me, my heart's pumping quite vigorously right now.

GOTTSCHALL: You're excited. We're all excited for you. Why, before four o'clock this morning, Julia was already up and out of bed, fixing breakfast, getting Pauline into a new outfit. Julia's very fond of you, Son.

JERRY: I wouldn't be here today if she hadn't been so supportive.

GOTTSCHALL: She—I shouldn't tell you this.

JERRY: What?

GOTTSCHALL: *(Laughing.)* Well, she... She is something. And she plays to win, as you well know from the licking she gave you at Scrabble.

JERRY: Yes.

GOTTSCHALL: Well, she... *(Laughs.)* You know, membership in her Sunday School class is harder to come by than membership in any country club in Houston. There's a lot of big deals have been made out of relationships forged in that class. Big deals. You ask Ross Perot, he'll tell you. And she...she told Bucky Buckholz to tell his committee that if they didn't quit talking to Chuck Bissonette and start talking to you, she'd kick the whole bunch of them right out of her class. She plays to win.

JERRY: I didn't know she'd done that.

GOTTSCHALL: Son, you had me, Julia, God and George Bush on your side.

JERRY: President Bush? I'm...I'm astonished. I was under the impression—

GOTTSCHALL: Spinach trees! He loved that, made him look at broccoli in a whole new light. In fact, a couple of days after you preached on that, he was having dinner at the Petroleum Club—Bucky was there, he told me this story, God's honest truth—and the President thought, why not try it, broccoli, see if it tastes like spinach after all. George Bush ordered broccoli! Well, jaws and menus fell all over the club. The Secret Service man about had a stroke on the spot and sent iced tea flying every which way.

JERRY: And did Mr. Bush like the broccoli?

GOTTSCHALL: Hated it. But you got him to do something his mother, his wife, and every broccoli farmer in the country couldn't do. You got him to at least give it another try. He's coming to the ten o'clock.

JERRY: I'm…I'm honored.

GOTTSCHALL: Now, you watch Julia. She'll spoil your boys, treat them like grandkids. She'll spoil them worse than she spoils our Pauline—the boys, you, and your pretty little Melody.

JERRY: She's already got Melody on a dozen committees…

GOTTSCHALL: Good, good.

JERRY: …and teaching kindergarten Sunday School.

GOTTSCHALL: People are crowding in out there because they *want* to know you. The flock follows the shepherd because they know him, they know his voice.

JERRY: I want to know them, too.

GOTTSCHALL: Good, good, Son. Preaching the eight-thirty every Sunday's a good start, gives you a chance to…to—

JERRY: To establish credibility with the congregation.

GOTTSCHALL: That's right. But I want you to have high visibility on campus as well. High visibility. Mrs. Neville typed up a schedule for you of all the events in the coming couple of weeks where you're expected. *(Finds it.)* Here.

JERRY: Did she check schedules with my secretary?

GOTTSCHALL: This will keep you out of the way while they're finishing the custom work on your office.

JERRY: About that: are bulletproof windows really necessary?

GOTTSCHALL: Carved bookcases and gold bathroom fixtures aren't necessary, either, but they want you to have them. So leave all that up to the committee and Nellie Winslow; she's decorated two Ritz Carltons and the Mexican ambassador's house. She knows what she's doing. *(Looking at the schedule.)* Tomorrow morning you start with the senior swim club and you go right on through the week—dedication for the new bowling alley, recovery groups…

JERRY: *(Reads the list.)* Bucky's Fellowship of Success lunch group—

GOTTSCHALL: Oh, that's a mistake. I offer the blessing there, do it every week.

JERRY: I'll trade you that one for the Women's Weight Loss Ministry Jello Jubilee.

GOTTSCHALL: Just get out there. The people will come to know you. *(Jerry is lost.)* What's on your mind? Too much for the first week?

JERRY: No. No, I'm ready.

GOTTSCHALL: What, then? San Antonio?

JERRY: No. Well, I suppose, of course… All my time there, years of building and teaching.

GOTTSCHALL: Of course.

JERRY: Promises made… But, I feel God's called me to do his work here.

GOTTSCHALL: He has. You're famous now.

JERRY: Yes.

(Hugo enters.)

HUGO: Excuse me, Pastors.

GOTTSCHALL: Where is the girl?

HUGO: On the way. She went to the hospitality center for coffee during the eight-thirty, and she's crowd-surfing her way back here. It's worse than the Christmas Light Parade out there. *(He stares at the trophy as he listens on the headset.)* Yeah, Dave… I copy… Will do… Fifteen. Out. *(To the pastors.)* On the air in fifteen.

GOTTSCHALL: Get the girl! Let's get this show on the road.

HUGO: Will do, Pastor. *(To Jerry.)* Pastor.

(Hugo exits. Beat.)

GOTTSCHALL: You are thinking something.

JERRY: Yes, I was thinking… Nothing.

GOTTSCHALL: Jerry, I'm your pastor. I don't want you carrying a burden in your heart. Especially not when the ten o'clock is about to start and the TV cameras are looking right at you. I want you out there full of light!

JERRY: I'm fine. I'm excited. So much to think about.

(Beat.)

GOTTSCHALL: Join me in prayer. *(They pray.)* Lord, your servant, here, loves you. On this, the greatest day in his life of service in your name and the sweet redeeming love of Jesus, he gives praise to you before the world. But, just as the shepherd is happier with the one little sheep from the flock which was lost and found again, Jerry would be more gratified with the praise of one man… *(Jerry looks up at Gottschall.)* …than in the thousands, the millions whose eyes will be upon him today. Bring peace to Jerry's heart on this, Lord. In Jesus' name, we pray. Amen.

JERRY: Amen.

GOTTSCHALL: Wherever your daddy is, I do hope he's watching TV at ten o'clock. Now let's get some color on that face!

SCENE TWO

The pulpit a few minutes later. The orchestra plays as the TV Announcer's voice-over booms over the church orchestra's thrilling prelude.

TV ANNOUNCER (V.O.): From magnificent Rock Baptist Church Houston, RBC Media Ministries brings you *Reverend Philip Gottschall's Mighty Hour of Praise and Glory.* Today's message: "The Hand Upon the Shepherd's Shoulder." With the RBC symphony orchestra, the RBC Voices of Jubilee, America's mightiest pipe organ, and Dr. Gottschall's special guests, the legendary Clint Black and Lisa Hartman Black.
(The TV lights intensify on the pulpit. As the orchestra and organ thunder, and the 300-voice choir triumphantly sings, Gottschall and Jerry take their seats. The song ends and Gottschall steps to the pulpit.)

GOTTSCHALL: We come to you, Lord, offering all praise and glory to your name. Hallelujah, hallelujah! All praise and glory to our Redeemer, Christ the King. Amen. Amen. My heart overflows with joyfulness this morning as I introduce to you the young man who, after an exhaustive search, has been selected to co-pastor with me, to provide for an orderly transition as I…well, I may appear to be indestructible, but no man is immortal. As you know, I am a firm believer in our doctrine that a congregation selects its pastors. Although I had absolutely no wish whatsoever to interfere in the work of the pastoral search committee, had the decision been mine to make, I would have unequivocally chosen the same servant of God selected by our committee. Please welcome with me a man who is a preacher, a scholar, a professor, an author, a devoted husband and father, one of the true stars in the firmament of our denomination: Dr. Jeremiah Mears.
(Gottschall holds out an arm to welcome Jerry to the pulpit, then steps back and sits. Jerry's hands feel the carving of the pulpit's wood, he gazes at the congregation and savors the moment. He has reached the mountain-top at last. As he opens his mouth to speak, Gottschall rushes up beside him.) This does not mean I will not be preaching to you anymore. No, no, not at all. Not at *all!* This is not the announcement of my retirement. No, sir. The Lord has kept me sharp and fit, and I will preach his revealed word with

every last ounce of life in my body until the day he takes me from mortal life. Praise his holy name!

(The orchestra and organ swell as lights fade.)

SCENE THREE

Jerry's appearances at activities and meetings on campus.

(At the bowling alley.)

JERRY: Lord, as we begin this evening in your name, we thank you for the blessing of six new lanes and computerized scoring. We thank you for providing a safe place where families can come together, to have fun, and enjoy...um...all-you-can-eat popcorn.

(At the singles ministry.)

JERRY: Lord, bless the Christ-centered men and women of this wonderful singles ministry as they come together in your name for a day of fellowship and football. We also ask that you bless our Aggies with victory today as they face off against the Texas Christian University Horned Frogs.

(At the High on a Higher Power Alcoholism Recovery Ministry.)

HUGO: Pastor.

JERRY: You're in this group?

HUGO: I'm in every recovery group on campus.

JERRY: *(Suddenly remembers.)* A woman called my office on Monday, looking for you. Sorry, I forgot to tell you...

HUGO: A woman?

JERRY: *(Checking pockets.)* Been so busy...I might have stuffed the message... said it was personal. She saw your name in the credits on the broadcast, and...couldn't find your number listed... *(Finds the message.)* Brenda Lopez.

HUGO: Never heard of her.

(Hugo crumples the message and tosses it aside. Jerry's pager beeps. He checks it and sighs.)

JERRY: Don't you want to find out what she—

HUGO: Pastor, that woman's either a new problem, or a problem from a time I don't half recall. Either way, I got enough problems just dealing with today.

JERRY: Right. *(The meeting begins.)* Will you all join me in prayer? Lord, bless your servants here who have turned away from drugs and alcohol to get "High on a Higher Power."

(At the Women's Weight Loss Ministry.)

JERRY: Lord, through prayer, fellowship and vigorous exercise these ladies have shed so many unwanted pounds, and for that we give all praise and thanks to you. *(Quickly checks a "cheat sheet" in his pocket.)* We ask especially for you to give Rowena Martin strength during the hours she's at work; help her to know that every Grand Slam breakfast she serves is not temptation on a plate, but a reminder, a call to be vigilant, and trust that faith and fitness will lead her to walk the path you have chosen for her, a more slender Christian.

SCENE FOUR

The Ministers' Room, weeks later; as the final triumphal strains of the closing hymn of the eight-thirty fade, Hugo pours tea for Gottschall, who will preach the televised ten o'clock.

GOTTSCHALL: It's the young people.

HUGO: Yes, sir.

GOTTSCHALL: They're the lifeblood of a church.

HUGO: We got the biggest youth ministry in the country.

GOTTSCHALL: But it's not getting any bigger. I had hoped a younger co-pastor would bring the youth in.

HUGO: Young people watch TV.

GOTTSCHALL: Out of the question—

HUGO: If he could do the ten o'clock now and then, get some TV exposure—

GOTTSCHALL: You, too?

HUGO: Say, what?

GOTTSCHALL: Bucky Buckholz has been bugging me… No, no, it's out of the question. The viewers would cry bloody rebellion if I wasn't in their living rooms every Sunday morning.

HUGO: Just an idea. *(Beat.)* Numbers are up for the eight-thirty, way up.

GOTTSCHALL: Numbers? Look at the numbers that come in envelopes after the broadcast. Look at the numbers on Mastercard and Visa that get called in to the prayer partners when I'm on TV. Those are *numbers. (Beat.)* Did he tell you to ask me about doing the ten o'clock?

HUGO: Dr. M.? No. I was just thinking on my own.

GOTTSCHALL: Thinking is not in your job description. *(Beat.)* Wire me up.

(Hugo does his audio.)

HUGO: I'm sorry, Pastor. You know I can't help making dumb comments now and then. Sorry.

GOTTSCHALL: God has a job description for all of us, Son. Every now and then we need to be reminded what it is.

(Jerry enters.)

JERRY: Good morning.

GOTTSCHALL: Morning. It went well, I trust?

JERRY: I must have had over two hundred walk the aisle when I made the call. That's the size of my entire first congregation!

GOTTSCHALL: Praise God. Two hundred!

JERRY: At the eight-thirty.

GOTTSCHALL: Hugo, did we have any spikes at the eight-thirty?

HUGO: No, we stopped spiking a couple weeks ago. Dr. M.'s been doing fine without 'em.

JERRY: You've been spiking the call?

GOTTSCHALL: Just to get things off to a good start, help you make a good name for yourself.

HUGO: It worked real good when you preached that month of guest sermons, before—

JERRY: Why wasn't I told?

GOTTSCHALL: The worship committee makes these decisions.

HUGO: The marketing boys get in on it, too.

JERRY: I should have been told.

GOTTSCHALL: Don't get all huffy. It's not as if we hired actors to do it.

HUGO: No, they're folks that already called in to accept Jesus as their personal savior.

GOTTSCHALL: They just come to the service instead of being saved on the phone by a prayer partner.

HUGO: They kind of hold it for a day or two. Makes them really want to run down that aisle when you make the call.

GOTTSCHALL: It's more meaningful for them to come to Jesus in church.

JERRY: I had no idea…

GOTTSCHALL: Well, you wouldn't want to make the call and have nobody answer, would you?

JERRY: I want that stopped. Right now.

GOTTSCHALL: It's been stopped.

JERRY: It's dishonest, it's not how God works.

GOTTSCHALL: I know how you feel, Jerry. Dishonesty, secrets, little deceptions—
not God's way at all. *(Beat.)* Hugo, could you…?

HUGO: Yes, sir.

(Hugo removes Jerry's audio.)

JERRY: Oh, Brenda Lopez left four or five messages for you this week. Please,
just call her back so she stops calling me.

HUGO: *(On headset.)* Yeah, Dave… Got it. Out. *(To Jerry.)* They're waiting on
you at the Promise Makers breakfast.

JERRY: Pastor… *(Jerry checks a printed list and sighs.)* Three breakfasts, lunch, and
two prayer coffees… Pastor, could you and I meet this afternoon, before
the spaghetti supper hymn-sing? There are a couple of things we should—

GOTTSCHALL: *(Overlapping.)* No time today, lad. None at all.

JERRY: I've been speaking with Bucky and a few of the deacons about—

GOTTSCHALL: I know all about your secret meetings.

JERRY: They're not secret.

GOTTSCHALL: Was I informed before they occurred?

JERRY: I'm trying to tell you right now.

GOTTSCHALL: Right now, before I preach?

JERRY: All right, then, this afternoon—

GOTTSCHALL: Bucky's already spoken to me.

JERRY: Oh. About the numbers?

GOTTSCHALL: What about them?

JERRY: Well, we're doing very well at the eight-thirty, but it appears, by analyz-
ing the numbers, that it's at the expense of the ten o'clock.

GOTTSCHALL: People just want to get a good look at you. Once they're satisfied, they'll go back to sleeping an hour later and coming in for the ten.

JERRY: Bucky thinks I should start doing the ten o'clock. *(Beat.)* At least, some
of the time. The majority of deacons feel the same way.

GOTTSCHALL: Oh? There's been a *vote*?

JERRY: No, no. Informal discussions. To be frank, there's great concern about
the budget, and the report from Marketing—

GOTTSCHALL: They don't know Thing One about running a church.

JERRY: They say it's not a matter of message, it's a matter of demographics.

(Hugo listens on his headset.)

GOTTSCHALL: Look at you: pasty, worn-out, flabby. You got to start taking
better care of yourself.

HUGO: *(Overlapping.)* Yeah, Dave… I copy… Will do. Out.

JERRY: When can we talk?

HUGO: Pastor? *(Both Jerry and Gottschall look at Hugo.)* Dr. M., I mean. They're still waiting on you.

JERRY: Fine, fine. I'm on the way.

HUGO: *(On headset.)* Hugo to Dave, do you read me? Over.

JERRY: We have to talk. So many things—

GOTTSCHALL: We'll talk. But not now.

HUGO: En route. Five minutes…I copy. Out.

GOTTSCHALL: Come work out with me tomorrow over at the Houston Club, you can use my locker.

JERRY: Why not right here at the Family Life Gym?

GOTTSCHALL: Half of the pledges that built Gottschall College were made in the steam room at the club. If you want to do the ten o'clock someday, you get some color in your cheeks and you start working the movers and the shakers.

JERRY: Tomorrow's so busy, but—

GOTTSCHALL: You pray on it. If God wants us to talk, he'll give us time to do it. *(Frustrated, Jerry starts to leave.)* Jerry…

JERRY: Yes?

GOTTSCHALL: Work up a special service for the youth ministry, something they'll want to bring other young people to hear.

HUGO: Only thing kids want to hear about is sex.

GOTTSCHALL: Whatever, just get the young people in the church. It's critical, demographics-wise.

JERRY: I'll do something.

GOTTSCHALL: They like you, but they're not following you.

JERRY: I need to establish more credibility with them, I guess.

GOTTSCHALL: Good, good, lad. I'm pleased with what you're doing here. I am very pleased with you.

(Gottschall has uttered the magic words—and knows it. Satisfied that the last word has been his, he flies out of the room.)

SCENE FIVE

Jerry addresses a Youth Ministry group of teenagers.

JERRY: I know how you feel. I was a teenager myself. We know how hard it is sometimes to be both a teenager and a Christian at the same time, don't we? My father told me once it's like being a Christmas tree, and every now and then, without any warning whatsoever, your blinker lights start twinkling and flashing. When my father told me that in the most understanding and sympathetic way you could imagine, somewhat unfortunately for me, he was speaking in his customary big loud voice, and the boys my age *in the house next door* heard every word. For years after that, every time they saw a light come on in our bathroom window, they'd burst into a chorus of "O, Christmas Tree." *(Beat.)* Beware the flashing colored lights. They're almost always warning lights: traffic hazards, train crossings. Think of the gaudy streets of Las Vegas, millions and millions of flashing colored lights; whether they're the Devil's lure or God's warning to us, Christians are not seduced by such gaudy displays. Christians resist the temptation. Christians run in the opposite direction, toward a greater light, the light that John wrote about in his gospel: "In him was life, and that life was the light of men…the true light that gives light to every man." *(Beat.)* When your lights start blinking and flashing, you think about that greater light. And thank God for the precious gift of your life. And you'll know what to do.

(The meeting ends. Hugo brings Jerry his jacket and helps him put it on.)

HUGO: Wish I could have heard preaching like that when I was a teenager. Took me twenty years to find the "Off" switch for my blinker lights. *(Jerry puts his jacket on gingerly.)* Pastor, you okay?

JERRY: Just a little stiff from my workout today with Dr. Gottschall.

HUGO: He whooped you.

JERRY: The bicycles, then the rowing machine, then the weights, and the sit-ups and what-have-you. If I did ten, he did twenty. If I did twenty, he did fifty. The man's amazing, he'll live to be a hundred. Praise God. *(Beat.)* He was right about the steam room.

HUGO: Say, what?

JERRY: When they're sitting right next to you stark naked, they're vulnerable. Don't kick 'em when they're down, close 'em!

HUGO: And you closed Dr. G.?

JERRY: Starting week after next, we alternate the ten o'clock.

HUGO: Hallelujah! It's about time. *(Jerry starts to speak, but giggles instead.)* Now that is the first time I have ever, in—what is it now? Nine, ten months?—and I finally see you laughin'.

JERRY: The picture: the co-pastors of the biggest Protestant church in the world, talking in utter seriousness about the future of this church, as we sit in our birthday suits in a room full of steam.

HUGO: That's the picture they should have run in *Time* magazine.

JERRY: It's still going to be called *Reverend Philip Gottschall's Mighty Hour of Praise and Glory.*

HUGO: All in all—and I'm speaking here as someone who has worked at Dr. G.'s side for a long, long time and seen it all—he's doing pretty good, having you co-pastor.

JERRY: You see it that way?

HUGO: Yes, sir, I do. This church may have thirty thousand members on the books, but it's his church, his rock. You know that. He's still here. And if he wanted to look at things in a certain light, he could view giving you this service, and that meeting, and this program, and that class…well, those are pieces of his rock.

(Beat.)

JERRY: Is Accounting's computer system up and running again?

HUGO: Yes, sir, it is.

JERRY: Good. Last week, I didn't get my Sunday numbers until Tuesday.

HUGO: Well, there's a new policy.

JERRY: What new policy?

HUGO: Well, instead of giving me the numbers…now Accounting takes them directly to Pastor's office.

JERRY: No. I don't care where Dr. Gottschall wants his delivered, or when, but I want my copy right away on Sunday.

HUGO: Well, that's not how Mrs. G. wants me to do it.

JERRY: Mrs. G. is not running this church.

HUGO: Now that, right there, is the funniest thing you said today.

SCENE SIX

The Ministers' Room a month later. The orchestra, choirs and congregation perform the final chorus of the hymn concluding the ten o'clock service. Gottschall looks through Jerry's open briefcase, glancing at documents, rifling through a daily planner, etc.

JERRY: *(Off.)* Not now, page me after the eleven-thirty.
(Gottschall quickly puts the things back where he found them, and starts out of the room, nearly colliding just outside the door with Jerry.)

JERRY: *(Continued.)* Pastor!

GOTTSCHALL: Whoa, there!

(Ad lib "Sorry, didn't see you, what's the hurry," etc.)

JERRY: I didn't realize you were still here. How was your eight-thirty?

GOTTSCHALL: Fine, fine. Good numbers. I told you they'd come back up once the congregation figured out we're alternating the ten o'clock.

JERRY: Numbers are up at every service.

GOTTSCHALL: The flock will follow the shepherd.

JERRY: Some tea?

GOTTSCHALL: No, just leaving.

JERRY: Oh. You weren't waiting for me? To discuss—

GOTTSCHALL: No, just…just resting my eyes, and I dozed off. Well! Pauline's birthday today. Julia's got a brunch all set up over at River Oaks Country Club. Mrs. Bush is coming, and she's bringing Lee Greenwood along to sing "Happy Birthday." How about that?

JERRY: I wish I'd known.

GOTTSCHALL: Julia would have invited you, but, of course, you've still got the eleven-thirty to finish.

JERRY: I'll have a gift sent over to Overbrook. *(Takes some papers out of his briefcase, reads.)* We're doing some retakes at the eleven-thirty; preaching without notes has its pitfalls when you don't have enough time in the week… *(Senses something.)* It was right here…

GOTTSCHALL: Well! On my way. There's some bee pollen and a couple bags of dried pitted prunes in the cupboard. Help yourself.

JERRY: Pastor?

GOTTSCHALL: Good for the memory. The TV boys never have to stick around for my eleven-thirties.

JERRY: Pastor?

GOTTSCHALL: Yes.

JERRY: About my memo…

GOTTSCHALL: I've seen no memorandum. Must run now.

JERRY: Mrs. Neville—

GOTTSCHALL: Yes.

JERRY: She's had my parking spot labeled, "Co-Pastor."

GOTTSCHALL: Of course.

JERRY: But yours still says, "Pastor."

GOTTSCHALL: I don't have time for—

JERRY: In my memo… Either both spots should be labeled "Co-Pastor," or—

GOTTSCHALL: Trivialities, lad. Inconsequential trivialities that have nothing

whatsoever to do with God's work. You learn your lines, now, get your
message down pat for the TV cameras.
(Gottschall flies out of the room.)
JERRY: Dr. Gottschall…
GOTTSCHALL: *(Off.)* Bee pollen, lad. Bee pollen and dried pitted prunes.

SCENE SEVEN

*Just before a meeting of the High on a Higher Power Recovery Ministry.
Hugo is twitchier than usual. Jerry comes up to him and speaks so no one else
can hear.*

JERRY: We've got a few minutes before the rest of the group gets here.
HUGO: Recovery meetings don't need any of this mystery, thank you very much.
JERRY: I'm sorry about that, but it's serious, Hugo. Very serious.
HUGO: That woman?
JERRY: Brenda Lopez. She came to my office today.
HUGO: I don't know her.
JERRY: I canceled a meeting with the Christmas Electrical Parade Committee,
even though that's already thirty thousand over budget. I had to spend
time with Brenda, once she told me—
HUGO: *(Jumps.)* Whatever she's claiming, don't—
JERRY: Hugo, she does know you. Or did.
HUGO: How do you know?
JERRY: You knew her very well when you were in Albuquerque.
HUGO: No, don't think so.
JERRY: She knows you've got "Jesus wept" tattooed on the right side of your
rear end.
HUGO: Albuquerque…
JERRY: Twelve, thirteen years ago?
HUGO: Yeah, maybe.
JERRY: Hugo, you're a father.
HUGO: No.
JERRY: You and Brenda have a son.
HUGO: No!
JERRY: He's twelve years old.
HUGO: That is a lie, a lie, a lie! I swear on a stack of Bibles—
JERRY: You have a son, and he needs you.

HUGO: I do not!

JERRY: How do you know you don't?

HUGO: How do you know I do?

JERRY: I believe this woman.

HUGO: You are so gullible, Pastor. Any woman off the street comes in here, and—

JERRY: She knows you, Hugo. She described you. That tattoo!

HUGO: I don't remember any woman in Albuquerque! I don't half-remember Albuquerque! All due respect, but please, just butt right out of my business, and quit believing every lie any stray dog tells you.

JERRY: I believe Brenda. She's in Houston now. She's a Christian. I prayed with her today.

HUGO: I'm not seeing her.

JERRY: The boy needs his father.

HUGO: Yeah, well, I needed a father once.

JERRY: Don't do to him what your father did to you. A fatherless boy feels like he doesn't really exist in this world. You know that.

HUGO: You don't know—

JERRY: You felt so worthless you nearly killed yourself. Do you want that to happen to this boy someday? He's your son. It's your job to be his father.

HUGO: I'm sick of everybody telling me what my job is! *(Jerry waits.)* Is she still fat?

JERRY: So you do remember her.

HUGO: There was a fat girl in Albuquerque I recall somewhat.

JERRY: She was a prostitute. She told me. And she sold drugs.

HUGO: We weren't country club material. Okay, say she's got a kid, and she got pregnant around the time I was in Albuquerque, that does not prove that I'm the kid's father.

JERRY: She says she's sure.

HUGO: What does that prove?

JERRY: Hugo, I know how you feel. I know you're scared.

HUGO: Tell her you couldn't find me.

(Hugo tears off, but Jerry is quick, and stops him. Hugo struggles in Jerry's grip.)

JERRY: This kid's in trouble. He needs a father. He needs a role model.

HUGO: Role model?

JERRY: Yes.

HUGO: I'm a role model for a car wreck.

JERRY: Twelve years old, that's all he is. And he sneaks out, gets drunk...burglary, arson. He idolizes the neighborhood crack dealer.

HUGO: Well, the apple don't fall very far from the tree.

JERRY: You can save this boy. You can be responsible for him. But if you reject him, you're handing him a death sentence. You and I know, it'll just be a matter of time. And you don't have the right to do that. Do you hear me? Only God had the right to sacrifice his son, and he did it so that we may have eternal life, our sins washed away by the blood, the suffering of Jesus. You accepted Jesus as your savior. You turned your life over to him. He brought you here. And now he's brought your son to you. You reject this boy, that's...that's rejecting Jesus. *(Hugo stops struggling.)* Your son...he has a name.

HUGO: Don't say it!

JERRY: Victor. Your son's name is Victor.

(Hugo sobs, a defensive little boy.)

HUGO: You're just doing this 'cause you're still mad at your daddy for walking out on you.

JERRY: He didn't walk out.

HUGO: Your daddy...he could look you in the eye and know what you're thinking, feel how you're hurting. Make you feel safe. That's a father. I can't be that.

JERRY: You can be more than he ever was. You've mythologized him based on one night's experience on a street corner in El Paso.

HUGO: He saved me.

JERRY: No, God saved you. You saved yourself. But Dad...Dad wasn't God. He loved God, but he was a closer. He didn't know where the selling stopped and the saving began. He looked you in the eye because that's what salesmen do. Good eye contact establishes control. Then he told you, "I know how you feel." He was establishing credibility, see? Then he uncovered your needs, didn't he? "You feel lost, Son, don't you? Sure you do. Your life is like being in the passenger seat of a car doing eighty miles an hour, and nobody's at the wheel, isn't that right? A dead man for sure. I *know* how you feel." Then he'd go on to the features of his product. "Son, you have eternal life with Jesus, do you know that?" Then the benefits, "You'll wake up every morning, knowing that somebody's there for you, looking out for you; somebody with a plan for your life." Need, feature, benefit. Then, the close, "Will you pray with me now? I'll be right here with you. I'm Christ's rabid dog, and I won't let you go. Pray with me." Sound familiar, Hugo?

HUGO: You're jealous of him!

JERRY: I believe you can be a better father than he was.

HUGO: Jealous!

JERRY: You can be there for your son. My father couldn't do that.

HUGO: I feel sorry for you. No matter how hard you try, no matter what heights you climb to, you can never be bigger than your old man, can you?

JERRY: Hugo, that's not—

HUGO: *(Not stopping.)* Because try as you will to tear him down, he's always going to be as big and as powerful as he was the day he walked out on you. And you'll always be the squinty-eyed kid who never measured up in the old man's eyes. It must be sad, dang sad, to be your age and still need so much approval.

(Beat.)

JERRY: I know how you feel. Hugo, I do. But this isn't about me. Or you. It's about a twelve-year-old boy named Victor who desperately needs his father's approval.

(Beat.)

HUGO: Well…I'm his father.

JERRY: Yes. You are. You're responsible for this boy.

HUGO: I do such a piss-poor job of being responsible for me, how can I—?

JERRY: I'll help you. We'll get him enrolled here at Rock, get him away from the criminal element.

HUGO: Have you seen him?

JERRY: No.

HUGO: Oh. I was just wondering if he…

JERRY: Brenda wants me to call her tonight. She's bringing him to the ten o'clock tomorrow morning.

HUGO: Oh, Lord. Oh, Lord! I'm gonna see him. My kid. My boy. *(Beat.)* What if he don't want to see me?

JERRY: Hugo, believe me, he wants to see you.

HUGO: Be with me. You doing the ten tomorrow?

JERRY: Yes. I'll be right there with you.

HUGO: One thing, Pastor.

JERRY: Yes?

HUGO: Don't say anything to Dr. G. about this.

JERRY: Why? He wouldn't—

HUGO: I know him better than you. You and God may be okay with bringing Brenda here, and my…my son. But I don't know how okay I am with all of this yet. So, if it's all the same to you, I'd like to be the one to tell Dr. G., you know, once I get used to it all.

JERRY: Fine. I won't say a word.

HUGO: So…tomorrow after the ten o'clock? *(Beat.)* Okay. All right. Well…Pastor, you got a room full of recovering Christian alcoholics in there who could really use a prayer from you right now to get the meeting going. Don't mind me if tonight I just sort of hang out behind the back row. I'm feeling a little shaky.

(Jerry moves to where the meeting is starting, and leads a prayer.)

JERRY: Heavenly Father, we come before you tonight, your children, with full faith in You and Your presence in our lives.

SCENE EIGHT

The Ministers' Room, that Sunday, following the eight-thirty service. It is the last Sunday of Advent. Gottschall enters quickly as the final music of the organ postlude ("O Come, O Come, Emmanuel") fades. He pours a cup of tea and grabs a bag a dried pitted prunes, devouring them as he gathers his things to leave. He checks his watch—geting late!—fumbles with his microphone, and finally hollers in exasperation.

GOTTSCHALL: Hugo! Where in Creation are you?

HUGO: *(Off.)* Coming!

GOTTSCHALL: I got meetings to get to!

(Hugo flies into the room, wearing a new jacket and tie, nervously touching his freshly-combed hair.)

HUGO: Sorry, Pastor. I was in the men's room.

GOTTSCHALL: What are you all slicked-up for?

(Hugo removes Gottschall's microphone pack.)

HUGO: Um… Nothing special. I try to look presentable for the ten o'clock. In case the TV cameras pick me up in the background, or something.

GOTTSCHALL: All slicked up for Dr. Mears' ten o'clock.

HUGO: I'm gonna slick myself up for all the ten o'clocks now. New policy.

GOTTSCHALL: Lots of new policies around here.

HUGO: Yes, sir! You can feel the old excitement coming back to Rock, can't you?

GOTTSCHALL: I'll tell you what I feel, Hugo. And I'm telling you this because I know, and Mrs. Gottschall knows, every word you hear goes right back to Dr. Mears and his cronies. *(Hugo stunned, stammers, unable to answer.)* Sides are being taken, and I will not have it. I will not have dissension. I am still Pastor of this church, do you hear me? Whisperings, secret meetings, secret plans. Every day a new program, new policy, new major expenditures about which I was not informed—not even consulted! Memoranda, mountains of memoranda, yes! All of it after the deeds are done!

HUGO: But, you're Pastor, you should be—

GOTTSCHALL: Don't deny your role in this…this conspiracy.

HUGO: Say, what?

GOTTSCHALL: "A false witness will not go unpunished, and he who pours out lies will not go free."

HUGO: Pastor, do you think I'm lying to you? I'm not. I swear!

GOTTSCHALL: Don't swear to me. That's between you and God, Son. You and God.

HUGO: Pastor, you know I'm completely devoted to you. I'll do anything you ask.

GOTTSCHALL: What's most heartbreaking is that Mrs. Gottschall no longer feels she can trust you. She needs to know what's happening on campus. I cannot be everywhere at once, and we've relied upon you. As Paul relied upon Silas!

HUGO: I'm still her eyes and ears everywhere! I tell her everything!

GOTTSCHALL: Everything?

HUGO: Everything!

GOTTSCHALL: Did you tell her about your meeting last night with Dr. Mears?

HUGO: What meeting?

GOTTSCHALL: Hugo. "Devise not evil against thy neighbour."

HUGO: Last night? Dr. M. gave the blessing at High on a Higher Power.

GOTTSCHALL: You're denying, then, that you and he met privately before the meeting?

HUGO: We just said, you know, what's new and what-have-you.

GOTTSCHALL: You're denying he was attempting to recruit you for—?

HUGO: We just said *hello*.

GOTTSCHALL: I was told the two of you were—

HUGO: Told by who? What is going on around here?

GOTTSCHALL: I will not have plots, and secrets. I will not! We are here to serve God, glorify his holy name and bring souls to Jesus. There is no place here for plotting, and whispering, and secrets!

HUGO: All right! Okay, about that meeting: I hope you won't think too much less of me for what I'm going to tell you, but it has to do with something stupid I did I ain't proud of.

(Hugo summons the courage to reveal his parenthood to Gottschall, but before he can speak, Jerry enters, and senses the tension in the room.)

JERRY: Good morning. Pastor. Hugo.

GOTTSCHALL: Good morning.

JERRY: The eight-thirty…?

GOTTSCHALL: Record numbers for the last eight-thirty in Advent. Record numbers, lad!

JERRY: *(Attempting humor.)* Well, I hope a few thousand are left to show up for my ten o'clock.

(Beat.)

GOTTSCHALL: I'm due at a meeting. Hugo, you give Mrs. Gottschall a call and give her a complete report right now on what we were just discussing. Will you do that?

HUGO: Yes, sir, I will.

GOTTSCHALL: Jerry, I'll see you tonight for the Christmas Electric Light Parade.

JERRY: Yes.

HUGO: I'll take you two up to the Pastor's Float at six-fifteen.

GOTTSCHALL: Don't forget to make that call, Hugo. God bless you, lads.

(Gottschall exits.)

JERRY: And what was all that?

HUGO: *(Pouncing.)* Are they here?

JERRY: I put Brenda and Victor in the second pew, center aisle, left side.

HUGO: Lord, get me through this morning.

JERRY: I assigned an usher to bring them back here after the service.

(The organ and bell choir prelude to the ten o'clock service begins, "O, Little Town of Bethlehem," played with sensitivity and grace. Hugo leans in to Jerry.)

HUGO: Does he… *(Almost a whisper.)* The kid, does he…

JERRY: Yes, quite a bit. Especially the eyes. The resemblance is remarkable.

HUGO: Oh, Lord.

JERRY: Fidgety. He's got a tattoo, but at least it says, "Mother."

(Gottschall returns, pausing at the door as he sees Jerry and Hugo deep in intense conversation. At first they don't see him.)

HUGO: *(Deep breath.)* Did she say if she wants to—

JERRY: It's all right, go ahead and ask.

GOTTSCHALL: I hope I'm not interrupting something private.

JERRY: No.

HUGO: No, nothing.

GOTTSCHALL: What are you two whispering about?

JERRY: We were… Frankly, Pastor, I've been counseling Hugo about a…a situation, a burden he's been struggling with.

GOTTSCHALL: Hugo, I'm your pastor. If your heart's burdened, you come to me, unless you'd rather—

HUGO: No! I mean, I would, but this particular burden came to Dr. M. and he brought it to me, and—

GOTTSCHALL: *(Retrieves his bag of dried pitted prunes.)* I'll leave you two alone now to get your story straight.

JERRY: Pastor—

HUGO: It's not what you think. *(Gottschall waves them off and leaves in a fury. Hugo listens on his headset.)* Yeah, Dave…I copy. Two minutes. Out. *(To Jerry.)* I got to do your audio.

SCENE NINE

The organ and bell choir hymn from the last scene becomes a digital, almost carnival-like, "electronic music" version of "O, Little Town of Bethlehem" for the Christmas Electrical Parade.

The Ministers' Room, 6:15 that evening. Gottschall waits, dressed in a suit, no topcoat, no scarf, no gloves. Jerry enters, wearing a long overcoat, gloves and wool scarf. The parade music plays in the distance, repeating itself continuously.

GOTTSCHALL: Well, lad… The parade just goes down Post Oak Boulevard, not all the way up to the Yukon Territory.

JERRY: Aren't you wearing an overcoat?

GOTTSCHALL: Not at all, lad. Not at all.

JERRY: It's pretty bitter out there.

GOTTSCHALL: Never had so much as a head cold since the day I took the pulpit. I'm not so easy to knock down. No, lad. It's not bitter *outside*. *(Beat.)*

JERRY: Shouldn't Hugo be here by now?

GOTTSCHALL: No, Hugo should not.

JERRY: Yes. He's supposed to take us up to the Pastor's Float.

GOTTSCHALL: Hugo Taney is no longer an employee of this church.

JERRY: What?

GOTTSCHALL: His employment, regretfully, had to be terminated.

JERRY: When? On what grounds? What the—? Who—?

GOTTSCHALL: His employment was terminated by the operations manager this afternoon.

JERRY: I was here all afternoon. Why wasn't I consulted?

GOTTSCHALL: Insubordination. We cannot tolerate insubordinate—

JERRY: You did this! This was you—

GOTTSCHALL: Collusion, plotting, working against the best interests of this church… We cannot have it.

JERRY: What collusion?

GOTTSCHALL: How you've changed since you came to Rock. I should have seen it coming, but I trusted you. But that's my nature, to be trusting.

JERRY: What did you do to Hugo?

GOTTSCHALL: I pray for you, Jerry. Julia and I both pray for you. We pray that this unbridled lust for power by which Satan's attempting to corrupt your soul—

JERRY: What did you do to Hugo?

GOTTSCHALL: He had to be let go. His behavior was destructive to the best interests of the church.

JERRY: That's not good enough.

GOTTSCHALL: I'm not surprised losing your little spy's made you go off the deep end.

JERRY: You're delusional.

GOTTSCHALL: Son, I'm sharp as a chisel. And I'm not the only one who's seen you two, whispering, making secret plans, plotting to render me irrelevant to my own church. *(Jerry starts to leave.)* Where are you going?

JERRY: I've got to find him.

GOTTSCHALL: You've got to lead this parade, young pup! You're on the Pastor's Float! This is history! The first time since they started this thing anyone's up on the Pastor's Float beside me! There are over two hundred thousand people out there waiting to view this historic moment, stuffing their faces with popcorn. And snow cones. Every TV station in Texas has a camera crew shivering out there, waiting for you.

(Beat. Jerry doesn't leave.)

JERRY: He loves you. He'd have done anything for you, anything.

GOTTSCHALL: At one time, yes, that was true. Before his loyalty was corrupted.

JERRY: His loyalty—my loyalty to you, for that matter—has never been corrupted.

GOTTSCHALL: "These six things doth the LORD hate:

JERRY: *(Talking over Gottschall.)* He's lost without this church. He can't handle his life without this church! And you drove him from it!

GOTTSCHALL: *(Continuing over Jerry.)* "A proud look, a lying tongue, and hands that shed innocent blood, an heart that deviseth wicked imaginations,

JERRY: He won't survive. You've sacrificed him to your own glory, your vanity!

GOTTSCHALL: *(Thundering. The final words.)* "Feet that be swift in running to mischief, a false witness that speaketh lies, and he that soweth discord among brethren."

JERRY: You've sacrificed Hugo. Sacrificed him, and his son.

(Beat.)

GOTTSCHALL: Hugo has no son.

JERRY: Yes, he does. He met him for the first time this morning, right after the ten o'clock. *(Jerry lets this sink in.)* The mother saw Hugo's name in the credits on the broadcast, my first Sunday here. The day you presented me as your co-pastor. She called me, and I was able to bring them together.

GOTTSCHALL: She called *you*?

JERRY: Yes.

GOTTSCHALL: She called the *co-pastor*.

JERRY: Hugo was afraid you'd think less of him for having fathered, and abandoned, a son. He didn't know there was a child, by the way, until last night. I told him, in private, just before High on a Higher Power started. *(Beat.)* He so wanted you to be proud of him, to be pleased with him.

GOTTSCHALL: He shouldn't have been afraid.

JERRY: That sorry, abused, wretched, little soul was clinging to your mighty rock for life itself.

GOTTSCHALL: He would have shared this burden with me if you hadn't poisoned him with your whisperings.

JERRY: Your approval was his life. Your rejection will likely be his death.

GOTTSCHALL: Well, then, go find him. Go look in every beer bar and dope den in Houston. I'll do the parade. The TV boys can get their historic two-pastors-on-the-float pictures next year.

JERRY: Next year?

GOTTSCHALL: The parade's an annual event.

JERRY: Pastor…Pastor, God brought me here to lead this church.

GOTTSCHALL: I brought you here, and God's been making me pay dearly for it ever since.

JERRY: You have got to allow God's plan to unfold.

GOTTSCHALL: How do you know what God's plan is? He's told you? I thought he hasn't spoken to you in a long time. We've all heard you whine about that often enough.

JERRY: He led me here. You know that.

GOTTSCHALL: If he led you here it was to test me, to prove that I am still completely capable of pastoring this church without the so-called assistance of—

JERRY: *(Overlapping.)* I was brought here on the understanding that after a brief transitional period, you would retire. You promised me —

GOTTSCHALL: I recall no such promise. I said we'd see what God does. In God's time.

JERRY: Are you waiting for God to strike you dead? Step aside now, enjoy your retirement—

GOTTSCHALL: *Step aside?* I'm stepping up on to the Pastor's Float. I gotta go holler, "Happy Birthday, Jesus!" Amen!

SCENE TEN

On the Pastor's Float in the Christmas Electrical Parade. The digital "O, Little Town of Bethlehem" continues, louder and more annoyingly. Jerry and Gottschall wave to the cheering crowd, a blinding array of twinkling colored lights reflect on their frozen smiles.

JERRY: This is the first thing that's going to go. This carnival.

GOTTSCHALL: Membership recruitment, lad. People want to be part of the excitement.

JERRY: Big numbers.

GOTTSCHALL: Big numbers make big deeds possible. God's work.

JERRY: Where is God in all this?

GOTTSCHALL: God is in every face in that crowd. Look at that! Praise Jesus! *(Shouts.)* Happy Birthday, Jesus!

JERRY: Is this what Jesus envisioned when he told Peter he would build his church upon a rock? A church built on a dinner theater and two swimming pools?

GOTTSCHALL: You have no vision, you have no sense of the greatness of God.

JERRY: The greatness of Dr. Philip J. Gottschall…

GOTTSCHALL: I thought you had what it would take to lead this church someday.

JERRY: What this church needs is to be a church, not Las Vegas.

GOTTSCHALL: What's happened to you?

JERRY: The church is not the rock. You're not the rock, I'm not the rock. Jesus is the rock.

GOTTSCHALL: You, who were so eager to work with us—

JERRY: I was eager—I *am* eager—to do God's work. Not to bless bowling alleys and ride in parades.

GOTTSCHALL: You came here for the same reason you do anything: so you can say, "Hey, Daddy! Look at me!" *(Shouts.)* Happy Birthday, Jesus! Praise his holy name!

JERRY: Then why did you hire me in the first place? To be the son you never had? So you could keep up with the rest of the big-timers, putting their sons in their pulpits? Sons, in the image of the fathers. It's not succession, it's not continuity, it's immortality.

GOTTSCHALL: *(Shouting.)* Happy Birthday, Jesus!

JERRY: You never wanted a successor. You wanted me to be your son. Your obedient son.

GOTTSCHALL: No, lad. That's not what I wanted. That's what *you* wanted. *(Beat.)*

JERRY: You're never going to let me lead this church, are you?

GOTTSCHALL: It's in God's hands.

JERRY: You promised me—

GOTTSCHALL: I made no such—

JERRY: You haven't answered my question. Are you ever going to—

GOTTSCHALL: You're a whiner, lad. Whining, whining about hearing God's voice. Why in Creation would God want to talk to a whiner?

JERRY: And God speaks to you?

GOTTSCHALL: Every day, Son. Every day.

(The music and cheering grow louder.)

JERRY: *(Shouting.)* How can you hear him over all this noise?

GOTTSCHALL: *(Shouting.)* Happy Birthday, Jesus! *(To Jerry.)* TV cameras. Big smile!

(The music and cheering are deafening. The lights flash faster. Gottschall waves and smiles. Jerry, like a wild animal seconds before it becomes road-kill, freezes, then leaps off the float and all is darkness.)

The persistent, shrill digital music of the Christmas Electric Light Parade becomes a solitary electronic keyboard playing the old hymn, "Faith of Our Fathers."

A rural swap meet, Sunday, several months later, about an hour before the doors open to the public. Jerry, in shirtsleeves, gazes outward. Hugo joins him.

HUGO: Pastor?

JERRY: Are we all set?

HUGO: Yeah, we got a good crowd today. A lot more dealers came in to do their set-ups early so they could join in. Oh, and Loretta Fink remembered to bring her grandson's keyboard in to play the hymns on. We're big-time religion now.

JERRY: Sounds fine.

HUGO: One of the churches in town sent over some hymn books for us. The preacher saw the story in *Time* magazine.

JERRY: Good.

HUGO: Victor and your boys got the tables all pushed back at the barbecue stand, and the crowd's waiting, so if you want to get started…

JERRY: Thank you.

(But Jerry doesn't move.)

HUGO: Swap meet doors open to the public in an hour. Pastor?

JERRY: Sorry. I was just…listening.

(Hugo leaves Jerry alone. Jerry continues to listen. The electronic keyboard "Faith of Our Fathers" is drowned out by the Rock orchestra and choir concluding the same hymn as lights come up on Gottschall at the Rock pulpit.)

GOTTSCHALL: In these last few months I have been asked many times to comment on the departure from this church of Dr. Mears. I have not wished to do so publicly. I've shared my thoughts with God, in prayer, and in private. But now, after all the newspapers, and the *Time* magazine story, I will say a few words, but only here, at our eight-thirty, when it's just us "family." *(Beat.)* My beloved Julia and I pray every day for Dr. Mears. We don't know why he left so suddenly. I'm sure he believes he was called. *Time* magazine seems to think it's an obscene waste of talent for him to be selling vitamins at a swap meet somewhere way out in the country. But I know his daddy was a salesman who served God in his own way, and I suspect… Well, like father, like son, as they say…in his image. *(Beat.)* We pray on Paul's message from Corinth to the emerging church in Rome. He wrote, "We know that all things work together for good to them that love God, to them who are *called*." *(Beat.)* And about Dr. Jeremiah Mears, I shall say no more. Except to say, God be with him.

(Lights fade, except for a warm pool of light on Jerry.)

JERRY: Elijah, hiding in the cave, heard God's whisper. God promised Elijah he would reveal himself to him. And though wind swept through the desert, fire raged and earthquake thundered, God was not in them. God came, God spoke, to Elijah in a *whisper. (Beat. Jerry speaks in a big voice now, his father's voice.)* It is possible that God was revealing himself to Elijah the whole time. But how could Elijah hear God's whisper over the deafening sound of the wind, and the fire and the earthquake? *(Quietly.)* How could God's whisper be heard? *(Beat.)* Jesus said, "What I tell you in the dark, speak in the daylight; what is whispered in your ear, proclaim from the roofs." Proclaim! Shout! BIG voice! "What is whispered in your ear…" What God whispers in your ear. *(Beat.)* Lord, I pray… I pray… I pray to you, let me hear your sweet voice, your whisper. I will proclaim. I will shout! I will proclaim your love, and your salvation, and your gospel. I have never in my life felt closer to you, my Father, my Father in Heaven, than I do right now. Right here. In this quiet place. Whisper in my ear, and I will proclaim. I will. *(Quietly.)* Lord? Lord I'm listening. I'm listening. *(Beat. Jerry suddenly looks Heavenward. He whispers.)* Amen. *(Lights fade.)*

END OF PLAY

Life Under 30
An evening of ten-minute plays

*"Those who tell you that youth needs an ideal are idiots.
It has one already, which is youth itself and
the wondrous diversity of life…."*
Jean Anouilh

Life Under 30

Life Under 30 is the umbrella title for eight ten-minute plays which premiered during the 1999 Humana Festival of New American Plays. Selected by Jon Jory—with input from ATL's literary staff that included, at the time, three persons under the age of thirty—these works introduce eight talented young playwrights to an international audience. Finding a venue to showcase young playwrights, as well as young actors and directors, was a major part of this year's Humana Festival. "From the quality of their work," wrote critic Dick Kerekes, "I realized and am pleased to announce that the future of the theatre seems to be bright if these talented playwrights are any indication."

While no group of eight plays can speak to all concerns of a generation, this group does highlight several important aspects of life under thirty. Themes addressed include cultural/generational heritage, the value (or not) of work, and the loss of innocence. The plays are also highly theatrical, taking place in such evocative settings as a '76 Maverick on an LA freeway, a rooftop in Minneapolis, and the middle of the South Pacific. In addition, the project brought an exciting generational continuity to the Humana Festival, since many of the *Life Under 30* playwrights have studied with former Humana Festival playwrights, including Marsha Norman, Eduardo Machado and Elizabeth Wong. The eight playwrights were joint recipients of the 1998 Heideman Award.

—Ilana M. Brownstein

The running order of *Life Under 30* was as follows:

Slop-Culture by Robb Badlam
Mpls., St. Paul by Julia Jordan
Drive Angry by Matt Pelfrey
Just Be Frank by Caroline Williams

—Intermission—

Dancing with a Devil by Brooke Berman
Forty Minute Finish by Jerome Hairston
The Blue Room by Courtney Baron
Labor Day by Sheri Wilner

Slop-Culture
by Robb Badlam

BIOGRAPHY

Born and raised in the northern climes of Ogdensburg, NY, Robb Badlam graduated with a BA in English Literature from Colgate University in 1992, and received his Masters of Fine Arts Degree from the playwriting program at Rutgers University's Mason Gross School of the Arts in May of 1998. He's written numerous plays, including the full-length drama *Will* that interprets William Shakespeare's sonnets to explore the desperate love triangle between a dark mistress, a beautiful young man and the tortured soul behind the greatest poetry in history. (*Will* was selected as a semi-finalist in 1999 for the Chesterfield Film Company's Writers' Film Project.) In addition to *Slop-Culture*'s selection as a Heideman Award Co-Winner and inclusion in 1999's Humana Festival, a second ten-minute play of Robb's, *Guys*, was selected as a finalist in ATL's National Ten-Minute Play Contest the same year. His writings have been published by Samuel French, Inc., *Dramatics Magazine*, and *American Theater Magazine*. Among his many jobs, Robb works for the independent film company Artisan Entertainment as a script reader, evaluating scripts for potential production. Currently he is busily developing several new plays and screenplays of his own.

HUMANA FESTIVAL PRODUCTION

Slop-Culture premiered at the Humana Festival of New American Plays in March 1999. It was directed by Maria Mileaf with the following cast:

Brian	Bryan Richards
Dylan	Derek Cecil
Danielle	Monica Koskey
Cindy	Carolyn Baeumler

and the following production staff:

Scenic Designer	Paul Owen
Costume Designer	Michael Oberle
Lighting Designer	Mimi Jordan Sherin
Sound Designer	Darron L. West
Properties Designer	Mark Walston
Stage Manager	Heather Fields
Assistant Stage Managers	Dyanne M. McNamara & Alyssa Hoggatt
Dramaturgs	Amy Wegener & Sara Skolnick
Casting	Laura Richin Casting

CHARACTERS
BRIAN
DYLAN
DANIELLE
CINDY

TIME & PLACE
The present. New York.

Derek Cecil and Bryan Richards in *Slop-Culture*
by Robb Badlam

23rd Annual Humana Festival of New American Plays
Actors Theatre of Louisville, 1999
photo by Richard Trigg

Slop-Culture

Dylan and Brian, a pair of 20-somethings wearing their finest bumming-around-the-house clothes, are on the couch, in the midst of a heated discussion.

BRIAN: Oh, come on!

DYLAN: Can't do it.

BRIAN: That's my answer!

DYLAN: Inadmissible.

BRIAN: But it's true!

DYLAN: Our judges have spoken: The Pillsbury Dough Boy cannot be your role model.

BRIAN: Why not? Poke me in the stomach! Go ahead! I'll giggle!

DYLAN: Judges say: "Talk to the hand, girlfriend."

BRIAN: *(Very put out.)* Man!

(Pause.)

BRIAN: What about Fred from *Scooby-Doo?*

DYLAN: That, we'll accept.

BRIAN: Why Fred and not Pop'n'Fresh?

DYLAN: It's really for your own good.

(A pause. A grin creeps across Brian's face.)

BRIAN: *(Nodding.)* Dude…Daphne.

DYLAN: *(Complete agreement.)* Aaaww yeah. You know Fred was givin' her the business in the back of the Mystery Machine.

BRIAN: Aaaaaww yeeeaah. *(Beat.)* *(Impressed.)* Fred, man. He was one smooth operator. Had his own sense of style.

DYLAN: Not too many guys could pull off the white shirt and ascot and still look tough.

(They nod a moment. A pause.)

BRIAN: You think Shaggy and Velma ever hooked up?

DYLAN: *(With certainty.)* When they were drunk.

(Danielle enters. She has a packet of papers in one hand. She is dressed professionally, but she is very jittery and nervous.)

DANIELLE: Hey guys. Cindy here?

BRIAN: *(Calling over his shoulder.)* Cindy! Your lawyer's here!

DANIELLE: *(Instantly paranoid.)* Shit! Do I really look like a lawyer? Shit! I need to look like a personnel coordinator! A lawyer? Shit! Really?

BRIAN: You could be Marcia Clark's twin.

DYLAN: Twin? Dude, that's cold.

BRIAN: Oh, sorry. You'd be the younger, less weathered twin.

DYLAN: *(To Danielle.)* So what's with the new look? Witness Relocation?

DANIELLE: I'm applying for a job.

DYLAN: Whoa! Whoa! Whoa! I object, Your Honor! *(Steps onto a chair.)* Hear now these words I say: Under no circumstances...I say again for emphasis...*no circumstances*...are you to maintain or operate a frozen yogurt dispenser. Learn from my mistakes, Danielle...I have permanent scars. Let this be a lesson...look on my twisted form and learn...

(He starts to undo his pants.)

DANIELLE: No!

DYLAN: My life is nothing if not cautionary example.

DANIELLE: It's an office job!

(Pause.)

DYLAN: No frozen yogurt?

DANIELLE: No!

(Pause.)

DYLAN: Soft serve?

DANIELLE: Dylan! It's an office.

(Pause.)

DYLAN: *(Contemplative.)* I see. *(Pause.)* So...no dessert or snack vending of any kind?

DANIELLE: *(Emphatic.)* It's an OFFICE!

BRIAN: *(Offering.)* I got my hand caught inside the VCR once. *(Beat.)* I got it out.

DANIELLE: *(Frustrated, to Dylan.)* Is...your sister...home!?

DYLAN: Shower.

(He points vaguely down the hallway. Much on her mind, Danielle exits in that direction.)

DYLAN: Okay. One line. Summarize the show. *Dukes of Hazzard.* Go.

BRIAN: "Kew! Kew! Kew! Fuck you, Duke boys!"

DYLAN: Rosco never said "fuck."

BRIAN: That was his subtext. You go. *Gilligan's Island.*

DYLAN: "Gilligan! Drop those coconuts!" BONK! "Oow!"
  (*Pause.*)
BRIAN: Whoa. (*Pause.*) Nice. (*Pause.*) I could see the coconuts.
DYLAN: It's a gift.
  (*Cindy enters, bathrobe, towel, drying her hair. She is late and in a hurry. Danielle, like a small yap dog, is hot on her heels.*)
CINDY: Danni, I can't do this now. I'm late as it is. If I'm late one more time, the agency is going to fire me. Do you realize how difficult it is to get fired by a temp agency?
  (*Cindy brushes her hair in front of a mirror. She continues dressing and preparing throughout.*)
DANIELLE: I need your help!
CINDY: (*Resigned.*) Talk.
DANIELLE: They want me to answer this essay question...
CINDY: What's the question?
DANIELLE: ...And I don't think my answer is going to be what they're looking for...
CINDY: What's the question?
DANIELLE: ...In fact, I'm sure it's not what they're looking for...
CINDY: What's the damn question!?
DANIELLE: Cindy, did you ever go to church as a kid?
CINDY: That's the question?
DANIELLE: No. I'm asking. Did you ever go to church?
CINDY: Nope. My Sunday afternoons started with Abbott and Costello, and ended with Godzilla. God bless Channel 11. Why?
DANIELLE: Just curious.
CINDY: Thinking of finding Jesus?
DYLAN: And the conversation turns to matters of great import.
BRIAN: I met a Jewish guy once.
  (*They look at him.*)
BRIAN: (*Deflated.*) I don't really have a story to go with that.
  (*The conversation swerves back to Danielle.*)
CINDY: Ignore that man behind the curtain. Why do you ask, Danni?
DANIELLE: Sometimes I... (*Unsure, but pushes ahead.*) ...Well....there's this Baptist Church...in my neighborhood...and...sometimes I go...I just...I sit outside and listen.
CINDY: To what?
DANIELLE: The singing. It's nice.

CINDY: Why don't you go in?

DANIELLE: I couldn't. I don't…I don't belong.

CINDY: *(Stops. Looks at her.)* Are you okay, Danni?

DANIELLE: They've got something. I can't put my finger on it, but…
(Searching for words.)…It's…I don't know. They've got—

DYLAN: Milk?

BRIAN: The music in them?

DYLAN: The fever for the flavor of a Pringle?

CINDY: *(Threatening them.)* Don't make me turn this car around.

BRIAN: *(Intimidated.)* We'll be good.

(Pause.)

DANIELLE: They've got a past.

(Pause.)

CINDY: How do you figure?

DANIELLE: A past. A history. They came from somewhere.

CINDY: Did we spontaneously self-generate this afternoon, Master Yoda?

DANIELLE: It's different. It's something we don't have. It's a sense of…I don't know…community?

CINDY: What was college?

DANIELLE: Yeah, but don't you see? College pulls you out of one community, changes you and forces you into a new one. Then, as soon as you get comfortable, that new community is jerked out from under your feet after four years.

BRIAN: Six years.

DANIELLE: And where does that leave you? You're a different person now. You can't go backwards. You can't go back home. Because home isn't where you left it. It's different. *You're* different. You don't really fit in anymore. You don't have anything to hang onto. It's like you're…I don't know…marooned.

DYLAN: *Gilligan's Island.*

CINDY: *(Scolding.)* Dylan.

DYLAN: *(Onto something.)* No, I'm serious. That's the reason the Professor could build a satellite out of coconuts and twine, but couldn't patch the hole in the boat. They're spiritual castaways. They can't go back to the mainland because they don't belong there anymore. The island has changed them fundamentally. They *are* home. They just won't accept it because they can't see it. Where they most want to go, they already are. It's very Zen. They hate the island, but it's part of them. They can't deny it. You can take the boy away from the coconuts but you can't take the coconuts away from the boy.

BRIAN: Coconuts. The great social equalizer.

(Pause.)

CINDY: Dylan?

DYLAN: Yes?

CINDY: Never speak again.

DANIELLE: *(Producing paper.)* What's your earliest and fondest childhood memory?

CINDY: What?

DANIELLE: That's the question. "What's your earliest and fondest childhood memory and what impact do you think the experience has had on you as a person?" *(Beat.)* I need yours. Mine sucks.

(Pause.)

CINDY: *(Thinking.)* Hmm. McDonald's cheeseburger. *(Beat.)* Fridays used to be the big night. Mom would take us to McDonald's as a treat. We'd get all dressed up. She'd put those Happy Meals in front to us and we thought we were at the Ritz Carlton having caviar.

DYLAN: Uh-huh. And you used to tell me that Shamrock Shakes were made out of Grimace's brain juice. I've never forgiven you for that.

CINDY: I'd have been derelict in my duties as Older Sister if I didn't terrorize you.

BRIAN: My folks got divorced when I was three. I don't remember it. I always used to wish Fonzie was my real dad. *(Beat.)* Then I'd cry because the Cunninghams made him live in the garage. So I'd leave cookies in our garage. Then the raccoons came…

CINDY: So what's your memory, Danni?

DANIELLE: I can't…

CINDY: Come on.

DANIELLE: It's totally wrong!

CINDY: What is it?

DANIELLE: Do you remember in the opening credits for *Tom & Jerry*? When Tom's sticking his tongue out? And the big bulldog pounds him on top of the head and makes him bite his tongue off?

CINDY: Yeah. *(Danielle is quiet.)* That's IT? That's your earliest and fondest memory?

DANIELLE: *(Smiles.)* Tom looks so embarrassed about it!

CINDY: I could be wrong, but I think that's probably on that big list of things NOT to write on your job application.

DANIELLE: I know! *(Beat.)* But it's true. *(Pause.)* Cindy, when my mom was my age she was cooking huge Sunday dinners with her entire family…all the aunts and uncles and cousins and grandparents…they all lived right there in the same neighborhood! Like their own little Sicilian embassy in the middle of Brooklyn! *(Beat.)* But then my mom moved away and got married and started her own family…and I grew up in the suburbs. *(Beat.)* I was a kid eating Crunch Berries over *Schoolhouse Rock* at the same age when my mom and my great-great-great-grandmother were making… *(Searching.)*…baklava!

CINDY: Isn't baklava Greek?

DANIELLE: See! *(Beat.)* Cindy, I'm half Italian, and I need help ordering spaghetti at the Olive Garden!

BRIAN: If it helps, I've lost touch with my Viking heritage, too.

CINDY: *(To Brian.)* Don't make me come over there.

DANIELLE: So what do I do? I can't write down the truth. They'll think I'm four years old. I mean, I AM! I might as well be! I feel totally out of place going into an office! Like I've snuck in with my mom's blazer and my dad's briefcase. Petrified they're going to find me out! That they're gonna suddenly look up at me and say, "Silly rabbit! Jobs are for grown-ups!"

CINDY: So you want my advice?

DANIELLE: YES!

CINDY: Lie.

(Cindy moves swiftly off in the direction of the back bedroom.)

DANIELLE: No shit! How? *(Following her halfway.)* I wanted to use yours, but cheeseburgers and…and…Fonzie's brain juice aren't on *Fortune* 500's big list of "do's" either!

(Cindy re-enters, dressed and ready. Bag in hand, she is out the door.)

CINDY: I really wish I could be more help, sweetie, but if I don't leave right now, I'll be filling out job applications too. Relax. Be creative. Good luck.

(A quick peck on the cheek and Cindy is gone. A pause. Danielle stares at the door. Then, lets out a frustrated scream.)

DYLAN: Don't deny the island, Danni.

DANIELLE: What?!

DYLAN: Your past. Your history.

BRIAN: Your coconuts.

DYLAN: Where the castaways most want to go, they already are. The island. It's part of them. Like it or not.

BRIAN: Dude, didn't Gilligan get arrested for dope?

DYLAN: You're not helping the metaphor.

BRIAN: Sorry.

DYLAN: So what if our cultural heritage is only twenty-five years of bad TV. It's not much, but it's something. Embrace it. Its ours.

BRIAN: *(Serious.)* Gilligan, drop those coconuts.

DYLAN: *(Serious.)* Bonk.

BRIAN: *(Serious.)* Ow.

(Pause.)

DANIELLE: *(With a faint smile.)* Yeah.

DYLAN: Be proud, Danielle. You go right ahead and bite off that cartoon cat's tongue.

BRIAN: Hear! Hear!

DYLAN: *(To Brian.)* I think our work here is done. *(Motions to door.)* Shall we?

BRIAN: Indubitably!

(Brian and Dylan get up and start out.)

BRIAN: Dude, we got nowhere to go.

DYLAN: *(Without breaking stride.)* Doesn't matter.

(They're gone. Danielle, alone, sits thinking. Then takes up her pen and begins to write—with confidence. A smile creeps across her face. For the first time, she is relaxed. A weight's been lifted—more than the application.)

DANIELLE: *(Laughing.)* No way I'm getting this job.

(She keeps writing. Blackout.)

END OF PLAY

The Blue Room
by Courtney Baron

BIOGRAPHY

Courtney Baron received her MFA from the Columbia University Playwriting Program in May of 1998. Her play *The Good Night*, produced at Theatre for the New City in NYC, was a finalist for the 1998 Princess Grace Award's Playwriting Fellowship. Other productions include: *You Are Not Forgotten* (workshopped at the Royal Court Theatre, London), *Love As a Science* (Seattle Fringe Festival), *Clip* (Frontera Fest, Austin) and *The White Girl and the Sheep* (Theatre Three, Dallas). Her play *Dream of Heaven and Hell*, inspired by William Blake's *The Marriage of Heaven and Hell*, received a production by Reverie Productions in New York City in 1999.

HUMANA FESTIVAL PRODUCTION

The Blue Room premiered at the Humana Festival of New American Plays in March 1999. It was directed by Maria Mileaf with the following cast:

Woman . . . . Carla Harting
Sailor . . . . Bruce McKenzie

and the following production staff:

Scenic Designer . . . . Paul Owen
Costume Designer . . . . Michael Oberle
Lighting Designer . . . . Mimi Jordan Sherin
Sound Designer . . . . Darron L. West
Properties Designer . . . . Mark Walston
Stage Manager. . . . . Heather Fields
Assistant Stage Managers. . . . . Dyanne M. McNamara &
Alyssa Hoggatt
Dramaturgs . . . . Amy Wegener & Sara Skolnick
Casting . . . . Laura Richin Casting

CHARACTERS

WOMAN
SAILOR

TIME & PLACE

The middle of the South Pacific, coordinates: 48° 30'S/ 125° 30'W.

Bruce McKenzie and Carla Harting in
The Blue Room by Courtney Baron

23rd Annual Humana Festival of New American Plays
Actors Theatre of Louisville, 1999
photo by Richard Trigg

The Blue Room

*Lights up. The middle of the South Pacific, coordinates: 48° 30'S/ 125° 30'
W. A blue room rocks steadily, twilight casts shadows of waves on the walls. A
woman in a blue slip lightly drags her finger in a blue tub of water, moving a
tiny blue toy boat. A sailor kneels on the upper deck of his ship, looking out
into the ocean. He scrubs the deck with a brush. He remembers the woman,
she remembers nothing but the moment of his memory.*

SAILOR: She dreams of me.
(The woman dreams.)
She loves the water.
(She puts her feet in the tub and smiles.)
She loves the water, I think sometimes she may be a seal. I can picture her
smiling, lips pulled back and I see her teeth, her gums are fleshy like
salmon, I think sometimes she is a seal.
(The woman pours water into the tub.)
What do you love?
WOMAN: *(Testing the tub water.)* Water.
SAILOR: She comes to the locks to watch the ship come in. When the salmon
spawn they get caught in the locks and seals congregate because the catch
is easy, like pink gold. They swat and catch enough to be full in an hour.
We men try to keep them at bay but they always return. It's like trying to
keep a kid out of a candy store. She says something, something that
would make anyone fall in love, but really she just says…
WOMAN: *(As if she's heard a noise.)* Hello?
SAILOR: And I can't help myself because she would make a good catch for any
man. And I don't know anything about her before the ship comes in and
we're married before I set sail again. She dies while I'm away and I
remember her into the sea. And without knowing it, she's trapped in the
blue room where we spent our first night together. I trap her there with
too much remembering. And as the tale goes, the sailor who remembers
love too strongly, who thinks too hard will find nothing but the woman

trapped in the memory, out to sea, in the middle of the sea. Too far for anyone to swim safely and there are no seals out here.

(The sailor jumps ship. He lands on the periphery of the blue room.)

SAILOR: Just the blue motel room. And she tells me she loves the water, and I tell her I will have to leave and she tells me she married me because she loves the sea and wants me to take her along. But I can't and she tells me I'm her last chance. And I say that chance is never worth depending on and when I leave in the morning, she spits and says that she will get there one way or another. And so she does. Because she is well versed in the game of memory. In the lore of sailors. And in the middle of the sea she gets what she wants without begging. And I sail for money, because it is a job. Because the ocean is only the traveling—land is the arrival. And she loves the water. She loved me, maybe. Married me, to be out at sea, where land is a memory, I think she is a seal.

(The sailor enters the blue room.)

WOMAN: Here is my sailor.

SAILOR: She is my wife.

(The sailor slides into the tub. The woman giggles.)

WOMAN: I'll give you a bath, it's what a dirty sailor needs, wash the grit.

(He kisses her and she shies away.)

Look what I've brought you!

(She holds up the toy boat.)

For my sailor! Tell me about the sea.

(He tries to kiss her again, she laughs and splashes him.)

SAILOR: Come here.

WOMAN: Tell me about the boat, the sails…

SAILOR: It's cold and lonely and smells of fish.

WOMAN: Ha! My sailor!

SAILOR: We spend the days barefoot, socks mold to our feet if we leave them on while we work.

WOMAN: You've made the sea here, taste the water. From the salt between your toes.

(She washes him with a cloth in the tub.)

SAILOR: You can't drink seawater.

WOMAN: I know a place where you can, just where it feeds into the Amazon, off the coast of South America, in the Atlantic a hundred miles before the shore, the water there is fresh, you must have been there.

SAILOR: No.

WOMAN: No?

SAILOR: No.

WOMAN: I would go there and drink the ocean. Like the story of the five Chinese brothers, all identical, with different talents. The first brother could swallow the entire ocean. Hold it all in his mouth. Full and smiling. I would be full and smiling if I drank the ocean.

SAILOR: You would dehydrate and die.

WOMAN: Have you ever washed behind your ears?

SAILOR: I'll buy you a house. You can fill it with flowers.

WOMAN: Buy me a boat, I'll be happy then.

SAILOR: There are no flowers on boats. It's bad luck to bring them aboard. Nothing grows there but moss and longing.

WOMAN: My father was a farmer, the only thing he grew was dirty root vegetables, potatoes and turnips, he died and I said I would never grow a damn thing. So, I came to coast, everything is under the surface of the water…I never learned to swim and the first time I saw the sea I knew I didn't need to know how.

SAILOR: You have to swim, to be a sailor, you have to.

WOMAN: My father found nothing but bitterness in the ground.

SAILOR: When I'm at sea, do you know what I think of?

WOMAN: Freedom?

SAILOR: Land. All day I look out to see hard dry earth. I crave it. I've gotten to where sand won't do, I prefer grass, hard dirt. I miss mud. Clean things. A woman to hold onto.

(He pulls her in close.)

WOMAN: But at night, do you follow the stars?

SAILOR: Sure.

WOMAN: And see the red meteors?

SAILOR: Mostly we see nothing. Just waves and more waves. The night, the day, the day, the night, the clouds and the flying fish. I'm getting out.

WOMAN: What?

SAILOR: Of the bath. Come to bed.

WOMAN: But the water is just right.

SAILOR: Why did you pick me?

WOMAN: Pick you?

SAILOR: A whole crowd of us and you came up to me.

WOMAN: Get back in.

SAILOR: You're beautiful.

(He stands up, dripping wet, he pulls her close. He looks her in the eyes, she looks above him and then grabs one of his hands.)

WOMAN: Your hands are like barnacles.

SAILOR: Sailing is my trade, only a job.

WOMAN: Funny, my father's hands were like potatoes, eyed with calluses.

(He finally kisses her hard and she goes limp. He lays her down.)

SAILOR: Barnacles make cement, stick to anything they touch, won't let go.

WOMAN: And you won't let go.

SAILOR: In the morning.

WOMAN: Take me with you.

SAILOR: I can't.

WOMAN: I want to live on the ocean.

SAILOR: I'll be back. You have the ring, my promise.

(She pulls away, stands, back to the sailor.)

WOMAN: Do you know that there is gold in the sea? I want that. I want to be a sailor.

SAILOR: You're a sailor's wife.

WOMAN: I will follow you.

SAILOR: You'll make us a home. We'll have children to keep you company.

(He hovers over her and kisses her. He starts to undress her.)

WOMAN: I picked you because I could smell it on you, see it in your watery eyes, I knew that you would love me enough to want—

SAILOR: I want you on the shore.

WOMAN: —to take me with you.

SAILOR: I became a sailor because I had nothing to come home to. And if you come with me, what then?

WOMAN: You'll be home.

(The woman pulls away.)

SAILOR: No. It moves too much. No matter what you've heard, everyone gets sick. You'd get sick. All of that damned back and forth, everything gets lost. Your sense of taste, of smell. Everything. And your skin never feels right.

(They exchange a look, the woman seems to resolve something, she falls back into the sailor's arms.)

WOMAN: Then you'll dream of me and I will follow you.

(The sailor closes his eyes. He returns to the deck of the ship and resumes his scrubbing. He speaks while the woman does the following: The woman returns to the position she was in at the start of the play. She replays her movements from the beginning until the point of the sailor's entry: The

woman dreams. She puts her feet into the tub and smiles. The woman pours water into the tub.)

SAILOR: The night, the day, the day, the night, the clouds and the flying fish. She died the afternoon I left. They sent word and I dreamt of her. I put her out to sea. And at that point in the South Pacific where land is farthest away on both sides, the blue room appeared. I passed it once, I knew she was there. But she is stuck in the memory and doesn't know that I have given her a home on the open sea. Rocking back and forth. Her skin is slick now from the mist and waves. Her hands are like nothing and I try to remember her differently, give her something else, to let her know that I have given her the sea and I have no reason to touch land again. I think maybe she is a seal, stuck in the blue room where we spent our wedding night. And it floats there.

(The sailor jumps, the sound of splashing water.)

WOMAN: Here is my sailor.

(The sailor slides into the tub. The woman giggles.)

I'll give you a bath, it's what a dirty sailor needs, wash the grit.

(He kisses her and she shies away.)

Look what I've brought you!

(She holds up the toy boat.)

For my sailor! Tell me about the sea.

(He tries to kiss her again, she laughs and splashes him.)

END OF PLAY

Dancing with a Devil
by Brooke Berman

BIOGRAPHY

Brooke Berman is a writer and performer based in New York City. Her full-length play *Wonderland* is the winner of the 1998 Francesca Ronnie Primus Prize for women playwrights. Ms. Berman's plays have been read at the Denver Center Theatre Company, Dance Theater Workshop, La Mama Galleria and the Juilliard School, where she was recently a playwright-in-residence. Her plays have been produced at HERE, One Dream, New Georges, Naked Angels and nada. She is a recipient of a Lila Acheson Wallace American Playwrights Fellowship at the Juilliard School, a Lecompte du Nouy Award (in both 1998 and 1999) and an Independent Artist Challenge Grant, the latter of which allows generative artists money to problem-solve issues in the arts community at large. Originally a solo performer, Ms. Berman trained as a performer with Anne Bogart and has studied playwriting with Marsha Norman, Christopher Durang, Jon Robin Baitz and Maria Irene Fornes. Her fiction and nonfiction have appeared on The Knot (www.theknot.com) and Maxi Mag (www.maximag.com). Ms. Berman is a member of The Dramatists Guild.

HUMANA FESTIVAL PRODUCTION

Dancing with a Devil premiered at the Humana Festival of New American Plays in March 1999. It was directed by Abby Epstein with the following cast:

Woman . . . . Carolyn Baeumler
Younger Woman . . . . Monica Koskey
Man . . . . C. Andrew Bauer

and the following production staff:

Scenic Designer . . . . Paul Owen
Costume Designer . . . . Michael Oberle
Lighting Designer . . . . Mimi Jordan Sherin
Sound Designer . . . . Darron L. West
Properties Designer . . . . Mark Walston
Stage Manager . . . . Heather Fields
Assistant Stage Managers . . . . Dyanne M. McNamara &
                                                                                Alyssa Hoggatt
Dramaturgs . . . . Amy Wegener & Sara Skolnick
Casting . . . . Laura Richin Casting

CHARACTERS

WOMAN

YOUNGER WOMAN

MAN

TIME & PLACE

Here. Now.

Monica Koskey and C. Andrew Bauer in
Dancing with a Devil by Brooke Berman

23rd Annual Humana Festival of New American Plays
Actors Theatre of Louisville, 1999
photo by Richard Trigg

Dancing with a Devil

A woman is on the stage. Another woman, who is the younger version of herself, is with her. The first woman talks to the audience. A man in a black turtleneck and black pants listens.

WOMAN: This is how it happens. I will tell it in the present tense so that you can be there with me. I will tell it in the present tense as if there were a way to reverse the story, to change the ending, so we can all hope together that it will be different.

YOUNGER WOMAN: I hate it when you tell it. It makes me feel afraid.

WOMAN: I am twenty-four years old and I live in New York City.

YOUNGER WOMAN: I really hate when you tell it. But I like the part before it happens. I like being young in New York.

I am twenty-four years old, and I live in New York City. My life is shiny and new and just barely discovered. I am an emerging something or other, waiting tables and writing stories. I go to parties with people whose skin sparkles and whose names are known. I like to tell stories about how I am twenty-four and still a virgin, deconstructing the relationship between my heart and my skin and my sex.

WOMAN: I was a virgin.

YOUNGER WOMAN: I like to dance, to feel air inside my body. I think that dancing will save me from pain. The music will Earth me and the beat will bring me to the ground. I go dancing in gay bars with funny names. I take great pleasure being a girl in a boy-bar, enjoying the fact that no one will try to pick me up. My life is safe. I play outrageous, but my life is safe. I have made it that way. Just enough outrage and lots of safety nets.

I live in an old apartment building in Soho, where the artists are, across the hall from a Mafia widow and next door to an idiot with a loud dog. I listen to the dog howl whenever he is alone. The sound of this drives me crazy and I complain about it but the owner does not listen.

On the first day of the new year, I write down a list of my dreams and goals. I have many dreams—the foremost of which is this: "I want to be transformed." I write it down, "I want to be transformed," because that is what I want.

I look for my transformation anywhere I can. I look for it in the eyes of other people, but do not see it there. I look for it in the mountains in New Mexico, in the water of the hot springs, in the air of New York City and in the words that come to me while I dream. I dream that I am leaving an old city and moving to a new one and going to film school and leaving my mother.

It is June, and I am twenty-four, and I am about to be transformed.

WOMAN: It is June, June 9th to be precise, just barely after midnight, and I am about to fall asleep in my safe bed, in my safe Soho fourth-floor walk-up.

It is four in the morning and I open my eyes, certain that Sarah, my old roommate, has come home, though she moved out months ago and this makes no sense, I am sure that Sarah is in the apartment and I open my eyes, fully believing that I will see her there.

But I don't see Sarah. I see someone I do not know. I open my eyes to a stranger standing at the foot of my bed wearing a little black half-mask and a black turtleneck, looking a little bit like Zorro or like an existentialist Lone Ranger and I cannot understand how this stranger has penetrated my sleep or entered my apartment.

YOUNGER WOMAN: I don't like this part.

WOMAN: The stranger just stares at me. He doesn't move. He says, "Good evening."

MAN: Good evening.

WOMAN: And I say, Don't hurt me.

YOUNGER WOMAN: Don't hurt me.

WOMAN: And the stranger moves toward me, very very slowly like in slow motion and I understand everything that is about to happen. I understand it in my mind before he even touches me. I think, this can't happen to me. I think, this can't happen to me because I am very smart. I have read Roland Barthes and I know how to deconstruct sexuality. I am a virgin and I am very smart and things like this are not supposed to happen to people like me.

YOUNGER WOMAN: I really don't like this part.

MAN: I won't hurt you.

(The younger woman and the man start to dance—a very slow ballroom dance. They dance throughout the next beat.)

WOMAN: He shows me the knife by running it across my ass so that I will feel that it is sharp and yet it leaves no mark. He leaves no mark. I will be taken to the hospital within an hour but there will be no mark that anything has happened to me.

YOUNGER WOMAN: But it is the present and I am not at the hospital yet. I am dancing with the devil right now in time that lasts longer than ordinary time. I say, "Please don't hurt me," and no one talks after that.

MAN: I won't hurt you.

YOUNGER WOMAN: I'm a virgin. I'm like the Virgin Mary. This can't happen to the Virgin Mary. And I think, You knew all along that this would happen to you. Who else were you saving yourself for?

MAN: You were saving yourself for me.

WOMAN: Maybe I was. How could I have known?

MAN: Everything will change now. Everything about you will change. You will no longer be who you were. You will have to become someone else to even understand this, to even put it behind you. You will leave your friends, your home, your family, in order to become the person who can put this behind herself. I am the answer to your prayers. I am giving you what you asked for. I am giving you the gift of transformation.

YOUNGER WOMAN: But I don't want to transform. Not like this. I don't want to go through with it.

MAN: You have no choice. You can fight me, or you can live through this.

WOMAN: I am light and light I shall remain. That is what I was told to say.

YOUNGER WOMAN: I am light and light I shall remain. I am in a time and place in which this event is not occurring. I am not in my body, and so you cannot touch me. You are filling me with your pain, with your body, but you are not touching me. You are not even near me, you are nowhere near me. I am held in the arms of angels and I am light, and light I shall remain.

(The man and the younger woman stop dancing. The man bows to the woman and leaves the stage.)

WOMAN: It was over quickly. It seemed to take a long time but I know that in the reality we will call reality, it happened within the span of ten, maybe fifteen minutes. He turned me over like some object and covered my head with a pillow and stuck his pain and his rage and his dick all inside me, and then it was over, and he was gone, as quietly and mysteriously as he came. He came out of the night and went back inside of it and was never caught.

YOUNGER WOMAN: He disappears. He is never caught. I run through the halls of my apartment building half-naked looking for help.

WOMAN: I do not want to see women get raped anymore. Not in the movies, not in the theater, not on TV and not in my bedroom. I do not want this experience. I do not want to see it and I do not want to relive it.

YOUNGER WOMAN: I am light and light I shall remain.

WOMAN: That's what the spirit guides told me to say. I am light and light I shall remain. I cannot be hurt. But I was hurt.

I have taken the pain of some man that I do not know inside of me. I have taken it inside and transformed it, inside. I have gone to rape crisis centers and to therapy and to psychic healings in order to transform the pain that you stuck inside me one morning, me a stranger. I carry energy inside of me, some of which you deposited there, and rapists do not use condoms.

But I am not a repository for some stranger's suffering. Do you hear me? I DON'T WANT YOUR SUFFERING. YOU CAN JUST PUT IT SOMEWHERE ELSE. AND I HOPE THAT YOU SUFFER TILL THE END OF TIME, TILL THE END OF EVERYTHING, MAY YOUR SOUL KNOW WHAT YOU HAVE DONE TO ME AND MAY YOU BE…. May you be healed.

YOUNGER WOMAN: I want to go home now.

WOMAN: We're almost done. We're almost at the end.

YOUNGER WOMAN: I'm hurt, and I want to go home.

WOMAN: I am going to tell it again.

YOUNGER WOMAN: Everything will change, he said. And it did. I did. Please don't tell it. I don't want to remember.

WOMAN: Everything will change, he said. Although he didn't really speak at all.

(The man reappears.)

MAN: Good evening…

YOUNGER WOMAN: I want to go home now.

WOMAN: I am not twenty-four years old anymore. I do not know the people I knew then. My friends are different. My work is different. I have lived in seven different apartments in the span of three years. Everything has changed. I have changed.

YOUNGER WOMAN: Except that I still wake up at four in the morning expecting to find him there.

(The man moves towards her.)

MAN: You are one of the statistics. You are about to become a statistic. One of the numbers. How many women in ten?

YOUNGER WOMAN: I don't want to dance with you.

WOMAN: I'm not going to tell it again.

YOUNGER WOMAN: I just want to go home.

WOMAN: I am twenty-eight years old, and I still live in New York. I sleep with a nightlight. I do not live alone. I stay at other people's houses when my roommates are away. I do not watch movies in which women are tracked, killed, hurt, maimed, terrorized or raped. This means I do not watch a lot of movies. I meet young women who remind me of myself before it happened, and they scare me. I am afraid that something might happen to them too that will cause them to leave a piece of themselves behind forever. I hope this is not the case. I wish them well.

END OF PLAY

Forty Minute Finish
by Jerome Hairston

BIOGRAPHY

Jerome D. Hairston was featured twice in New York's Young Playwrights Festival with his plays *Live from the Edge of Oblivion* (1993, Playwrights Horizons) and *The Love of Bullets* (1994, The Public Theater). His play *L'eboueur Sleeps Tonight* received a reading at La MaMa E.T.C. (Shenandoah International Playwrights Retreat) and was presented at Playwrights Horizons (Black Ink reading series, directed by Marion McClinton). The Public Theater commissioned Mr. Hairston to write a full-length play entitled *Carriage*, which recently won the Kennedy Center/American College Theatre Festival's National Student Playwriting Award. *Carriage* was presented at the Kennedy Center in Washington D.C. and was part of the Public Theater's New York Now! staged reading series (directed by Robert O'Hara). Mr. Hairston received his undergraduate degree from James Madison University, and continues his studies under playwright Eduardo Machado in Columbia University's MFA playwriting program.

HUMANA FESTIVAL PRODUCTION

Forty Minute Finish premiered at the Humana Festival of New American Plays in March 1999. It was directed by Maria Mileaf with the following cast:

Ike	Derek Cecil
Terry	Nick Garrison

and the following production staff:

Scenic Designer	Paul Owen
Costume Designer	Michael Oberle
Lighting Designer	Mimi Jordan Sherin
Sound Designer	Darron L. West
Properties Designer	Mark Walston
Stage Manager	Heather Fields
Assistant Stage Managers	Dyanne M. McNamara & Alyssa Hoggatt
Dramaturgs	Michael Bigelow Dixon & Ilana M. Brownstein
Casting	Laura Richin Casting

CHARACTERS

IKE: a young grocery store clerk
TERRY: a young grocery store clerk

TIME & PLACE

A grocery store. The present.

Derek Cecil and Nick Garrison in
Forty Minute Finish by Jerome Hairston

23rd Annual Humana Festival of New American Plays
Actors Theatre of Louisville, 1999
photo by Richard Trigg

Forty Minute Finish

Two mop buckets. Two mops. Two guys in smocks.

IKE: They're still out there. What the hell could they be talkin' about? The ambulance pulled out of here, what, 7:15. It's like an hour later they're still over there yip yappin' away.

TERRY: These things take time I guess.

IKE: I'm trying to make out the words but their lips are too small. Like trying to make sense out of flapping bologna. Can you make out anything?

TERRY: No.

IKE: C'mon, look for real. Can you read what they're saying?

TERRY: Maybe. I don't know.

IKE: Oh, hold back, man. Don't astound me with the eagle eyes.

TERRY: It's none of our business.

IKE: When the hands are feeling any part of eight o'clock on a Sunday and I'm still sporting this smock, it's totally my business. *(Looking one last time.)* Hell with it, let's just go.

TERRY: Aren't you gonna help me?

IKE: Help you? Help you what? There's nothing left.

TERRY: We might have missed something.

IKE: Let's inspect. *(To the floor.)* What am I seeing? I'm seeing me. I'm seeing you. I'm seeing us. A reflection. The floor's spotless. What's the problem?

TERRY: I don't know. Feels disrespectful. How old do you think that guy was? Sixty? Sixty-five?

IKE: He was old.

TERRY: Exactly my point. He was old.

IKE: Yeah. And old people have strokes, that's what they do.

TERRY: But they usually don't crack their heads open in the process. I mean, you think he's dead?

IKE: I don't know. How would I know?

TERRY: What I'm saying is, people bleed, yeah. But to see it like that. To watch his life spread down the aisle. Somethin' about it. Just didn't seem…human, you know?

IKE: Well, humans bleed. That's what they do.

TERRY: How can you be like that?

IKE: How am I like, Terry?

TERRY: This is something here. What me and you witnessed.

IKE: We really didn't see anything. He was on the floor before we got here.

TERRY: So, it doesn't bother you?

IKE: What do you want? You want me to squirt a few? I didn't even know the man.

TERRY: You know how long it took to clean up?

IKE: What's that have to do with anything?

TERRY: Forty-two minutes.

IKE: It was longer than that.

TERRY: Forty-two, I checked the clock.

IKE: And you're callin' me distracted?

TERRY: 7:32 we started. First change of water 7:46. Last change eight o'clock. Bringing us up to now. The water's hardly red. Forty minutes. To clean up sixty-year-old blood.

IKE: It was a pain.

TERRY: That can't be possible, right?

IKE: Like a tipped stack of egg cartons.

TERRY: To erase somethin' that old that quick. There's something wrong in that, isn't there?

IKE: You want to give it another once over, what?

TERRY: You're missing the point.

IKE: No, I'm missing the game. And I can't punch out until you do. So if it's going to take us sliding the mop fifty times more, then let's do it.

TERRY: You have to know what I'm talking about.

IKE: What is it we're supposed to do? Turn the clock? Split inside the guy and fix his stroke? We're here to bag groceries. Mop floors. Not place a Band-Aid on the order of the fucking universe.

TERRY: I just feel we have to own up to the event somehow.

IKE: Did we do it? Did we slam his head into the tile?

TERRY: We cleaned up.

IKE: So that's supposed to tie a knot between us and this guy? You even know this guy's name? I can hardly remember what the man was wearing and I'm supposed to light a candle right here in the middle of the bread aisle.

TERRY: What *was* he wearing?

IKE: Huh?

TERRY: I can't remember what he was wearing.

IKE: Who cares?

TERRY: Somebody does. Somebody's going to want to know what he looked like right before he…you think he's dead?

IKE: Maybe. Who knows. And if he is, what can you do?

TERRY: I could've paid attention. I mean, I would've never noticed the guy at all if he didn't hit the floor. That's all I'm going to remember.

IKE: That's all you can remember. Look, you're tired. You're freaked. But it's over.

TERRY: Yeah. Finished.

IKE: Let's go, huh? We'll watch the game. Throw a few down. Sleep solid. What do you say?

TERRY: Something just won't let me move, you know. Feel like something should be said.

IKE: *(Pause.)* Brown pants. Grey sweater. Baby blue zigzags.

TERRY: What's this?

IKE: What he was wearing.

TERRY: You remember what he looked like?

IKE: Yeah. Black dude. Grey beard. Kinda looked like Grady from *Sanford and Son*.

TERRY: *(Small laugh.)* Get outta here.

IKE: He did. Spittin' image. Almost asked for an autograph when he first stepped in.

TERRY: You know, it is possible. You think it might have been him?

IKE: Nah.

TERRY: Stranger things have been known to happen. You don't think that there's even a chance?

IKE: Nah.

TERRY: You really think he's dead?

IKE: *(Pause.)* Yeah. *(Silence.)* Punch the clock for ya?

TERRY: Sure. *(Pause.)* Some night, huh?

IKE: Some night.

(Lights fade.)

END OF PLAY

Mpls., St. Paul
by Julia Jordan

BIOGRAPHY

Julia Jordan won the 1997 Francesca Primus Prize out of Denver Center Theatre Company for her play *Tatjana in Color*, which was featured in their 1998 U. S. West Theatre Fest. *Tatjana* was shortlisted for the Susan Smith Blackburn Award and published by Smith & Kraus in their volume *Women Playwrights: The Best Plays of 1997*. It was produced in 1999 at the Contemporary American Theater Festival. Ms. Jordan's other plays include: *Smoking Lesson* which was workshopped at the Sundance Playwrights Lab, the Intiman Theatre New Voices Festival and the Cleveland Play House Next Stage Festival; and *3 - 1/2 Catholics*, which was also developed at Cleveland's Next Stage Festival. Ms. Jordan recently completed her first screenplay, *Satin Doll*. A former playwright-in-residence at Juilliard, she recently received her Masters of Philosophy in Creative Writing at Trinity College, Dublin.

HUMANA FESTIVAL PRODUCTION

Mpls., St. Paul premiered at the Humana Festival of New American Plays in March 1999. It was directed by Abby Epstein with the following cast:

Mel . . . . Erica Blumfield
Billy . . . . C. Andrew Bauer

and the following production staff:

Scenic Designer . . . . Paul Owen
Costume Designer . . . . Michael Oberle
Lighting Designer . . . . Mimi Jordan Sherin
Sound Designer . . . . Darron L. West
Properties Designer . . . . Mark Walston
Stage Manager . . . . Heather Fields
Assistant Stage Managers . . . . Dyanne M. McNamara &
                                                Alyssa Hoggatt
Dramaturgs . . . . Michael Bigelow Dixon &
                                                Adrien-Alice Hansel
Casting . . . . Laura Richin Casting

CHARACTERS

BILLY
MEL

TIME & PLACE

1985. A rooftop in Minneapolis or St. Paul.

Erica Blumfield and C. Andrew Bauer in
Mpls., St. Paul by Julia Jordan

23rd Annual Humana Festival of New American Plays
Actors Theatre of Louisville, 1999
photo by Richard Trigg

Mpls., St. Paul

Billy and Mel are climbing out a window onto the roof.

BILLY: I did!

MEL: Bull-crap.

BILLY: And Stinson was wailing away. I turned…

MEL: Lie.

BILLY: He was wailing away on that guitar…

MEL: *(With her hands over her ears.)* Na-na-na-na-na-na—Can't hear lies. Don't hear little boy lies.

BILLY: Just because you weren't there…

MEL: Neither were you.

BILLY: …doesn't make it not true.

MEL: Yes it does.

BILLY: In your mind. I sang with The Replacements last night at 7th St. Entry. End of fuckin' story. And you're jealous.

MEL: I don't want to sing with The Replacements.

BILLY: Sure you do.

MEL: No. I don't.

BILLY: You wanna get close to them. And I got closer than you'll ever get. I got inside the best song from the best rock album ever released, which just happens to be by The Replacements.

MEL: Who's Alex Chilton?

BILLY: An influence.

MEL: Yeah, but who?

BILLY: I don't know.

MEL: 1967, he was sixteen, his band, the Boxtops, had a Number One with "The Letter." At nineteen he formed Big Star and they released *#1 Record*, which never went near Number One. Then *Radio City*. They never played Radio City. And *3rd Record*. But no one cared. So he recorded his fuck-you album, *Like Flies on Sherbet*. The Replacements love *Flies on Sherbet*. One critic said it sounded like a "bunch of drunken louts running amok…"

BILLY: Your brother told you that.

MEL: No. I just know. I was born knowing. He's not their biggest fan. I am.

BILLY: He's their fattest fan. Maybe he was there. The fat slob standing at the back so as he won't get hurt and all of a sudden who's on stage singin' his favorite song, "Favorite Thing"? Me. That's who. Me.

MEL: You better stop tellin' your tired old lie or I'm gonna push you off the roof.

BILLY: Girl, if you wanna touch me you don't have to come up with an excuse like that. You wanna touch the man that sang with The Placemats?

MEL: Shut up.

BILLY: I haven't bathed.

MEL: Ugh.

BILLY: Still got their sweat on my skin. Rock sweat. Mine and Paul Westerburg's. He was right next to me. This close. He handed me the microphone with his SWEAT on it. Hand to hand. You know what I'm sayin'? And then Bobby spun round and a whole truckload of it whipped 'cross my chest. Which do you want to touch first? Hand or chest? What do you want first? Mine and Paul's sweat? Or Bobby's and mine?

MEL: Only Paul's. Thanks.

BILLY: We should start our own band. You can be the singer.

MEL: Can't sing.

BILLY: We could write the songs together and I'll play the guitar.

MEL: You don't know how to play the guitar.

BILLY: Anybody can play the guitar. It ain't easy but it ain't hard. The Replacements don't know how to play.

MEL: Yeah, but you suck.

BILLY: Bobby Stinson sucks.

MEL: I mean *really*.

BILLY: Tommy Stinson really sucks.

MEL: Yeah, but The Replacements are geniuses at sucking. You suck…generally.

BILLY: You could be Chrissie Hynde.

MEL: I don't want to be Chrissie Hynde.

BILLY: Who do you want to be then?

MEL: Paul's girlfriend.

BILLY: Well, you're not. You're mine.

MEL: I am not.

BILLY: We spend every day together. We sleep together when your 'rents are out of town.

MEL: Do we fuck?

BILLY: You're a virgin.

MEL: So are you. So I'm just a girl and your friend. Like that. I'm gonna be Paul's *girlfriend*.

BILLY: You wanna fuck Paul?

MEL: You taken that Mensa test yet?

BILLY: How do you know you want to, when you don't even know what it is, the thing you say you want to do.

MEL: I know.

BILLY: How?

MEL: I know because when he sings, "you're my favorite thing bar nothin'," I can feel him singin' it to me.

BILLY: He doesn't sing it, he yells it.

MEL: I get this shudder.

BILLY: He's already got a girlfriend. She's in a band.

MEL: Her time's up.

BILLY: If you and me were in a band, we could open for them. Meet them.

MEL: I don't want to be in a band. Who wants girls in a band?

BILLY: What do you have against rock chicks?

MEL: I got nothin' against them. I just don't want to fuck them.

BILLY: Well, I do.

MEL: Well, it's not gonna happen, even if I was in a band.

BILLY: I was talking about the Go-Gos.

MEL: That's not gonna happen either.

BILLY: But you're gonna do Paul Westerburg.

MEL: Right.

BILLY: How?

MEL: The old-fashioned way. Jump him.

BILLY: My friend Paul? We're friends now. Me and Paul. Yep. After the Entry we all went over to Liquor Lyles, me and Paul, Tommy, Bobby, and Chris Mars and all our hangers-on…bunch of girls like you that we ignored. We all went over there and met up with Paul's super hot-*rocker*-girlfriend. Not girl and friend. Like that. But *girlfriend* as in the only girl he wants to fuck.

MEL: O.K. First of all. How could you get into the Entry anyway? You're underage.

BILLY: Back door when the bouncer stepped away. Hid in the boiler room from four in the afternoon till ten-thirty. Which is when I heard the beatific tones of "Gary's Got a Boner" and slyly segued my underage ass into the crowd and pushed my way up, front and center.

MEL: Uh-huh. And how did you get into Liquor Lyles? They card at the door.

BILLY: They don't card when you come in with God and they don't card when you come in with The Replacements. Impressed now, huh? You wanna touch me now?

MEL: The Replacements don't hang out at Liquor Lyles. If you were a true fan, you'd know that. They hang out at the CC Club. "The bar with casual elegance." Even my brother knows that.

BILLY: O.K. Fine. We didn't go to Liquor Lyles. But I did get into the Entry and I did jump up on stage and I did sing. I sang "Favorite Thing." And when I got to BAR NOTHING, Paul stood back 'cause I was doin' him proud and Bobby…Bobby Stinson just wailed away on that guitar. For one song. One rendition, in their hometown, of the best song off the best album of rock ever released, and ever to be released, and I was in the band. I was a Replacement.

MEL: So…you don't know if he has a girlfriend or not.

BILLY: I know it's not you.

MEL: Well, it's gonna be.

BILLY: How come you do that, huh?

MEL: Do what?

BILLY: Shoot me down.

MEL: I'm just sitting here. Wanna get high?

BILLY: NO! I'M TALKING HERE ABOUT OUR RELATIONSHIP WHICH HAPPENS TO BE VERY IMPORTANT TO ME. WELL, O.K., BUT LATER. It's important to you too, isn't it?

MEL: 'Course. My brother's gonna be home by six and it'll take a good half hour to find it. He rehid it. I think he's weighing it. We gotta get slyer.

BILLY: It'll take twenty minutes tops to find it. So listen to me…

MEL: All right you've got ten minutes.

BILLY: I don't know that I have ten minutes worth to say. It's just…

MEL: What?

BILLY: I don't like it when you talk about them like that.

MEL: Who?

BILLY: The Replacements.

MEL: Like what? Like I love and adore them? Like sometimes when people, like my fat brother, really piss me off, I mean really, like there'll never be another fun time in my whole life, ever, like they save me a little? A LOT.

Like they are a huge massive part of my life and always will be? Like that? Like when I talk about them like that? You don't like that? Like how the fuck do you think you sound?

BILLY: When you say you want to fuck Paul. I don't like that.

MEL: You said you wanted to do the Go-Gos and don't go thinkin' I don't know exactly which one you mean.

BILLY: I'm not lettin' her stand between us.

MEL: Her who? Go-Go Jane?

BILLY: I said shut up.

MEL: Jane far, far away in Califor-ni-ay?

BILLY: I'm being serious.

MEL: So am I. I'm real serious about Paul. *He lives here.* In reality. Someday I'll walk down the street and bang, smack into him. I could just bang into him.

BILLY: If you had any balls, you'd just take the bus downtown to the Entry…. Why can't we sleep together?

MEL: We do.

BILLY: You know what I mean.

MEL: Fuck?

BILLY: Don't use that word with us.

MEL: Because.

BILLY: Because why?

MEL: Because I love you.

BILLY: What?

MEL: You're my best…my…well…you just are. It's true. Can we get high now?

BILLY: You're not making any sense.

MEL: Oh fuck off. I said it didn't I?

BILLY: You never said it before. I thought that's why…. Because you didn't. Every time before when I said it. When I said it to you. All you said back was "thank you."

MEL: I was grateful.

BILLY: But you did? All along?

MEL: I don't know about "all along." I don't know when it started. It just sort of occurred to me. After it was already there. Sorta.

BILLY: Why didn't you tell me?

MEL: I just did! Can we get high now? My brother's gonna be home soon.

BILLY: But we're not gonna…

MEL: No.

BILLY: Why not?

MEL: 'Cause that would seal the deal and I've got things to do before I sign on any dotted line.

BILLY: I'm not askin' you to sign anything.

MEL: Yes you are.

BILLY: No I'm not.

MEL: I have things to do.

BILLY: Like Paul Westerburg.

MEL: And other things. All sorts of things.

BILLY: Without me.

MEL: I'm never gonna find anybody else. Not like you. I'm never gonna be able to say to anyone else, "Remember? Remember when we used to get high up on the roof and talk about, you lie about, The Replacements?" Nobody but you. You'll always be my favorite. This will always be my favorite time. We're never gonna forget this. 'Cause it's so stupid and great. Mythic even. To us at least. And that's enough. That'll be enough to pull us back together after we get our alone stuff done. That's what I think. So that's why. I'm gonna go find his pot. Thank God he still lives at home at the age of twenty-four. Beller when you see the fat bastard's car.

(Mel climbs back in through the window.)

BILLY: I'm her favorite thing. Bar nothin'. Fuck Paul. I sang it better than he ever did. He knew it.

(Lights dim, then "rock star moment" lights up as Billy rocks out to the memory.)

END OF PLAY

Drive Angry
by Matt Pelfrey

BIOGRAPHY

Matt Pelfrey's play *Gore Hounds* has been produced at the American Theatre of Actors in New York, the Stark Raving Theatre in Portland and the Non-Prophet Hatching Co. in Los Angeles. Mr. Pelfrey studied playwriting with Silas Jones in the Wordsmith Playwriting Program. His other plays include *Honkies With Attitude* and *Cockroach Nation*. He presently toils in Los Angeles.

HUMANA FESTIVAL PRODUCTION

Drive Angry premiered at the Humana Festival of New American Plays in March 1999. It was directed by Abby Epstein with the following cast:

Chemo-Boy . . . . Bryan Richards
Rex the Mex . . . . Derek Cecil

and the following production staff:

Scenic Designer . . . . Paul Owen
Costume Designer . . . . Michael Oberle
Lighting Designer . . . . Mimi Jordan Sherin
Sound Designer . . . . Darron L. West
Properties Designer . . . . Mark Walston
Stage Manager . . . . Heather Fields
Assistant Stage Managers . . . . Dyanne M. McNamara &
Alyssa Hoggatt
Dramaturgs . . . . Michael Bigelow Dixon & Ilana M. Brownstein
Casting . . . . Laura Richin Casting

CHARACTERS

CHEMO-BOY: Male, 20s.
REX THE MEX: Male, 20s.

TIME & PLACE

Night in Los Angeles. A thundering '76 Maverick.

Bryan Richards and Derek Cecil in
Drive Angry by Matt Pelfrey

23rd Annual Humana Festival of New American Plays
Actors Theatre of Louisville, 1999
photo by Richard Trigg

Drive Angry

Rex the Mex behind the wheel. Chemo-Boy rides shotgun.

REX THE MEX: Concrete, concrete, concrete...

CHEMO-BOY: My dad stopped by yesterday...

REX THE MEX: ...lights, neon, billboards...

CHEMO-BOY: ...out of nowhere. Just, like, I'm chillin', then KNOCK KNOCK KNOCK, I'm like, "Oh, shit, who's that..."

REX THE MEX: ...rich cars, poor cars, ugly cars, dented cars, cars with tint, cars with out-of-state plates, cars with vanity plates...

CHEMO-BOY: ...so I open the front door and there's my oldster, and he gets in my face, he's like, "How you doin' kiddo?"

REX THE MEX: ...cars with loser zoos, cars with stupid bumper stickers, cars with no bumpers, hot rods, jeeps, vans, busses...

CHEMO-BOY: And I swear to Christ, I almost pass out—his breath smelled like seaweed...

REX THE MEX: Asian dudes, Armenian dudes, Arab dudes, black dudes, brown dudes, white dudes...everyone mixing, merging, honking...

CHEMO-BOY: ...like there was this sick, repugnant *stew* brewing in his mouth...

REX THE MEX: Like this freeway is just a big concrete bloodstream full of mechanical germs...angry mechanical germs...

CHEMO-BOY: So he comes in and we talk, same old shit, then he asks me if I've got any soup...and I tell him I got plenty of soup. So now he's there for like, five minutes only and he already wants me to cook for him. So I tell him I got Minestrone and I got Fiesta Bean, but that's not good enough, he wants Vegetable Beef. I'm like, "Man, just have the Minestrone," and that's what I cook up. So I give him a bowl with some crackers, and he just clams up. Stops talkin'. He just sits there, staring at his soup, brooding. Y'know? Just like, in a funk. This hideous soup-funk. So I said, basically, unless you got money to help me with my medical bills, you can fuckin' get lost. So that's what he did. He split. Didn't touch his soup. Swear to Christ, I wanted to beat him over the head with his prosthetic arm.

REX THE MEX: I know you don't want to hear this, I know you want me to be on your side here and all, but, honestly, your dad sounds like a total fucking stud. I mean, come on! He's all corroded and raspy and tweaked out…

CHEMO-BOY: He's lived in a motel for two years.

REX THE MEX: So? He's a desperate, volatile maverick! He's on the edge!

CHEMO-BOY: But it's by choice…

REX THE MEX: What is?

CHEMO-BOY: His motel life-style. He has settlement money from the accident. I know he does.

REX THE MEX: So wait—he's holding out on you? He's got loot?

CHEMO-BOY: I think so.

REX THE MEX: See, *that* I got a problem with.

(They drive in silence for a moment.)

CHEMO-BOY: I hear some scientist in Seattle found Sasquatch hairs.

REX THE MEX: Fuck's a Sasquatch hair?

CHEMO-BOY: Sasquatch is another name for Bigfoot.

REX THE MEX: And some scientist has its hair?

CHEMO-BOY: Well actually, they think they're pubes…

REX THE MEX: Hold on. Sasquatch is covered, head-to-toe, in hair. Correct?

CHEMO-BOY: Yes.

REX THE MEX: Then follow me here: how do you know which hairs are his normal hairs, and which are his pubes?

CHEMO-BOY: When experts say they got Bigfoot's pubes, you take a statement like that at face value. *(Beat.)* Check it: initial tests show it's definitely some sort of non-human primate.

REX THE MEX: *(Repeating to himself.)* …primate…

CHEMO-BOY: A primate's an ape.

REX THE MEX: I know what a fucking primate is…

CHEMO-BOY: That's so cool. I hope it exists.

REX THE MEX: Bigfoot?

CHEMO-BOY: Yeah.

REX THE MEX: Why would you give a shit if Bigfoot exists or not?

CHEMO-BOY: I'd hunt it.

REX THE MEX: Get outta here…

CHEMO-BOY: No, man, I would. Chase its ass, blow it away, skin the bastard, make a cool rug. Sell the meat to Burger King or Arby's. *(Pause.)* Can you give me a lift tomorrow?

REX THE MEX: Where to?

CHEMO-BOY: Where do you think?

REX THE MEX: What time?

CHEMO-BOY: Gotta be there by nine.

REX THE MEX: *(Slightly annoyed.)* Yeah, I can give you a ride.

CHEMO-BOY: Hey, I don't want to put you *out* or anything...

REX THE MEX: Just wanted to sleep in.

CHEMO-BOY: So fuck off. I'll find a ride.

REX THE MEX: I'll drive you.

CHEMO-BOY: No, really...

REX THE MEX: ...said I'd drive you...

CHEMO-BOY: Hey, you got *sleeping* to do.

REX THE MEX: I said I would fuckin' drive you, okay? Stop sniveling.

CHEMO-BOY: I'm not sniveling.

REX THE MEX: You are. You're sniveling like some kinda *victim*.

CHEMO-BOY: Shut up...

REX THE MEX: Little Chemo-Boy suffering from cancer. Waaa!

CHEMO-BOY: Fuck off.

REX THE MEX: You're not even losing your *hair*.

CHEMO-BOY: What's that supposed to mean?

REX THE MEX: You know what it means.

CHEMO-BOY: No. I don't. Fuckin' tell me.

REX THE MEX: I mean, you know, what kind of wimpy cancer you got that your chemo doesn't make you go bald? You know? On TV, all the cool cancer patients go bald.

CHEMO-BOY: My stuff doesn't do that.

REX THE MEX: ...'Cause you got pussy chemo.

CHEMO-BOY: I implore you to fuck off. You're being a dick.

REX THE MEX: I'm chemo for your manhood.

CHEMO-BOY: You're what?

REX THE MEX: You heard me. I'm like, chemo for your, whatever, yeah, your manhood. I won't let you become one of those people who start to feed off their disease. My uncle got pancreatic cancer, and that's what he became. Pancreatic Cancer Man. Everything was about his disease. How he's "bravely battling cancer." All that disease hype. The whole time, I'm thinking, what's so fucking brave about battling something that you have no choice about? You got cancer. You deal with it. It's like how we treat cops and firemen. They save someone, they catch a killer, and, yeah, that's great, but it's their *job*. It's not like some civilian that risks his life to intervene and save someone. A cop or fireman has no choice. Doing that shit is no more than what's expected. It's their job. They're not being heroes, they're earning a paycheck and enjoying a privileged position in society.

CHEMO-BOY: Whatever.

REX THE MEX: *(Pause.)* What you goin' in for?

CHEMO-BOY: Like you care.

REX THE MEX: Stop brooding…

CHEMO-BOY: *(Pause.)* You ever get a CAT scan?

REX THE MEX: Fuck no.

CHEMO-BOY: Dude, they give you a bottle of this shit, it's like, this white, creamy stuff, you gotta drink it before going in, so your insides will show up when they take the picture…

REX THE MEX: …yeah…

CHEMO-BOY: …stuff, I'm not kidding, is like drinking *moose semen*.

REX THE MEX: …not that you know what drinking moose semen is like…

CHEMO-BOY: I'm using poetic imagery so a puny mind like yours can grasp the horror and complexity of what I'm saying.

REX THE MEX: I think I appreciate that.

CHEMO-BOY: You fuckin' better.

REX THE MEX: So…

CHEMO-BOY: …so that's what they're doing tomorrow. I'm drinking a pint of moose cum, then they're shooting iodine into my veins to find out if I got any creepy shit hiding out.

REX THE MEX: That's fucked up.

CHEMO-BOY: Yeah it is…

(Pause. Rex thinks about something.)

REX THE MEX: Let me ask you a question. Let me pose a thought to you…

CHEMO-BOY: Please do.

REX THE MEX: Why did you get cancer?

CHEMO-BOY: *(Slight pause.)* I don't know.

REX THE MEX: But what did the doctors tell you?

CHEMO-BOY: It could be any one of five hundred reasons.

REX THE MEX: But at your age, ass cancer is rare.

CHEMO-BOY: Extremely.

REX THE MEX: So why did this shit grow inside of you?

CHEMO-BOY: I just told you—I don't fuckin' know.

REX THE MEX: Yeah? Well, I *do*.

CHEMO-BOY: Oh, great.

REX THE MEX: I do, man. I really do.

CHEMO-BOY: There is no way on God's green earth you know anything my doctors don't know.

REX THE MEX: What you continually fail to grasp, my diseased little friend, is that I am not burdened by over-education. I haven't spent eight years after high school getting taught how to think or what pre-packaged crock of shit to spout so that I appear smart at parties and espresso bars. I actually think. I have forced myself to remain open to the Cosmic Whatever.

CHEMO-BOY: "The Cosmic Whatever?"

REX THE MEX: That's right…

CHEMO-BOY: Alright—what's your diagnosis?

REX THE MEX: Existential pollution.

CHEMO-BOY: What the fuck is that?

REX THE MEX: All the shit out there. All the shit that pisses you off and eats at you day in and day out. All that shit has crawled up inside your ass and died like a sick rat. And that got everything infected.

CHEMO-BOY: And the shit is…?

REX THE MEX: Well, as I touched on already—all the chicks that piss us off, our bullshit jobs, our fucking parents and especially the psychotic, selfish, assholic drivers who plague us every day of our lives. You see, all these elements are out there, like secondhand smoke—like *smog*—it's drifting, hanging in the air, contaminating our world. That's why our enforcement, our roadway counteroffensive against the scumbag fuckers of the world—that's why it's so important.

CHEMO-BOY: Hmmm…

REX THE MEX: Am I right? You know I am.

CHEMO-BOY: It's food for thought.

REX THE MEX: It's a fucking all-you-can-eat buffet and it's all true.

CHEMO-BOY: Yeah it is.

REX THE MEX: *(Something grabs his attention.)* Here we go…

CHEMO-BOY: Where?

REX THE MEX: Next lane over.

CHEMO-BOY: Red truck?

REX THE MEX: Uh-huh.

CHEMO-BOY: What's the crime?

REX THE MEX: Merges like an a-hole, then cut across three lanes of traffic without signaling.

CHEMO-BOY: That is totally unacceptable behavior.

REX THE MEX: Agreed.

    (Rex accelerates. Chemo-Boy produces a pellet handgun from under the seat.)

REX THE MEX: How's the pellet supply?

CHEMO-BOY: Doin' okay.

REX THE MEX: We need more?

CHEMO-BOY: We're cool.

REX THE MEX: Just tell me when.

CHEMO-BOY: I know the game.

REX THE MEX: Anyone behind us?

CHEMO-BOY: No.

REX THE MEX: Don't do it until just before the next off-ramp.

CHEMO-BOY: Who do you think you're talking to?

REX THE MEX: We can't get careless.

CHEMO-BOY: Don't worry about it.

REX THE MEX: Here it comes...

CHEMO-BOY: It's time to administer some real medicine. Chemo for a tumorous city...

REX THE MEX: Concentrate on the job at hand.

CHEMO-BOY: Shut up. I am. Here we go.

    (Chemo-Boy leans out of the window, aims the pellet gun, fires three shots. Rex turns the steering wheel sharply towards the off-ramp. Glass shatters. Tires squeal.)

END OF PLAY

Just Be Frank
by Caroline Williams

BIOGRAPHY

Caroline Williams graduated from the University of Southern California School of Theatre shortly after *Just Be Frank* premiered. Since then, her work in playwriting has expanded to include writing for both film and television. She is a member of the Screen Actors Guild and the Dramatists Guild.

HUMANA FESTIVAL PRODUCTION

Just Be Frank premiered at the Humana Festival of New American Plays in March 1999. It was directed by Maria Mileaf with the following cast:

Diane.................................... Carolyn Baeumler
Charlene .... Monica Koskey
Jan .... Caitlin Miller
Secretary .... Erica Blumfield
Boss..................................... Todd Cerveris

and the following production staff:

Scenic Designer .... Paul Owen
Costume Designer .... Michael Oberle
Lighting Designer....................... Mimi Jordan Sherin
Sound Designer........................... Darron L. West
Properties Designer .... Mark Walston
Stage Manager.............................. Heather Fields
Assistant Stage Managers............. Dyanne M. McNamara &
                                          Alyssa Hoggatt
Dramaturgs .... Amy Wegener & Adrien-Alice Hansel
Casting .... Laura Richin Casting

CHARACTERS

DIANE

CHARLENE

JAN

SECRETARY

BOSS

TIME & PLACE

The present. A busy office.

Caitlin Miller and Monica Koskey in
Just Be Frank by Caroline Williams

23rd Annual Humana Festival of New American Plays
Actors Theatre of Louisville, 1999
photo by Richard Trigg

Just Be Frank

Lights up—morning in a busy office. Spotlights focus on two coworkers sitting at adjacent desks, downstage right. Behind them, other employees are periodically seen passing through, miming office business or huddled around the water cooler, upstage center. At stage left is a large reception desk and a freestanding closed door—later, the boss's office will be just beyond it.

In the spotlight: Charlene, an attractive, overbearing young professional, is wearing a garish, hot-pink suit and talking animatedly with her dull-looking colleague, Diane. In dress and posture, Diane is the mouse-like antithesis to Charlene's in-your-face confidence. It is clear who dominates both their work relationship and the conversation in progress.

CHARLENE: *(Striking a pose/modeling her new ensemble.)* It looks expensive, doesn't it? I won't say how much…but let me just tell you…if you even knew—you would die. *(Beat.)* Five hundred dollars. The saleslady said it looked incredible on me. You don't think it's too loud, do you? She said I'd definitely stop traffic…

DIANE: You *are* hard to miss. I mean, it is—*pink.*

CHARLENE: It's not *pink*, Diane, it's *salmon*. I want to look professional when I approach the boss. I really think this suit says, "I'm a woman. I'm not afraid to wear a salmon suit. I can be a valuable asset to this company." *(Beat.)* That promotion has my name written all over it. *(With a determined smile.)*

DIANE: You mean the Gaines Beefy-Treat account? I'm up for that promotion…I mean, I was thinking of applying. I thought since my proposal saved the Ferber Cheese-Stick account last year…

CHARLENE: Oh, that was *you*. Well. You should know that Ferber Cheese was *child's play* compared to Beefy-Treats. *(Smiling "helpfully.")* You wouldn't want to be in over your head.

DIANE: *(Dejected.)* I guess you *are* more assertive than I am…and confident… *(A beat. She looks at Charlene.)* …and you stand out…

CHARLENE: *(Condescendingly.)* Listen. Since you and I are friends—I'll be frank. *This* is the cutthroat world of business. *You* simply don't have any killer instinct and rarely do you ever have anything exciting to say. Not that those are *bad* qualities—you just lack *verve*.

DIANE: Verve?

CHARLENE: Don't worry—you still fulfill a very important role here. Where would people like *me* be without people like *you*? You're punctual and efficient and—meek.

DIANE: *(On the verge of tears.)* Mm-meek?

CHARLENE: *(Big, fake smile.)* In fact, you're LUCKY *we're such good friends* that we can be honest with each other because, for the most part, Diane, there is no place for honesty in business and not everyone will be as helpful as I am. Come to think of it, when I become president of this company, my first decree will be to have all of my people be *completely* honest—*all* of the time. *(She thinks.)* It will *revolutionize* the world of business. *(Beat.)* Sometimes my brilliance takes even me by surprise.

(Charlene is transfixed by her vision. Speechless, Diane stares at her in disbelief.)

CHARLENE: *(Emerging from her reverie, admiring herself.)* Anyway, my suit *is* sensational, isn't it? *(Turning toward the water cooler, she is out of earshot by the time Diane, her face contorting, manages to stammer.)*

DIANE: *(Under her breath.)* What do I know—I'm MEEK!

CHARLENE: *(Smiling over her shoulder, oblivious to Diane's mounting rage.)* No need to thank me—

DIANE: *(Calling after her, sarcastic/bitter.)* Oh yeah, THANKS!!

(Diane turns angrily back to her computer and furiously begins to type. Meanwhile, spotlights follow an obnoxiously cheerful Charlene to the water cooler where a fellow employee, Jan, is standing alone, looking paranoid. Dressed in typical middle-management attire [unflattering earth-tone blazer/skirt combo, "nude" pantyhose and incongruous stark white tennis shoes], Jan holds a paper Dixie-cup and speaks in a flat, nasal monotone. Her face is an expressionless mask of resigned irritation and nausea.)

CHARLENE: Good morning, Jan. How was your weekend?

JAN: Absolute crap.

CHARLENE: Excuse me—?

JAN: I got stood up, my minivan blew a tire and I have a yeast infection. Do you mind? I'm trying to look inconspicuous here and you're standing next to me like a flashing pink beacon.

CHARLENE: *(Confused.)* Actually this suit is not pink, *Jan*, it's salmon. What's gotten into you anyway? I'm counting on you to nominate me for the new account. You're the only one the old windbag ever listens to…

JAN: Actually, *Charlene*, I'd feel better about *myself* if you'd continue to earn substantially LESS than I do.

CHARLENE: *(Still confused.)* Are you trying to say you're not going to give me the recommendation?

JAN: Listen, I'll be blunt. I don't like you. I've never liked you. The way you are *constantly* waving at me from your desk—I have to pretend like I'm writing or looking for something just to avoid acknowledging you—but *you don't get it*…you wave, I ignore you and you keep flappin' away like…some kind of—large, flightless bird.

CHARLENE: Well! *Excuuse me*, JAN!

JAN: *(Continuing—she couldn't care less about Charlene's objections.)* And God help me if I ever sit next to you at a lunch meeting again…watching you eat could drive a person insane—it's like watching one of those pointy-faced rodents—incessantly pecking and pecking and…

CHARLENE: *(Seething.)* Of all the rude…

JAN: *(Continuing.)* …and *speaking* of chewing—your last presentation was so mind-numbingly boring I actually had to *work* to keep from gnawing off my own arm.

CHARLENE: I have heard just about ENOUGH thank-you-very-much! *(She turns to leave.)*

JAN: Oh, in that case—before you go, the next time I sleep with the boss in order to advance my own career, I'll be sure and let slip that you called him a windbag.… Good luck! *(She goes abruptly back to her desk.)*

CHARLENE: *(Calling lamely after her.)* If that's the way you feel, then FINE— I'll meet with him *myself!*

(Charlene stomps off to a large reception desk in front of a free-standing closed door inscribed with the word President in gold lettering. She addresses a perky, somewhat effeminate male Secretary who wears a constant obsequious smile. Everything he says is delivered with a cheerful voice and genuinely eager, helpful attitude.)

SECRETARY: *(Smiling warmly throughout.)* Hello, Ms. Parker. How can I kiss your ass today?

CHARLENE: Excuse me?

SECRETARY: Would you like some coffee? This is regular but if you'd like decaf I'll just leave and come back with the same pot—you'll never know the difference.

CHARLENE: *(Confused.)* Uh—no. I just want to make an appointment with Mr. Ross ASAP.

SECRETARY: *(Checks appointment book, then looks up, still smiling.)* I'm sorry but I don't think he can squeeze your big pink ass in today. *(Cheerfully.)* Is there anything else I can help you with? *(Charlene's face reddens with anger. She is about to speak when the phone rings.)* Just a moment.... *(He holds up a finger to silence Charlene who waits, fuming. Answering the phone.)* Burton and Ross, may I help you? ...Today? ...With Mr. Ross? ...How about 2:15? ...All right then, buh-bye. *(Back to Charlene.)* As I was saying, are you sure there isn't anything else? I could go fetch some Post-its? Your dry-cleaning, perhaps? *(Charlene looks at him blankly, speechless.)* After all, what am I here to do if not *your* mindless, tedious busywork? Whatever you and all your *over-educated* colleagues with reserved parking and big pink suits think you're just too good for. *(Big smile.)*

CHARLENE: *(Enraged.)* FOR-YOUR-INFORMATION the suit is SALMON and I don't know what your problem is but I thought you said Mr. Ross was *busy* all day— *(Points to phone accusingly.)* What was that!

SECRETARY: *(Explaining calmly, as if to a small child.)* No, I didn't say he was *busy*—I said I *couldn't squeeze you in.* He's actually free until *(Glances down.)* 2:15. But due to my inferiority complex and because this appointment book makes me drunk with power, I've decided to act out my passive-aggressive rage against you.

CHARLENE: *Excuse me* but I will *not* tolerate a secretary with that kind of attitu—

SECRETARY: *(Interrupting.)* That's *administrative maintenance engineer* and I would care what you were saying if you had any power at all in this company. Since you don't, I'll just smile and nod while I look for somebody important to suck up to.... Oh! There's an executive! If that will be all Ms. Parker... *(He grabs the coffee pot and rushes off.)*

CHARLENE: *(Disgusted, to no one in particular.)* What is *wrong* with you people?! *(She walks past the desk to the boss's door and knocks, opening it gingerly, flooding his "office" with light. Inside sits Mr. Ross, flanked by stacks of files, behind an imposing oak desk. He wears a dark three-piece suit, red "power tie" and is slightly overweight with short hair and kind features. His tone and demeanor suggest an unbearded corporate Santa Claus.)*

CHARLENE: Mr. Ross?

MR. ROSS: *(Looking up from his paperwork.)* Yes? Come in...

CHARLENE: Hi, I was wondering if I could talk to you for a few minutes about a possible promotion on the new dog-treats account? Last month you had mentioned how I was really up-to-speed and I was thinking, what with my...

MR. ROSS: *(Cutting her off, leaning back in his swivel-chair.)* Hmm—yes, the Beefy Treats. You know, this is quite fascinating. I don't doubt that you do, in fact, work here and I may, indeed, have commented on your work…. I just can't for the life of me seem to remember who in the hell you are. What department did you say you work in?

CHARLENE: Um…marketing and development.

MR. ROSS: Right, right—marketing. You must perform one of those benign tasks that, apparently, I see fit to dole out some measly, pissant salary for… *(Cheerfully.)* in which case I suppose I should hear you out. You were saying…?

CHARLENE: Uh…well, I had actually come in here about a promotion but maybe now's not exactly the right time…

MR. ROSS: *(Interrupting her with a sudden realization.)* Wait a minute! I do remember you—your desk is just across the way there. *(Gestures past the door.)*

CHARLENE: *(Excited.)* Yes! That's me! Did you recall how I typed up those reports last term?

MR. ROSS: *(Cheerful and professional.)* Heavens no! I do recall, however, that I quite enjoy looking down your blouse on my way in here each morning…and considering that my taxes alone are probably twice what you make in an entire year—I suppose it wouldn't hurt to hand over an account I'll probably take credit for anyway. Congratulations Miss…

CHARLENE: Parker…Charlene Parker.

MR. ROSS: Of course. Congratulations Miss Proctor, the promotion is yours. *(Earnestly.)* Good luck and nice ass.

(He gives her a friendly thumbs-up [think enthusiastic Little-League coach "nice catch!"] and promptly refocuses on his paperwork, effectively sending her on her way. Charlene is speechless. She walks slowly back to her desk, more than slightly disturbed.)

DIANE: *(Bitterly.)* So, how'd it go?

CHARLENE: *(Suddenly crazed.)* GREAT DI-ANE! As a matter of fact, WONDERFUL. *(Grotesquely enunciating each word.)* Did I not explain to you that a salmon suit like this would command RESPECT?

(Diane, startled, looks at Charlene like she is insane. After a moment they turn to their respective computers and get to work.)

END OF PLAY

Labor Day
by Sheri Wilner

BIOGRAPHY

Sheri Wilner is a playwright based in New York City whose works have been performed all over the country. Productions or readings of her plays include: *Hunger* at the Williamstown Theatre Festival (MA) and New Dramatists (NYC); *Relative Strangers* at New Georges (NYC), Pittsburgh New Works Festival, the Women's Project and Productions (NYC), The Open Eye (NY), and Organic Theater Company (NYC); *Hiding Places* at Columbia University's Horace Mann Theatre and *Sanctuaries* at the Thirteenth Street Repertory Company (NYC), Theatre Winter Haven (FL), Pegasus Theatre (Dallas), Theatre of Western Springs (IL), Art and Work Ensemble (NYC), Playwrights' Platform (Boston), New York University and Cornell University. She received her MFA in Playwriting from Columbia University and is a member of the Dramatists Guild and the Women's Project and Productions.

HUMANA FESTIVAL PRODUCTION

Labor Day premiered at the Humana Festival of New American Plays in March 1999. It was directed by Abby Epstein with the following cast:

One	Nick Garrison
Two	Erica Blumfield
Three	C. Andrew Bauer
Four	Monica Koskey
Five	Bryan Richards
Six	Carolyn Baeumler

and the following production staff:

Scenic Designer	Paul Owen
Costume Designer	Michael Oberle
Lighting Designer	Mimi Jordan Sherin
Sound Designer	Darron L. West
Properties Designer	Mark Walston
Stage Manager	Heather Fields
Assistant Stage Managers	Dyanne M. McNamara & Alyssa Hoggatt
Dramaturgs	Michael Bigelow Dixon & Ilana M. Brownstein
Casting	Laura Richin Casting

CHARACTERS

ONE, male or female, age 21-28
TWO, male or female, age 21-28
THREE, male or female, age 21-28
FOUR, male or female, age 21-28
FIVE, male or female, age 21-28
SIX, female, age 29

TIME & PLACE

The night before Labor Day, 11:50 p.m. A party.

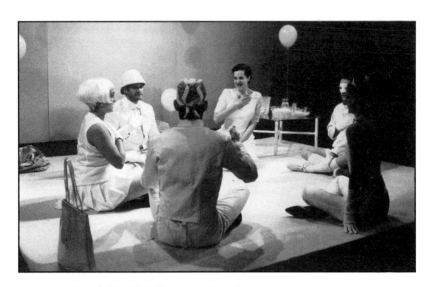

Erica Blumfield, Nick Garrison, C. Andrew Bauer, Carolyn Baeumler,
Bryan Richards and Monica Koskey in
Labor Day by Sheri Wilner

23rd Annual Humana Festival of New American Plays
Actors Theatre of Louisville, 1999
photo by Richard Trigg

Labor Day

Labor Day Eve, 11:50 P.M. A nondescript room, save for some white decorations. Six friends, all dressed completely in white, sit in a circle. Characters One, Two, Three, Four and Five range in age from 21 to 28. Character Six is 29. They are playing a party game and strike their chests with their hands before speaking. [Note on the game: Although individual casts and directors are encouraged to create their own unique ways to play this fictional game, a particularly effective method was discovered for this production. After each player called out a word and hit his or her chest, the other players, one at a time in clockwise order, would hit their chests as well. The next word was not called out until a complete round of "chest-hitting" had been completed. This method created a ritualistic rhythm and set a good speed for the game.]

ONE: *(Hits chest.)* Sale.

TWO: *(Hits chest.)* Noise.

THREE: *(Hits chest.)* Pages.

FOUR: *(Hits chest.)* House.

FIVE: *(Hits chest.)* Collar.

SIX: On rice.

ALL: One word!

SIX: Close enough.

ONE: It is not. No way.

THREE: And you didn't tap your chest.

SIX: *(Hits chest.)* On rice.

FOUR: It's not one word and you didn't tap your chest.

SIX: *(Hits chest repeatedly to get a "reverb" effect.)* O-o-o-o-n-n-n r-i-i-i-c-c-c-e.

FIVE: You're out.

SIX: It's just a game.

FIVE: Right. And you lost it. Sit over there.

SIX: It's my white party and I'll sit where I want to. Sit where I want to. Sit where I want to.

> *(They watch her in silence as she chooses a location for herself. It is off to the side and near a white table covered with an array of white foods.)*

ONE: Actually, it's my white party.

SIX: Obviously. If it were my WHITE party, I wouldn't serve WHITE wine.

FIVE: *(Hits chest.)* Wine.

SIX: White wine is white in name only.

ONE: *(Hits chest.)* Head.

TWO: *(Hits chest.)* Out.

THREE: *(Hits chest.)* Face.

SIX: Anyone want more Wonder Bread balls? Popcorn? Milk?

ALL: No.

(They continue with their game, ignoring her while she speaks.)

FOUR: *(Hits chest.)* Russian.

SIX: *(Shrugs.)* More for me.

FIVE: *(Hits chest.)* Wash.

(Six pours herself a glass of milk.)

ONE: *(Hits chest.)* Wedding.

SIX: *(She raises her glass.)* Here's snow in your eye. *(She drinks.)*

TWO: *(Hits chest.)* Meat.

THREE: *(Hits chest.)* Fish.

SIX: What will you miss the most?

FOUR: *(Hits chest.)* Christmas.

FIVE: *(Hits chest.)* Cap.

SIX: Me, I'll miss the danger. The terror felt at every forkful, at the possibility that a dozen

ONE: *(Hits chest.)* Lines.

SIX: dots of marinara will spray onto your chest. Or that a fist-size clump of chocolate ice cream will lean off its cone

TWO: *(Hits chest.)* Chocolate.

SIX: and fall right into your lap.

THREE: *(Hits chest.)* Guilt.

FOUR: *(Hits chest.)* Man.

SIX: No, you can never feel safe wearing white. That's what I'll miss, believe

FIVE: *(Hits chest.)* Wall.

SIX: it or not. Somehow, it makes you more sensitive. More awake. More aware of every wave pattern in the atmosphere. Is that a rain cloud? A sticky-fingered child? Do I look like a nurse?

ONE: *(Hits chest.)* Bread.

SIX: My period was last week, right? In white, all your senses are heightened. You hear new sounds, smell more smells. You

TWO: *(Hits chest.)* Castle.

SIX: develop a whole new set of senses.

FOUR: *(Hits chest.)* Slavery.

FIVE: *(Hits chest.)* House.

ALL: Said it!

FIVE: No sir.

ONE: Yes sir.

FIVE: No way!

TWO: Yes way.

THREE: Oh please, of course someone said White House.

FIVE: Who did?

FOUR: I did.

FIVE: I didn't hear you.

ONE: I heard her *(or him)*.

FIVE: Well I didn't.

FOUR: I definitely said White House.

FIVE: When?

SIX: *(Hits chest.)* Sale.
> *(Hits chest.)* Noise.
> *(Hits chest.)* Pages.
> *(Hits chest.)* House.
> Fourth item called. Then *(Hits chest.)* collar, then the fatal *(Hits chest.)* on rice.

FOUR: *(To Five.)* Have a seat.

FIVE: I thought she said mouse.

ONE: *(Hits chest.)* Mouse.

TWO: *(Hits chest.)* Album.

THREE: *(Hits chest.)* Lie.
> *(Five walks over to the food area. Six offers Five a glass.)*
> FOUR: *(Hits chest.)* Trash.

SIX: Milk?
> ONE: *(Hits chest.)* Race.

FIVE: No thanks. *(Five pours a glass of white wine.)*
> TWO: *(Hits chest.)* Flag.

SIX: You're better off. It's a stupid game. Limited to one word. How much is
> THREE: *(Hits chest.)* Tie.

SIX: neglected because of that punishingly arbitrary rule? *(Hits chest.)* Sands of time. *(Hits chest.)* Cliffs of Dover.

FOUR: *(Hits chest.)* Flight.

SIX: "Hills Like *(Hits chest.)* Elephants."

FIVE: *(Hits chest.) Men Can't Jump.*

ONE: *(Hits chest.)* Knight.

SIX: That's actually not one I miss.

TWO: *(Hits chest.)* Owl.

FIVE: Ha! That's a good one! *(Hits chest.) Men Can't Jump.*

THREE: *(Hits chest.)* Supremacists.

FIVE: Hey, is there any more vanilla ice cream left?

FOUR: *(Hits chest.)* Lightning.

ONE: In the freezer. *(Hits chest.)* Fang.

FIVE: Excellent.

TWO: *(Hits chest.)* Diamonds.

(Five starts to exit.)

SIX: Wait!

THREE: *(Hits chest.)* Sox.

FIVE: What?

FOUR: *(Hits chest.)* Haired.

SIX: Tell me what you'll miss. The most. About wearing white.

ONE: *(Hits chest.)* Rabbit.

FIVE: I never wear white.

TWO: *(Hits chest.)* Water.

FIVE: This party every year is the only time I ever do. *(Five exits.)*

SIX: *(To group.)* Did you hear that?

THREE: *(Hits chest.)* Light.

SIX: *(Yelling after Five.)* You're not invited next year.

TWO: *(Hits chest.)* Market.

THREE: What the hell's a *(Hits chest.)* market?

TWO: I don't know. There's a black market. That means there must be a *(Hits chest.)* market, right?

ONE: No.

FOUR: Buh-bye.

TWO: Who's got a dictionary?

ONE: I do. But it's red.

THREE: Buh-bye.

TWO: Shit.

(Two sits down next to Six. Six offers Two a bowl.)

FOUR: *(Hits chest.)* Hot.

SIX: Mashed potatoes?

    ONE: *(Hits chest.)* Squall.

TWO: Yeah. Thanks. *(Two takes the bowl and a fork and begins eating.)*

    THREE: *(Hits chest.)* Pride.

TWO: Any salt?

    FOUR: *(Hits chest.)* Sauce.

SIX: Need you ask? *(Six hands Two a salt shaker.)*

    ONE: *(Hits chest.)* Mountains.

SIX: What will you miss? The most? About wearing white?

    THREE: *(Hits chest.)* Plains.

TWO: *(Thoughtfully ponders before answering.)* If you don't have a tan, it looks like you do. If you do have a tan, it looks even darker.

    FOUR: *(Hits chest.)* Rat.

SIX: I'll miss the possibilities.

    ONE: *(Hits chest.)* Satin.

SIX: There's nothing quite like that giddy post-Memorial Day moment when you open up your closet and think: "Anything. Absolutely anything."

    THREE: *(Hits chest.)* Pine.

SIX: There's no reaching for something and then stopping yourself. No fears, no hesitations. You thrust in your hand and can pull anything out.

    FOUR: *(Hits chest.)* Paper.

SIX: Absolutely anything.

    ONE: *(Hits chest.)* Tailed.

TWO: That's not true for me.

    THREE: *(Hits chest.)* Rage.

SIX: Why not?

    FOUR: *(Hits chest.)* Space.

TWO: I don't wear red in the summer. I could have the greatest tan,

    ONE: *(Hits chest.)* Hope.

TWO: but I put on red and some moron inevitably says, "Ouch, bad burn."

    THREE: *(Hits chest.)* Chapel.

FOUR: *(Hits chest.)* Gold.

ONE: *(Hits chest.)* Knuckled.

    (Five re-enters.)

FIVE: You guys know what time it is? It's 11:59.

    (Everyone but Six screams, stands and then runs around the room retrieving their white bags, purses and backpacks.)

FIVE: Man, if I didn't go into the kitchen—

ONE: Oh my god, where's my bag? Who's seen my bag?

TWO: What color is it?

ONE: Very funny. Where is it, where the hell is it?

TWO: Everyone, quick, get your stuff. Quick!

SIX: *(A quiet pronouncement.)* This year I won't do it.

THREE: *(Yelling at Six.)* You're standing on my strap, move!

SIX: This year I won't do it.

THREE: Get your stuff, hurry!

SIX: I won't do it. I won't give it up. The danger. The freedom. The possibilities. I won't give it up.

FOUR: You have to.

SIX: Why? Who says that I do? Who's issuing the order?

FOUR: Forty seconds to Labor Day!!

ONE: Thirty seconds. On your mark, get set…GO!

(Suddenly everyone but Six starts to take off their white clothes and quickly replaces them with colored clothes.)

ONE: Twenty seconds. Watch the clock.

TWO: *(Struggling.)* Shit. This button won't— !

THREE: Hurry. Hurry!

FOUR: *(To Six.)* Come on.

ONE: Ten seconds.

SIX: STOP!

(Time stops. They all freeze, except Six.)

SIX: Why does today feel like the saddest day of the year? It always has. From early on. I died a small death every September. Every first day of school. The feeling that something was over. Something glorious and light and free was over. Why do we follow clocks and calendars? Daylight Savings and New Year's? Why the divisions? Why the markers? Do we really have to make it so obvious that time is passing? That our sisters are now mothers, our parents now grandparents? That the last remnants of our childhood have all but slipped through our fingers? *(Beat.)* I am staying in these clothes. I am staying in these clothes and safe from breast cancer and ovarian cancer and all other diseases that ignore the young. My legs will stay smooth with thin, hidden veins. My parents will not turn sixty but stay the age they were when they each took a hand and lifted me over puddles. I will not allow another season to pass. I can't stop that blasted ball dropping on New Year's, but I will stop this.

(Time re-starts, they all resume changing clothes.)

ALL *(Except Six.)*: 10, 9, 8

SIX: Stop it.

ALL: *(Except Six.)* 7, 6, 5

SIX: I said stop it.

ALL: *(Except Six.)* 4, 3, 2

SIX: Stop it.

ALL: *(Except Six.)* 1! Happy Labor Day! *(They cheer, yell, hug and blow noise-makers.)*

SIX: EVERYBODY STOP IT!!

(They stop what they are doing and stare blankly at Six. On her hands and knees, she moves about the room gathering all of their white clothes, and in the process, one of the white balloons. She holds the clothes tightly to her chest and buries her face in them. Pause.)

FOUR: It's just pants and shoes. You can still wear white shirts.

ONE: Yeah, and there's always winter whites.

SIX: None of you know. None of you have any idea.

(Hits chest) I miss the freedom.

(Hits chest.) I miss the freedom.

(Hits chest.) I miss.

(Six releases the white balloon and watches it float up into the air.)

END OF PLAY

T(ext) Shirt Project

"Whether it acts as a camera of who we are and where we are going,
a commemorative calendar of dress, a dialectic across the gender line,
or even a simple assertion of the skin-shirt nexus,
the T-shirt is the canary in the coal mine of taste."
Alice Harris, *The White T.*, HarperCollins: New York, 1996

The T(ext) Shirt Project: An Introduction
by Kae Koger and Adrien-Alice Hansel

The Humana Festival's T(ext) Shirt Plays open a wide range of topics for exploration by fashion historians, theatre critics, students of American culture, and clothing mavens. These explorations begin quite simply with underwear. The history of the T-shirt in American culture begins in the mid-nineteenth century with the simple garment (known as a vest) intended to be worn under the shirt. Made of cotton, wool or silk, they were invariably white and rarely seen in public outside work settings like factories or farms. According to Richard Martin and Harold Koda, authors of *Jocks and Nerds: Men's Style in the Twentieth Century*, "In the early twentieth century, the Sears, Roebuck and Co. mail-order catalog advertised the T-shirt for its utility as an undergarment, but in the 1930s began to suggest the possibility of the shirt's exposure." Sears featured the "gob"-style shirt for the sailor, worn under the outer shirt during heavy work, helping to keep the outer shirt clean. Martin and Koda suggest that the "romantic association with the sea...allowed the T-shirt to emerge for limited use in its own right."

Undershirts (soon known as T-shirts because of their shape) began to appear as acceptable outerwear in the 1950s, notably with Marlon Brando's appearance in *A Streetcar Named Desire* (1951) and *The Wild One* (1954) and James Dean's starring role in *Rebel without a Cause* (1955). The Brando and Dean characters became symbols of youthful delinquency whose popularity made plain white T-shirts desirable casual attire for young men who aspired to adopt their rebellious images. Ironically, widely circulated photos of John F. Kennedy wearing a T-shirt while relaxing at home in Washington in the mid-1950s signaled the T-shirt as leisure-wear and sent a very different message, which Martin and Koda believe associated its "clean whiteness...with wholesome values."

In the 1960s T-shirts became a unisex garment, adapted by students in the Civil Rights and Vietnam War protest movements. Most fashion historians agree that the adaptation of the T-shirt as an almost universal garment for both sexes during the 1960s was a rejection of consumerism and materialism in American culture and an expression of a desire to "abandon fashion" by "dressing to suit oneself."

T-shirts printed with slogans also first appeared in the 1960s, although Jacqueline Herald dates the boom to 1973 when *Women's Wear Daily* announced that "the T-shirt is the year's number one counter-culture status symbol." Martin and Koda note that the "T-shirt had become not so much a sign in its own right as a signpost for the messages it carried.... In some sense an extension of the jersey worn by the college football team to reveal its identity, the T-shirt quickly became the bearer of advertisements, ideas, and judgments." Increasingly T-shirt slogans were used for educational and political purposes, promoting environmental causes like Greenpeace, as well as serving as an artistic extension of the music counterculture of the late sixties and early seventies.

Although it is impossible to date precisely the advent of advertising printed on T-shirts, in 1975 Budweiser Beer distributed printed T-shirts in Florida and California as souvenirs of Spring break. The potential for T-shirts as an artistic medium was first realized by artist Keith Haring in the 1970s when he "wrote poignant and pointed messages in which graffiti as a committed visual language was combined with moral judgments." London designer Katharine Hamnett printed a series of political statements on T-shirts in the 1980s and wore one protesting nuclear proliferation to a reception at Prime Minister Margaret Thatcher's residence. By the mid-1980s T-shirts had become a ubiquitous medium of advertising and self-expression.

Ironically, these garments which communicated the youth counterculture's disgust with consumerism and materialism in the 1960s have become testaments to conspicuous consumption and global product merchandising in the 1990s. And although it's impossible to explain why someone would pay a company for the privilege of wearing its advertising logo on their chest, it's equally unlikely that we would find a person in the United States today who doesn't own a printed T-shirt.

Marshall McLuhan's observation that "clothing, as an extension of the skin, can be seen a both as heat-control mechanism and as a means of defining the self socially" continues to be valid today. A T-shirt might attest to a special event a person participated in (their wedding, graduations, high school prom) or one that they didn't ("My grandma went to the Kentucky Derby and all I got was this lousy T-shirt"). A T-shirt may indicate a person's political affiliation, vocation, educational background, brand loyalty or sexual orientation. Or it might merely be the first thing the wearer pulled out of the drawer that morning in the rush to get out of the house. Despite our motivation for donning T-shirts, the messages they send reaffirm, in Martin and Koda's words, that "if the T-shirt is the natural tabula rasa of clothing, the statement T-shirt confirms the plausibility of clothing's own messages and acknowledges that the garment is, at skin's surface and the external world's approach, an innate and eloquent sign system."

The Humana Festival's T(ext) Shirt Plays exploit the possibilities of the T-shirt as a tabula rasa while extending the concept of the T-shirt as a means of artistic self-expression. The six playwrights whose work appears on the T-shirts have accepted the challenge to create plays which are short enough to be printed on the back of a T-shirt yet complex enough to communicate the self-reflective irony of the medium. Wendy Wasserstein's "To T or Not To T" juxtaposes the styles and ideas of famous playwrights from a wide range of historical periods in an ironic commentary on the act of writing a play for a T-shirt. In "Merchandising," David Henry Hwang comments upon how the strategies for selling a product or work of art have superseded the importance of the work itself. Jane Martin evokes the political roots of the printed T-shirt in her environmentally conscious "Stuffed Shirts."

A number of these plays comment on the body, or the fact of the medium itself. This self-reference decreases the differentiation between the subject of the play and the play itself. Naomi Wallace's "Manifesto" reminds us that in the 1990s the body itself has become a site of postmodern performance and demonstrates that, as Amelia Jones has written, "body art…places the body/self within the realm of the aesthetic as political domain." In dramatizing the troubled relationship between threads, Tony Kushner's "And the Torso Even More So" dovetails with Wallace's link between the body of the text and the body beneath the text. In "The Fez" Mac Wellman gives us another mainstay of the postmodern experience, the simulacrum. Where Hwang writes of buying a T-shirt as a replacement for an actual experience, Wellman gives us the description of a play as a substitute for actual dialogue. By choosing "a contemporary classic American or British play," Wellman offers us a tabula rasa on which to inscribe Something Strange, much as the T-shirt itself has submitted to the texts of these authors and the wearing of these T-shirts transforms the performance of their texts in a manner not unlike the Strange occurrence to which he alludes.

One stimulus behind this project is to give the wearer of the shirt "a sense of being a theater participant." The T(ext) Shirt Plays reshape some of the traditional constructions of viewing a performance and interacting with a text, shifting the relationship between author, actor, and audience. The author remains the playwright, who has been influenced by the medium. The person who wears the shirt becomes the actor, able to creatively fill the words, accessorizing with pearls or a dinner jacket as he or she sees fit, able to abridge the text as they will (with duct tape or magic marker, should a sentence or word prove offensive), but ultimately becoming a canvas for the playwright's words, the agent in the performance. The performance takes place when the shirt is worn (spending the rest of its time in a dresser/bookshelf); the performance space is wherever the "actor" is at the time the embodied text is present. The "actor" is a creative agent in this decision as well, since these plays have different resonance at an ecologist's conference and on the set of a movie.

The audience becomes those who see the shirt on a body. They, like audiences of a more traditional nature, are free to read some or all of the shirt, to remark on it, to ignore it altogether. This could prove a more interactive art form, with "actor" and audience conversing on the nature of the performance. It could also prove a more egalitarian one, since the "admission" has been paid previous to performance by the actor, who currently performs the play for all those standing behind him/her at the Winn-Dixie.

Given the history of text on T-shirts, which functions, in art historian John Neff's view, as a "painless tattoo, an intimate identification of the wearer with the shirt and its message," what then, does wearing a T(ext) Shirt Play suggest about its wearer? Certainly the "actor" is responsible for the content of the shirt in a different manner than the traditional actor or audience. This "actor" chooses the play and pays for its production, and cannot dismiss his or her personal investment in a certain piece of work because it was cheap to attend, or because it paid the bills for a while. With the T(ext) Shirt Plays, the actor stages the work at will, and is accountable for that decision throughout the day. Finally, the actor declares his or her affiliation with the Humana Festival and his or her participation in its cutting-edge development of new American plays.

BIBLIOGRAPHY

Hall, Lee. *Common Threads: A Parade of American Clothing.* Boston: Little Brown and Co., 1992.

Herald, Jacqueline. *Fashions of a Decade: The 1970s.* New York: Facts on File, 1992.

Jones, Amelia. *Body Art: Performing the Subject.* Minneapolis: U of M Press, 1998.

Martin, Richard and Harold Koda. *Jocks and Nerds: Men's Style in the Twentieth Century.* New York: Rizzoli, 1989.

McLuhan, Marshall. *Understanding Media: The Extensions of Man.* Cambridge: MIT Press, 1994.

Neff, Dr. John Hallmark."The T-Shirt." Detroit Institute of Arts, April 1975.

Rubinstein, Ruth P. *Dress Codes: Meanings and Messages in American Culture.* Boulder: Westview Press, 1995.

Storm, Penny. *Functions of Dress: Tools of Culture and The Individual.* Englewood Cliffs, NJ: Prentice Hall, 1987.

Merchandising
by David Henry Hwang

BIOGRAPHY

David Henry Hwang wrote both the screenplay and Broadway success *M. Butterfly*. His latest play, *Golden Child*, made its Broadway debut this year. Mr. Hwang is also the author of *FOB* (1981 Obie Award, Best New Play), *The Dance and the Railroad* (Drama Desk nomination, Guernsey's Best Plays of 1981-82), *Family Devotions* (Drama Desk nomination), *The House of Sleeping Beauties*, *The Sound of a Voice*, *Rich Relations*, *Bondage*, *Trying to Find Chinatown* and the Philip Glass opera *The Voyage*. He also collaborated with Philip Glass and designer Jerome Sirlin on *1000 Airplanes on the Roof*. Mr. Hwang also wrote the screenplay for *Golden Gate*, starring Matt Dillon and Joan Chen. He attended Stanford and Yale School of Drama.

T-Shirt design by Liz Nofziger.

Merchandising

Lights up on Marcus and Chuck sitting on parking lot pylons eating take-out commissary food. A cardboard box sits before them on the asphalt.

MARCUS: See, what Lucas did, which was amazing, is that he asked for the merchandising.

CHUCK: Today, it seems obvious.

MARCUS: Isn't that always the sign of true genius? And the assholes, what did they know? They gave it to him. And of course, the rest is history.

CHUCK: But nowadays, everyone does that.

MARCUS: Right. And the studios have wised up. That's why, nowadays, you gotta say, "Hey, screw the back end."

CHUCK: Hell, screw the front end.

MARCUS: Screw the goddamn movie altogether. I mean, don't even bother making it.

CHUCK: Which they never do anyway.

MARCUS: Right. So don't do me any favors. Don't even bother wasting your precious money on grips, or film stock, or writers—

CHUCK: Or actors.

MARCUS: Especially actors. Screw the movie. Just gimme the merchandising.

CHUCK: Yeah, the merchandising. Nowadays, that's where all the talent goes, anyway.

(They chew their food. Silence.)

CHUCK: Hey—sorry about your movie.

MARCUS: Ah, screw it. *(Beat.)* Want a T-shirt?

(Chuck shrugs, opens the box, rummages through promotional T-shirts. Fade to black.)

THE END

And the Torso Even More So
A T-Shirt Play in Sonnet Form
by Tony Kushner

BIOGRAPHY

Tony Kushner is the author of *A Bright Room Called Day*, *The Illusion* (freely adapted from Corneille); *Angels in America, A Gay Fantasia on National Themes, Part One: Millennium Approaches* and *Part Two: Perestroika*, and adaptations of Goethe's *Stella*, Brecht's *The Good Person of Setzuan*; and Ansky's *The Dybbuk*. His previous ATL premieres include *Reverse Transcription* (1996) and *Slavs!* (1994), which has now been performed in theatres around the United States, in London, Berlin, Vienna and Paris; and which won a 1995 Obie award. He is the recipient of the 1993 Pulitzer Prize in Drama and the 1993 and 1994 Tony Award for Best Play. A collection of recent writings, titled *Thinking About The Longstanding Problems of Virtue and Happiness*, was published by Theatre Communications Group, and a collection of his interviews, *Tony Kushner in Conversation*, has been published by The University of Michigan Press. Mr. Kushner was born in Manhattan and grew up in Lake Charles, Louisiana.

T-Shirt design by Liz Nofziger.

And the Torso Even More So

The Woof are the horizontal threads in the web of fabric, the Warp are the vertical threads.

WOOF: My dangling darling, whither gone? Withdrawn?

WARP: Depressed.

WOOF: Oh no, *Again*?

WARP: Mood indigo.
    My heart has plunged…

WOOF: Oh please, *please*, don't go on,
    You've got to see a shrink! TAKE PROZAC!

WARP: No.
    I am the Warp. My tight-wound soul descends;
    You'll never understand: I'm *deep, bereft.*

WOOF: You're *warped*, you solipsist. You've got no friends!

WARP: But I've got you. My Woof. My width. My Weft.

WOOF: I'm weary, baby, shuttling through this weave.
    I'd love to slip our ravell'd sleeve of care.
    The world's so wide…

WARP: Oh God, OH PLEASE DON'T LEAVE!
    Don't rend the veil! Don't leave the body bare!
    Thread-bare, and barren, naked flesh undressed!
    (They shudder. The Woof sighs.)

WOOF: I'll stay. For now. How do you feel?
    (Small pause.)

WARP: Distressed…

THE END

Stuffed Shirts
by Jane Martin

BIOGRAPHY

Jane Martin returns to ATL with her latest play following her premiere of *Mr. Bundy* in the 22nd Humana Festival. Her previous play, *Jack and Jill*, premiered in the 20th Humana Festival and won the 1997 American Theatre Critics Association Award for Best New Play. Ms. Martin, a Kentuckian, first came to national attention for *Talking With*, a collection of monologues that premiered at Actors Theatre in 1981. Since its New York premiere at the Manhattan Theatre Club in 1982, *Talking With* has been performed around the world, winning the Best Foreign Play of the Year award in Germany from *Theater Heute* magazine. Her other work includes *Middle-Aged White Guys* (1995 Humana Festival), *Cementville* (1991 Humana Festival), *Summer* (1984 Shorts Festival) and *Vital Signs* (1990 Humana Festival). Ms. Martin's *Keely and Du*, which premiered in the 1993 Humana Festival, was nominated for the Pulitzer Prize in Drama and won the American Theatre Critics Association Award for Best New Play in 1994. Most of her work has been published in a volume titled *Jane Martin: Collected Works 1980-1995*, published by Smith and Kraus.

T-Shirt design by Liz Nofziger.

Stuffed Shirts

ALEX: No, huh-uh, no, I don't hate sex, honestly, I just don't want you to take off your shirt. Really. Hey, look around you, we need as a nation to have sex without taking off our clothes.

VINNY: I…what? Why?

ALEX: Because, get real, we are seriously inaesthetic.

VINNY: But if we love each other?

ALEX: We're architecture. A serious person can't love an ugly building.

VINNY: That's weightist.

ALEX: Alright, I like the way you look, I just don't like the way you're shaped. Okay, the larger view. A body isn't apolitical, and I don't like the politics implied by your body. Shoot me. I don't like what it means for the earth.

VINNY: You are rejecting me sexually on an environmental basis?

ALEX: Hey, reality check, there is no difference between the personal and the political. Here's the deal: respect the earth, then you might get laid.

THE END

Manifesto
by Naomi Wallace

BIOGRAPHY

Naomi Wallace is from Kentucky. Her newest play, *The Trestle at Pope Lick Creek*, premiered at the 1998 Humana Festival and later played at New York Theatre Workshop. Her play *One Flea Spare* was commissioned and produced in October 1995 by the Bush Theatre of London and received its American premiere at the 1996 Humana Festival. *One Flea Spare* also received the 1997 Obie Award for Best New Play. Her film *Lawn Dogs*, produced by Duncan Kenworthy (*Four Weddings and a Funeral*), opened successfully in Great Britain, moved to the U.S. and won numerous film awards. Ms. Wallace is a published poet in both England and the United States. Her book of poetry, *To Dance A Stony Field*, was published in the United Kingdom in May, 1995.

T-Shirt design by Liz Nofziger.

Manifesto

Two figures speak to each other. It is almost dark.

RUINED BODY: Look at me. A piece of work. My throat's closed. Legs gone from standing. Arms I can't raise. God damn you.

SPECTRE: A spectre is haunting—

RUINED BODY: Stop playing the ghost. Show me your face.

SPECTRE: The history of all hitherto existing societies—

RUINED BODY: Come near to me. That's right. I can smell you now: the inside of a bird's nest, oranges, gasoline.

SPECTRE: —is the history of class struggle.

RUINED BODY: Stop talking. Shut your mouth.

SPECTRE: Two great classes directly facing each other.

RUINED BODY: Eye to eye. In yours I see myself awake. Listen.

SPECTRE: Abolition of property. Equal liability of all to labor.

RUINED BODY: Listen. Don't fucking move. You must kiss me where no one has ever kissed me. I'm still alive in that place. Put your hand inside me. We're awake now. Work with me.

SPECTRE: Overthrow of all existing social conditions.

RUINED BODY: Work with me. When my tongue moves across the roof of your mouth, I taste the smoke from the chimney.

SPECTRE: All that is solid melts into air. Work with me.

RUINED BODY: We're not abandoned. Someone is still at home.

RUINED BODY AND SPECTRE: And the face by the fire

RUINED BODY: It's still a good world

SPECTRE: to win. And the face by the fire, looks like

RUINED BODY AND SPECTRE: you, looks like me.

THE END

To T or Not To T
by Wendy Wasserstein

BIOGRAPHY

Wendy Wasserstein is the Pulitzer Prize and Tony Award-winning playwright of *The Heidi Chronicles* and *The Sisters Rosensweig*. Her other plays include *An American Daughter* and *Uncommon Women and Others*. She has written for PBS Great Performances and other television and film, including the screenplay for *The Object of My Affection*. She has also published work in *The New York Times*, *The New Yorker*, and *Slate Magazine*. Ms. Wasserstein authored the children's book *Pamela's First Musical*. She is a graduate of Yale School of Drama.

T-Shirt design by Liz Nofziger.

To T or Not To T

A boardroom.

PLAUTUS: What about "This T-shirt is definitely *not* a Prada"?

CHEKHOV: I think something with a place, like "Louisville, we've got to get to Louisville."

SHERIDAN: I like "I went to Louisville and all I got was this lousy T-shirt."

SHAKESPEARE: "Tomorrow and tomorrow and tomorrow." That should work.

WILLIAMS: Bill, we can't use anything from that Scottish play. Do "I rely on the kindness of strangers." At least that'll get some attention in a bar.

O'NEILL: It's a lousy pipe dream. T-shirt plays. A lousy pipe dream.

MOLIERE: Some people write for kings and others write for T-shirts. It beats the movie business.

RACINE: That's all you care about, money. What about love, death, and pity?

SHAW: The soul of the entire society is at risk.

LOPE DE VEGA: Fellas, as the author of 2,000,000 plays, I just want to get this done. What are we saying?

APHRA BEHN: The answer is simple. "WOMEN PLAYWRIGHTS AT LOUISVILLE—35 YEARS OF SCRIBBLING FOR EXCELLENCE. "

WASSERSTEIN: Gentlemen, I believe this meeting is adjourned.

THE END

The Fez
by Mac Wellman

BIOGRAPHY

Mac Wellman is the author of *Girl Gone, Fnu Lnu, The Damned Thing, The Sandalwood Box, Second-Hand Smoke, The Lesser Magoo* and *Infrared*. He also directed *I Don't Know Who He Was, and I Don't Know What He Said* as part of the four-month Mac Wellman Festival at House of Candles and elsewhere. He has received numerous honors, including both NEA and Guggenheim Fellowships. In 1990 he received an Obie (Best New American Play) for *Bad Penny, Terminal Hip* and *Crowbar*. In 1991 he received another Obie for *Sincerity Forever*. Three collections of his plays have been published: *The Bad Infinity* (PAJ/Johns Hopkins University Press), *Two Plays* and *The Land Beyond the Forest* (both from Sun & Moon). Sun & Moon also published *A Shelf in Woop's Clothing*, his third collection of poetry, and two novels: *The Fortuneteller* (1991) and *Annie Salem* (1996). In 1997 he received a Lila Wallace-Reader's Digest Writer's Award. He is a founding member of The Bat Theater.

T-Shirt design by Liz Nofziger.

The Fez

THE FEZ, a play, begins with: 22 minutes from the top of any of the better class of contemporary classic American or British play, a play properly inflated with moral updraft of a clear and paraphrasable kind. After the initial 22 minutes Something Strange happens: the actors drop out of their roles, and are astounded to find themselves on stage; some try to ignore the fact that the charmed spell of the theatre has somehow absented itself; others simply flee the emptiness of theatrical artifice in horror; still others bravely go on, although they have either forgotten how to act, or their lines, or both. 22 dwarves drag onstage an immense ceremonial wagon (as in the engraving by Albrecht Dürer) with appropriate fanfares, drones and chants which continue through the end of the play. All the dwarves wear red fezzes. Atop the ceremonial wagon is a gigantic fez, also red. The dwarves begin a sequence of strange dances: they do The Muscle Beach; they do The Fur-Lined Hangover; they do The Jamaican Car Service; they do The Hokey Locus; they do The Spinal Fusion. All the remaining actors stare at this and wonder, as do the dwarves who have been planted in the audience as shills. There is a 22-minute fade to black.

THE END

The Car Play

The Car Play

"Theater does not have to exist within the frame of buying a ticket to a two-hour event," explains Actors Theatre of Louisville Producing Director Jon Jory. "We have to seek other venues, forms and time limits to remain part of the contemporary lifestyle."

In this year's festival, one such experiment with venue, form and time was provided by Richard Dresser's *What Are You Afraid Of?*, a dramatic text that explores some possibilities of The Car Play. In this version of on-site theatre, audience members sit in the back seat of an automobile and watch the play performed by actors in the front seat. The familiarity of the setting evokes thoughts of voyeurism, déjà vu and audience participation. As Judith Newmark of *The St. Louis Post-Dispatch* explains, "The play challenges ingrained assumptions about what constitutes theater and about the audience's role in shaping it. Do we just sit back and say, 'Entertain me,' or can we alter the experience if we are more involved intellectually, emotionally, or, in this case, physically?"

What Are You Afraid Of? was presented at fifteen-minute intervals for several hours at a stretch by two different casts. The "set" was an old Lincoln Town Car parked outside the Actors Theatre of Louisville lobby—the car never left the curb. To enhance the play's expressionistic style, Dresser chose musical selections that were controlled by actors on the car's audio system. According to Dresser, "The limitations turned out to give the play its shape... [I had to] strip away everything that is not essential. Not an extra word, not an extra syllable."

—Sara Skolnick

What Are You Afraid Of?
by Richard Dresser

BIOGRAPHY

Richard Dresser's plays include *Below the Belt* and *Gunshy*, both of which premiered in the Humana Festival and were subsequently produced off-Broadway and at a number of regional theatres. Also *Alone at the Beach* (ATL 1988), *The Downside, Better Days, Bait & Switch, The Road to Ruin, Bed & Breakfast, At Home* and *Splitsville*, all of which are published by Samuel French. His newest full-length play, *Something in the Air*, opened the Bay Street Theatre's season in 1999. He has twice attended the O'Neill National Playwrights Conference, is a former member of New Dramatists and a current member of the HB Playwrights Unit. For television he wrote HBO's *Vietnam War Stories* and has served as writer/producer on such shows as *The Days and Nights of Molly Dodd, Bakersfield P.D., Public Morals* and *Smoldering Lust*. He currently resides in Los Angeles.

HUMANA FESTIVAL PRODUCTION

What Are You Afraid Of? premiered at the Humana Festival of New American Plays in February 1999. One cast was directed by Frazier W. Marsh:

Man . . . . Trip Hope
Woman . . . . Ginna Hoben

Another cast was directed by Stuart Carden:

Man . . . . Tudor Sherrard
Woman . . . . Jessica Jory

and had the following production staff:

Costume Designer . . . . Kevin McLeod
Sound Designer . . . . Malcolm Nicholls
Properties Designer . . . . Ben Hohman
Dramaturg . . . . Adrien-Alice Hansel

CHARACTERS

MAN

WOMAN

Trip Hope and Ginna Hoben in
What Are You Afraid Of? by Richard Dresser

23rd Annual Humana Festival of New American Plays
Actors Theatre of Louisville, 1999
photo by Richard Trigg

What Are You Afraid Of?

A man is driving by himself, grooving to the radio: "Sweet Hitchhiker" by Creedence Clearwater Revival. He stops the car, leans over, opens the door.

MAN: *(To himself.)* Yes! There is a God! *(A woman gets into the car.)*

WOMAN: Thanks. I thought I was going to be out there by myself forever.

MAN: *(Checking her out.)* You? I don't think so.

WOMAN: Most people are such jerks, trapped inside their own personal heads. They never even see me.

MAN: I don't usually pick up hitchhikers. You're actually my first. Aren't you afraid?

WOMAN: Of what?

MAN: Getting in a strange car. I could be anyone. I could be your absolute worst nightmare.

WOMAN: And I could be yours. *(A quick impression of a deranged lunatic.)* But you gotta take some risks sometime if you're gonna have a life, don't you? *(As their eyes meet, the music changes: "Don't Worry Baby" by the Beach Boys. The car is stopped. He puts his arm around her.)*

MAN: Beautiful isn't it?

WOMAN: Oh, you *like* toxic waste facilities?

MAN: No, you and me. Together. Can I kiss you?

WOMAN: I didn't think you brought me out here for the view.

MAN: I brought you here so we could be alone.

WOMAN: I guess all those "Danger" signs really do keep people away. *(He kisses her. She pulls away.)*

MAN: That bad?

WOMAN: No, I just swallowed my gum.

MAN: Bummer. I'll spring for another piece later on. *(He kisses her again. She stops.)* What?

WOMAN: In a *car*?

MAN: C'mon, it's just the two of us. There isn't another soul for miles. Nobody ever needs to know.

WOMAN: It's just a little…uncomfortable.

MAN: I've got an idea.

WOMAN: I bet you do.

MAN: Let's hop in the back. The seat folds down. It'd be like a night at the Ritz.

WOMAN: Just kiss me.

> (He kisses her. They slide down on the front seat, out of sight. A blouse flies into the back seat. Then a brassiere. They come up to a seated position. They both sigh.)

MAN: Wow.

WOMAN: My feelings exactly.

MAN: You're just…well, I've never…I mean…

WOMAN: What *do* you mean?

MAN: To be honest. I think I'm in…

WOMAN: What?

MAN: *(Struggles to say it.)* Lllll … As you've probably guessed, I have…

WOMAN: *What* do you have?

MAN: Strong feelings. Directed at you.

WOMAN: Gee.

MAN: You know what I mean.

WOMAN: Why can't you just say it?

MAN: Why do I need to say it if you know what I mean?

WOMAN: *(Teasing.)* C'mon, it's just the two of us. There isn't another soul for miles. No one ever needs to know.

MAN: It isn't that.

WOMAN: Then what?

MAN: I can say it.

WOMAN: When?

MAN: Soon. Don't rush me. *(Pause.)*

WOMAN: Tonight? This week? This year? I'm just trying to get a rough idea.

MAN: Hey, relax! I'm going to say it! *(Pause.)*

WOMAN: What are you afraid of?

> (As their eyes meet, we hear a tape of the homicide-inducing Barney song: "I love you, you love me, we're a happy family… ")

MAN: *(To the back seat.)* Would you kids shut up!

WOMAN: Please, honey, they've been in the car a *long time*. We've *all* been in the car a long time. *(To the back seat, sweetly maternal.)* Let's button our lips and throw away the key. Daddy's a little grouchy today.

MAN: Daddy isn't grouchy! Daddy's about to snap! Now what were those orders again?

WOMAN: *(Super-fast.)* Three Hamburger Happy Meals, two small Cherry Cokes, a large chocolate milk, I'll have Chicken McNuggets, medium fries, a Super-Size half-decaf coffee with Sweet'N'Low, don't forget to ask for straws and extra ketchup…and what do *you* want?

MAN: *(Aside.)* I want to kill myself. Then I want to kill Barney.

(He rolls down the window. Distorted electronic gibberish from a speaker.)

MAN: *(Continuing; to speaker.)* Excuse me?

WOMAN: Just tell him or her your order, honey. There are only about a billion cars behind us. *(Electronic gibberish.)*

MAN: Right. Okay. Three kiddie meals—

WOMAN: *(Calling toward speaker.)* Happy Meals!

MAN: Some drinks…

WOMAN: *(Calling toward speaker.)* Two small Cherry Cokes, one large chocolate milk, one Super-Size half-decaf with Sweet'N'Low—

MAN: She wants a chicken sandwich—

WOMAN: *(Calls toward speaker.)* McNuggets! *(Electronic gibberish.)*

MAN: *(To the speaker.)* Right back at ya!

WOMAN: You forgot to get something for yourself.

MAN: It's okay. I couldn't keep anything down with Barney around. *(Suddenly wheels around to back seat.)* Okay, who threw that?

WOMAN: Sweetie? You're supposed to pull up to the window and get our food.

MAN: *(Glaring at each person in the back seat.)* We're not moving till one of you tells me who did it! Who looks guilty?

WOMAN: *(Looks at people in back.)* If you ask me they *all* look guilty.

MAN: Then they're all gonna pay!

WOMAN: I'm sure it was an accident, dearest.

MAN: It hit me in the back of the head! It could have put my eye out!

WOMAN: Would you *please* pull forward and get our food?

MAN: *(Staring straight ahead, tense.)* I'm trying.

WOMAN: Is the car *supposed* to be making that sound?

MAN: No. It isn't.

WOMAN: *(Looking in back of car.)* Uh-oh. That black smoke isn't a good sign, is it?

MAN: Probably not, darling.

WOMAN: Oh, dear. What does it mean?

MAN: It means we can't go. We're stopped.

WOMAN: We can't be "stopped." We're blocking about a mile of traffic and we don't even have our food!

MAN: *(Suddenly wheels around to the back seat.)* Who said that? This is your last warning! Next time we get out of the car, I take off my belt and God help us all!

WOMAN: Honey? Shouldn't you get help?

MAN: I do not need "help." I need a vacation!

WOMAN: We're *on* a vacation, remember? I meant for the car.

MAN: Help for the *car*? Are you insane? What, you think I'm going to go up to another guy and ask for *help*?

WOMAN: Why not? What are you afraid of?

(As their eyes meet, the song changes back to "Sweet Hitchhiker." The Man and Woman are alone in the car, cruising along.)

MAN: So where exactly are you going?

WOMAN: I don't know.

MAN: How can you not know where you're going?

WOMAN: How can you *know* where you're going?

MAN: Look, if you don't have any particular destination...

WOMAN: Yes?

MAN: Well, I could take you...anywhere.

WOMAN: Where do you *want* to take me?

MAN: I don't know. Wherever you want.

WOMAN: *(Disappointed.)* Oh. Well. There's an on-ramp to the Interstate. I bet I could get another ride there.

(The car stops. She opens the door.)

MAN: Hey, I never even got your name.

WOMAN: All you had to do was ask. *(She gets out of the car.)*

MAN: *(Desperate.)* There are so many things I want to tell you! It seemed like there was really something between us. *(Thinks.)* But we were having such a nice time I didn't want to spoil it if you weren't interested and maybe once we got to know each other we'd find out we didn't have much in common and maybe we'd even grow to hate each other and this way, well, at least we both have a nice memory, right?

WOMAN: What are you afraid of?

MAN: Me? Nothing!

WOMAN: Okay. Well, thanks for the ride! *(She closes the door. She is gone.)*

MAN: *(To himself.)* Everything. *(The Man continues on his way, alone.)*

END OF PLAY

The Phone Plays

Audience members listening to The Phone Plays
in the lobby at Actors Theatre of Louisville

23rd Annual Humana Festival of New American Plays
Actors Theatre of Louisville, 1999
photo by Richard Trigg

The Phone Plays

When we're on the telephone, we use only one of our five senses—we listen. We listen for content, we listen for inflection, we listen for silence and any other clues that might help us piece together the unseen picture at the other end of the line. And how perfect that is for playwrights—a medium that relies on language, listening and the active engagement of an audience member's imagination to piece together a play.

So for this year's Humana Festival, we challenged five playwrights to exploit the dramatic potential of "The Phone Conversation." In response, they've given us an impressive array of confessions, revelations, propositions, arguments and threats—you know, the mainstays of compelling theatre.

While these phone conversations build on dramatic tradition, they also demonstrate how the medium affects the message—especially the portability of the medium. As we take our phones with us everywhere, our ability to reach out and touch someone becomes continuous, informal, and downright surprising. In fact, the more we use the telephone, the more transparent the technology becomes, revealing us fully in our glory and our shame. And what more could we ask of a three-minute play?

—Michael Bigelow Dixon and Amy Wegener

Will You Accept the Charges?
by Neal Bell

BIOGRAPHY

Neal Bell is the author of *Two Small Bodies, Raw Youth, Cold Sweat, Ready for the River, Sleeping Dogs, Ragged Dick, On the Bum* and *Somewhere in the Pacific*. His plays have appeared at Playwrights Horizons in New York and at regional theatres including the Berkeley Repertory, the Mark Taper Forum, South Coast Repertory, the La Jolla Playhouse and Actors Theatre of Louisville, where his ten-minute play *Out the Window* was a co-winner of the 1990 Heideman Award. Mr. Bell has been playwright-in-residence at the Yale Drama School, and has taught playwriting at New York University, Playwrights Horizons Theatre School, and the 42nd Street Collective. He is a recipient of fellowships from the Rockefeller Foundation, the National Endowment for the Arts and the Guggenheim Foundation. Mr. Bell was awarded an Obie in 1992 for sustained achievement in playwriting.

HUMANA FESTIVAL PRODUCTION

Will You Accept the Charges? premiered at the Humana Festival of New American Plays in February 1999. It was directed by Jon Jory with the following cast:

Bobby. . . . . Bruce McKenzie
Nan. . . . . Laurie Williams

and the following production staff:

Designer. . . . . Paul Owen
Sound Designer . . . . Jeremy Lee
Sound Engineer . . . . David Preston
Properties Designers . . . . Ben Hohman, Mark Walston

CHARACTERS

BOBBY
NAN

Will You Accept the Charges?

BOBBY: This connection is hell—you have to speak up.

NAN: *(Low.)* I can't talk now.

BOBBY: Are you in a meeting?

NAN: Yes.

BOBBY: I'm buried alive, and you've gone back to work already? *(Silence.)* Hello?

NAN: *(Muffled, to somebody else.)* I have to take this. Would you excuse me?

BOBBY: Hello?

NAN: *(In a more normal voice.)* Are you cold?

BOBBY: Can you talk *now*?

NAN: I was afraid you'd be cold.

BOBBY: No, the lining you picked out for my coffin is—what is it, silk?—it's very comfy. Soft, warm—

NAN: It's quilted.

BOBBY: Yes. I can feel that. DIG ME UP! *(Silence.)* The drug I took—how long was I out?

NAN: Three days. You said you'd call—

BOBBY: Three *days*? I've been in here—DIG ME UP!—oh god—the worms crawl in. NAN? HELLO?

NAN: I miss you. Curling around you at night—I had to wash your pillowcase. The smell of your hair—

BOBBY: I hang up, I go 9-1-1—

NAN: Do it. Tell them you faked your own death, to collect the insurance. *(Pause.)* I've been waiting for your call—I don't know. It hit me: "Mrs. Patterson, your dead husband, on Line 2."
(Pause.)

BOBBY: NAN, can you hear how hard my heart is beating? I smell—I'm so afraid, now—like I'm already rotting.

NAN: 9-1-1.
(Pause.)

BOBBY: You woke up one day, and you said, "I have to escape." And I said, "We need money for that." Do you remember? Waking up, that morning? You were trembling…. "I have to escape the rest of my life." That's what you said. We came up with a plan.

NAN: The worms crawl out…. If we needed the money this badly—we didn't escape. Did we? Hello? *(Silence.)* Hello?

END OF PLAY

Speech Therapy
by Rebecca Gilman

BIOGRAPHY

Rebecca Gilman is the recipient of the Roger L. Stevens Award from the Kennedy Center Fund for New American Plays for her play *Spinning Into Butter*, which premiered at the Goodman Studio Theatre in 1999 under the direction of Les Waters. She is also the recipient of the Scott McPherson Award, a $5,000 commission from the Goodman Theatre. Her play, *The Glory of Living*, which premiered at Circle Theatre in Chicago in 1997, received the American Theatre Critics Association's 1998 Osborn Award, a 1997 Joseph Jefferson Citation and an After Dark Award for New Work for the Chicago '96-'97 season. *The Glory of Living* opened at the Royal Court Theatre in London and in Vienna at Das Schauspielhaus in January of 1999. *The Glory of Living* has been published in English by Faber and Faber and in German by S. Fischer Verlag. Ms. Gilman's plays, *The Land of Little Horses* and *My Sin and Nothing More*, are both available from Dramatic Publishing.

HUMANA FESTIVAL PRODUCTION

Speech Therapy premiered at the Humana Festival of New American Plays in February 1999. It was directed by Jon Jory with the following cast:

Peter . . . . Matt Meyer
Lisa . . . . Andrea Clark

and the following production staff:

Designer . . . . Paul Owen
Sound Designer . . . . Jeremy Lee
Sound Engineer . . . . David Preston
Properties Designers . . . . Ben Hohman, Mark Walston

CHARACTERS

PETER
LISA

Speech Therapy

PETER: Well, I ran into Mary and she introduced me to that visiting professor from NYU and it turns out he's doing research on swallowing disorders.

LISA: Oh yeah?

PETER: Yeah. And I told him that you're a speech therapist, but I said, "My girlfriend is a speech therapist," and he said, "'Girlfriend?' Isn't that a bit archaic? Isn't it a bit, infantalizing?" You know. And, I thought, this is always going to be a problem. I know I'm not supposed to say "girlfriend," because it's not p.c. or whatever, but I just can't bring myself to call you my "partner."

LISA: I know. It sounds like we're filing articles of incorporation or something.

PETER: Exactly, but then, you know, what else is there? "Lover?" Every time somebody introduces me to their "lover" I just…I wince.

LISA: I immediately picture them having sex. Which is not always… exactly…appetizing.

PETER: It just…it functionalizes the relationship. Like that's all you do. Like the person just comes over for an hour every night and you have sex and then they leave.

LISA: Like a service contract.

PETER: Right, so I was explaining this dilemma we have, and Mary suggested "significant other," but I have real problems with that too.

LISA: It's too cute.

PETER: It's cute, and also, it's wrong.

LISA: Wrong how?

PETER: It's the "other" part. To me, it just…it differentiates you too much. I mean, of course you're your own person, as they say, but I still don't think of you as completely other than me. You know? Because I think of you as part of me too. As someone who is very much a part of me and very much informs me. *(Beat.)* So, to me, it would be very false to say you're my significant other because really, you're my significant other who is also a very significant part of me. *(Beat.)* And that's just…you know…too long to say.

LISA: You could make it an acronym. Significant other who…SOW…is also a...SOWIAA...also a very...SOWIAV...significant part of me. SPOM. SOWIAVSPOM.

(Small beat.)

PETER: I'm trying to say something serious here.

LISA: I'm sorry.

PETER: No, it's...I mean we talk about this like this but.... *(He trails off.)* It's okay. Just listen, okay?

LISA: Okay.

PETER: I left those guys and I was walking back to my office and thinking about it, and I was thinking that I don't want to worry about how to refer to you. You know? I don't want you to be off somewhere where I'm having to refer to you all the time. I want you to be with me. I love you and I want us to be together and I want you to be my...my SOWIAVSPOM forever. *(Small beat.)* So I'm...what I'm asking is, will you marry me? Will you let me call you my wife? *(Pause. She doesn't answer.)* Lisa?

LISA: I'm sorry. I just...I was having a little swallowing disorder of my own there.

PETER: Oh.

(Beat.)

LISA: Peter?

PETER: Yes?

(Small beat.)

LISA: Yes.

END OF PLAY

Them
by David Greenspan

BIOGRAPHY

David Greenspan is a playwright, director and actor. His plays include *Jack*; *The Home Show Pieces*; *2 Samuel 11, Etc.*; *Dead Mother, or Shirley Not All in Vain* and *The Myopia, an epic burlesque of tragic proportion*. These have been produced at the Public Theater in New York, The Royal Court in London, The Citizens Theatre in Glasgow and Stukke Theater in Berlin. Directing credits include *Gonza the Lancer*, a play by seventeenth century Japanese master Chikamatsu Monzaemon, and contemporary plays by Kathleen Tolan, Carlos Murillo and Nicky Silver. Recent acting credits include Richard Foreman's *Benita Canova*, Mac Wellman's *Second-Hand Smoke* and Mart Crowley's *The Boys in the Band* (Obie Award, Drama Desk Nomination). In January he appeared in Lee MacDougall's *High Life* at Primary Stages in New York.

HUMANA FESTIVAL PRODUCTION

Them premiered at the Humana Festival of New American Plays in February 1999. It was directed by Jon Jory with the following cast:

Voice 1 . . . . Preston Dyches
Voice 2 . . . . V Craig Heidenreich
Voice 3 . . . . Joanna Leah Buckner

and the following production staff:

Designer . . . . Paul Owen
Sound Designer . . . . Jeremy Lee
Sound Engineer . . . . David Preston
Properties Designers . . . . Ben Hohman, Mark Walston

CHARACTERS

VOICE 1: Younger than Voice 2, and his tone higher—a tenor, say, to 2's baritone. Voice 1 is the more imperative. If he becomes emotional as the piece progresses, he is never hysterical.

VOICE 2: Though more controlled than Voice 1, Voice 2 is by no means nonchalant.

VOICE 3: Should not be a child.

Them

The text should move at a good clip, convey a sense of urgency. It might be slightly hushed, but not whispered.

VOICE 1: Wait.

VOICE 2: What?

VOICE 1: Did I hear something?

VOICE 2: I don't know.

VOICE 1: Do you think they're listening?

VOICE 2: Who?

VOICE 1: Them.

VOICE 2: I don't know. They might be. They will be at some point.

VOICE 1: Are you sure?

VOICE 2: No.

VOICE 1: How will we know?

VOICE 2: What?

VOICE 1: If they're listening? Will we?

VOICE 2: What?

VOICE 1: Know if they're listening.

VOICE 2: No.

VOICE 1: Then they might—they could be listening now.

VOICE 2: They could. They might be.

VOICE 1: As we speak.

VOICE 2: Yes.

VOICE 1: What are they like?

VOICE 2: Who?

VOICE 1: Them. The ones listening. Potentially listening.

VOICE 2: I don't know. I imagine them all different.

VOICE 1: You've never seen them.

VOICE 2: Never. Not yet.

VOICE 1: Then you might at some point?

VOICE 2: Perhaps.

VOICE 1: I'm frightened.

VOICE 2: Why?

VOICE 1: Because I don't know them, and they could be listening—might be listening—right now. As we speak. Will they understand what we're discussing? Will it have any...? Will it make...sense to them?

VOICE 2: I don't know.

VOICE 1: I don't even know what they look like.

VOICE 2: Nor do I. But then, they have no idea what you look like. Or for that matter, what I look like. They have only our voices with which to imagine.

VOICE 1: Yes, but they...we...they.... We don't have their voices. So we...we imagine.... For us, it's pure imagination. Projection.

If only they could speak. With us. To us. Give us some idea—some impression—of who they are, what they are like. If they would say something—if we could hear it. At least the sound of their voice—voices—might tell us something.

VOICE 2: The unseen voice can be deceiving.

VOICE 1: True. How many times do voices—unseen voices—put—they put ideas into our heads—about the speaker that...they don't give the picture we would have if we could see.

VOICE 2: And even then, if we could see, what would we know? How much would we know?

VOICE 1: Looks *can* be deceiving. Still, if they could speak—would speak—say something, it would say something—tell us something.

VOICE 2: But even if they speak—would speak, you won't hear them. It's not designed that way.

VOICE 1: But still, maybe—perhaps they...they would hear something. As they spoke. If they spoke. Even if we can't hear them. They would hear themselves. Just—for just a moment. Hear the sound of their own voices—that singular music—as they might not generally.

VOICE 2: And perhaps hearing themselves in this context—this little pretend, it would remind them—

VOICE 1: Yes. That it is pretend. Just pretend.

Please. If you're there. If you're listening to this conversation—which is after all just a script recorded, we actors speaking words, a recording played over and over again—if you would say something.... Or better, ask a question. As though you could speak with one of us. For the sake of playing along.

VOICE 2: If they spoke, and I'm not saying they will, what question would they ask?

VOICE 1: Perhaps they might ask if anyone is listening.

VOICE 2: In other words—

VOICE 3: Do you think they're listening?

VOICE 1: Wait.

VOICE 2: What?

VOICE 1: Did I hear something?

VOICE 2: I don't know.

VOICE 1: Do you think they're listening?

VOICE 2: Who?

VOICE 1: Them.

VOICE 2: I don't know. They might be.

> They will be at some point.
>
> *(A momentary sound—to cap it off—the aural equivalent of Voice 1 looking up astonished. Then out.)*

END OF PLAY

Visitation
by Rebecca Reynolds

BIOGRAPHY

Rebecca Reynolds makes her ATL playwriting debut in this year's Humana Festival. Television and film credits for Ms. Reynolds and her writing partner Larry Brand include the films *Backfire*, Roger Corman's *Overexposed* and two HBO pilots. Other television credits include NBC's *Another World* and KET's *Graveyard Cleaning-Off Day* and *Borderlines*, winner of the Kentucky Humanities Council-Kentucky Arts Council Film/Video Project. Her play *Die Like a Dog in the Middle of the Road* was presented in 1999 at First Stage in Dayton, Ohio. Ms. Reynolds received her BFA in Acting from Southern Methodist University and her MFA in playwriting from Southern Illinois University. Acting credits include The Oregon Shakespeare Festival, The Acting Company, *Overexposed*, *Flo*, *Sheriff Lobo*, *B.J. and the Bear*, and *The Dukes of Hazzard*, where she kidnapped Loretta Lynn and forced Miss Lynn to hear her sing. A native of Mayfield, Kentucky, she lives in Leland, Michigan with her husband Jim Carpenter.

HUMANA FESTIVAL PRODUCTION

Visitation premiered at the Humana Festival of New American Plays in February 1999. It was directed by Jon Jory with the following cast:

Alline . . . . .Adale O'Brien
Teddy. . . . . David Weynand
MaryLizbeth . . . . Laurie Williams

and the following production staff:

Designer . . . . Paul Owen
Sound Designer . . . . Jeremy Lee
Sound Engineer . . . . David Preston
Properties Designers . . . . Ben Hohman, Mark Walston

CHARACTERS

ALLINE
TEDDY
MARYLIZBETH

Visitation

ALLINE: You moron.

TEDDY: Well, I am truly shocked.

ALLINE: Fine, you're shocked.

TEDDY: How long's all this been going on?

ALLINE: Five, six years. What difference does it make?

TEDDY: My God.... Will's a deacon in our church.

ALLINE: Was. Will was.

TEDDY: Hell, does everybody in town but me have a secret life...?

ALLINE: Everybody but you has a life.

TEDDY: Oh, God. Does Emily know?

ALLINE: If Emily knew, you think I'd be calling at one-damn-thirty in the morning?!

TEDDY: Hell, Alline, I sponsored him at the Moose Lodge. He never said a word.

ALLINE: Yeah, well y'all were real close. Now, hop out of the J. C. Penny Towncraft pajamas you wear every boring night of your life and put on a pot of coffee. We're coming over.

TEDDY: Sorry, Alline. I can't let you do that.

ALLINE: Teddy, get your butt downstairs and open that funeral home up right this minute.

TEDDY: Uh-uh. Visitation was over at eleven.

ALLINE: I'll drive up the steps and through the damn door if I have to.

TEDDY: *(Panicking.)* You're calling from your car?! Now, look, Alline, y'all can't come over here in the middle of the night! How's that gonna look?

ALLINE: MaryLizbeth wants to see Will, and dammit, she's gonna see him!

TEDDY: But she's not even family.

ALLINE: That's the whole point, you moron. All she wants is to say her good-byes. Okay, I'm making my turn here at Speedy Lube. You better hustle.

TEDDY: *(Desperate.)* Lord, what if Mother wakes up and sees two women sneaking in here...?!

ALLINE: We're just now passing the water and light office.

TEDDY: Don't do this to me, Alline. Please—!

MARYLIZBETH: *(Slurred.)* Hey, Teddy, doesn't Will have the cutest little butt?

TEDDY: *(Startled.)* MaryLizbeth…! I, uh…I am so sorry for your, uh, loss.

MARYLIZBETH: That stupid Emily told him it was too fat. You don't think it's too fat, do you?

ALLINE: That's enough, Hon. You lay back down.

MARYLIZBETH: *(Upset.)* Teddy, don't let 'em say Will's butt's too fat!

TEDDY: *(Grasping.)* Uh, yes well, uh, he was, uh…he will be sorely missed.

MARYLIZBETH: *(Sobbing.)* Oh, Alline, I'm gonna miss that little butt.

ALLINE: Give me the phone, MaryLizbeth. Look, Hon, see, here we are.

TEDDY: Alline, you are *not* bringing her in here like that! No way.

ALLINE: She's upset.

TEDDY: She's potted. *(Car horn honks.)* Alright, alright, drive on 'round to the back, to the hearse bay. *(Horn honks.)* Alright, dammit, the front door then. I'll be right down! Oh, wait, would you ask MaryLizbeth something?

ALLINE: What?

TEDDY: Don't upset her or anything…but would you ask if it's possible she has Will's front plate? It's just that Emily couldn't find them at the house, and they weren't in his hospital room.

ALLINE: His teeth…? You laid Will out in his coffin without his teeth?!

TEDDY: *(Offended.)* Well, Good Lord, no. Of course not. I put in Mother's.

ALLINE: You put your Mother's teeth in Will Tyler's mouth…?

TEDDY: Just temporarily.

ALLINE: Teddy…

TEDDY: Well, she hardly ever wears them anymore.

ALLINE: You moron. *(Horn honks.)* MaryLizbeth, Hon, don't do that—!

TEDDY: *(As car phone disconnects.)* Well, hell. *(Pause.)* Hello, Mother…

END OF PLAY

Happy Birthday Jack
by Diana Son

BIOGRAPHY

Diana Son is the author of *Stop Kiss, BOY, Fishes, R.A.W. ('Cause I'm a Woman)* and others. Her plays have been produced at the Joseph Papp Public Theater, La Jolla Playhouse, Seattle Repertory Theatre, Oregon Shakespeare Festival, Woolly Mammoth, Mixed Blood Theatre Company, New Georges, and the People's Light and Theatre Company. *Stop Kiss* has been published by *American Theatre Magazine* and as a trade paperback by The Overlook Press, Penguin Books. *R.A.W. ('Cause I'm a Woman)* appears in *Take Ten: New Ten-Minute Plays* published by Vintage Press and *Contemporary Plays by Women of Color* by Routledge Press. Diana is a member of New Dramatists.

HUMANA FESTIVAL PRODUCTION

Happy Birthday Jack premiered at the Humana Festival of New American Plays in February 1999. It was directed by Jon Jory with the following cast:

Bryan . . . . Jon Brent Curry
Jack . . . . V Craig Heidenreich

and the following production staff:

Designer . . . . Paul Owen
Sound Designer . . . . Jeremy Lee
Sound Engineer . . . . David Preston
Properties Designers . . . . Ben Hohman, Mark Walston

CHARACTERS

BRYAN
JACK

Happy Birthday Jack

*The sound of *69 being dialed followed by a ring.*

BRYAN: Hello? *(No response.)* Hello? *(No response.)*

JACK: …Bryan?

BRYAN: Yes? *(Pause.)* Oh. H-hi Jack.

JACK: Hi Bryan.

BRYAN: *(Tries to play it off.)* Funny you should call.

JACK: Funny how I should dial *69 and find out you called me—and hung up.

BRYAN: Yeah—funny.

JACK: So did you have something you wanted to tell me?

BRYAN: Huh? Uh…no, not in particular.

JACK: Are you calling and hanging up on all your old boyfriends or did you single me out special?

BRYAN: I—I'm drunk.

JACK: You're drinking again.

BRYAN: No! Not like that—I just, it's…my friend's birthday tonight and…we had a little wine at dinner…me and a bunch of friends.

JACK: Bryan, it's my birthday tonight.

BRYAN: Oh! What a—happy birthday. How old are you?

JACK: Bryan.

BRYAN: Thirty-five? Wow, I guess that makes me…still in my twenties! That means it's been…seven years since we last…since we—

JACK: Since I left you.

BRYAN: Right!

JACK: How've you been, Bryan?

BRYAN: Fine, great, happy. You happy?

JACK: Oh yeah. Things are going great for me. I'm an assistant professor of history at NYU. What are you doing?

BRYAN: Oh, well, I—well you may remember I was studying photography when we were together.

JACK: I remember.

BRYAN: Well I dumped that. Then I thought I'd go back to school but I couldn't decide what I'd want to study so I started working at this catering place and I really like it, you know, I thought I might like to become a chef—but then I realized that you have to work long hours and always smell like garlic so I quit that job but I thought I'd write a screenplay about all the interesting people I met and I did and I just sold it to Sony for two hundred and fifty thousand dollars.

JACK: Sure.

BRYAN: No, really, I did. So I just wanted to call you on your 35th birthday and say screw you, Jack, for being such a bad boyfriend and making me feel like I didn't deserve you. I have a new boyfriend now who loves me like you never could. Screw you, Jack, woo hoo!

(He hangs up. The sound of *69 being dialed. The phone rings. And rings.)

END OF PLAY

2/01

GAYLORD S